Charles Henry Hitchcock, Joshua Henry Huntington, S. A Nelson, A. F. Clough, Howard A Kimball, Theodore Smith, Luther Loud Holden

Mount Washington in Winter

The Experiences of a Scientific Expedition upon the Highest Mountain in New England

Charles Henry Hitchcock, Joshua Henry Huntington, S. A Nelson, A. F. Clough, Howard A Kimball, Theodore Smith, Luther Loud Holden

Mount Washington in Winter
The Experiences of a Scientific Expedition upon the Highest Mountain in New England

ISBN/EAN: 9783337258580

Printed in Europe, USA, Canada, Australia, Japan

Cover: Foto ©Andreas Hilbeck / pixelio.de

More available books at **www.hansebooks.com**

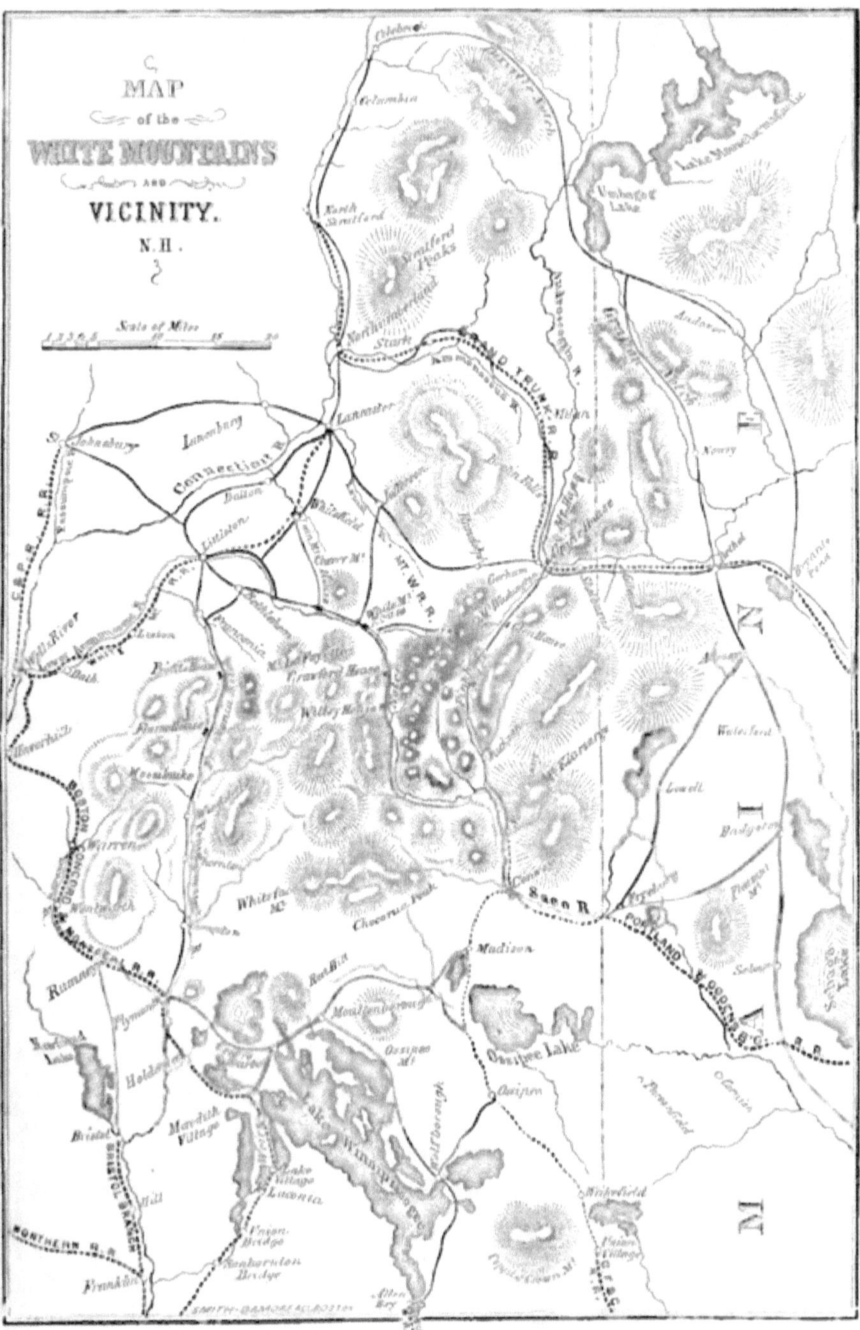

MAP
of the
WHITE MOUNTAINS
AND
VICINITY.
N.H.
Scale of Miles

MOUNT WASHINGTON

IN WINTER

OR

THE EXPERIENCES OF A SCIENTIFIC EXPEDITION UPON THE HIGHEST MOUNTAIN IN NEW ENGLAND — 1870-71

' The Lord hath his way in the whirlwind and in the storm, and the clouds are the dust of his feet."

" There are two voices; one is of the sea, one of the mountains; each a mighty voice."

BOSTON
CHICK AND ANDREWS
21 Franklin Street
1871

RIVERSIDE, CAMBRIDGE:

STEREOTYPED AND PRINTED BY

H. O. HOUGHTON AND COMPANY.

PREFACE.

All who have been connected with the Mount Washington Expedition have contributed to the preparation of this book. They address these pages, as their Official Report, to those friends who furnished the means for establishing this Arctic Observatory, whose names will be found in the Appendix.

C. H. Hitchcock has prepared the first four chapters and Part IV.

J. H. Huntington has prepared Chapters V., VII., VIII., XI., XII., Part III., the first and concluding portions of Chapter VI., and the first three pages of Chapter X.

S. A. Nelson has prepared Chapters XIII. and XIV.

A. F. Clough has prepared a part of Chapter IX.

H. A. Kimball has prepared the " Ascent of

November 30 " in Chapter **VI.** and the balance of Chapter IX.

Theodore Smith has prepared Chapter **X.**

The mountain was visited in the winter and spring by Mr. L. L. Holden, of the " Boston Journal," who has kindly contributed Chapter **XV.**

Each author is responsible for the subject-matter of the chapters here credited to him ; as much so as if there were as many separate books as there are authors.

CONTENTS.

PART I.

PRELIMINARY.

CHAPTER I.

PAGE

EARLY HISTORY OF THE EXPEDITION 1

CHAPTER II.

PHYSICAL CHARACTER OF THE WHITE MOUNTAINS . . 24

CHAPTER III.

EXPLORATION OF THE MOUNTAINS 36

CHAPTER IV.

THE APPROACHES TO MOUNT WASHINGTON 60

CHAPTER V.

MOOSILAUKE 87

PART II.

THE EXPEDITION AT WORK

CHAPTER VI.

THE ASCENT OF MOUNT WASHINGTON IN WINTER . . 101

CHAPTER VII.

A LOOK NORTHWARD AND EASTWARD 118

CHAPTER VIII.

A Look Southward and Westward 126

CHAPTER IX.

Photographing 132

CHAPTER X.

Telegraphing 146

CHAPTER XI.

Life at the Summit 155

CHAPTER XII.

Journal from October to December 163

CHAPTER XIII.

Journal continued 169

CHAPTER XIV.

Journal concluded 208

CHAPTER XV.

Mount Washington in May 251

PART III.

METEOROLOGY.

Introduction 281

CHAPTER XVI.

The Frostwork and Clouds 285

CHAPTER XVII.

The Wind 293

CHAPTER XVIII.

Storms 301

CHAPTER XIX.

PAGE

METEOROLOGICAL RECORD 309

PART IV.

WHAT THE WORLD SAID OF US 345

APPENDIX 358

PART FIRST.

PRELIMINARY.

CHAPTER I.

EARLY HISTORY OF THE EXPEDITION.

EARLY in the summer of 1858, a party of geologists started in a skiff from Burlington, Vermont, and gradually made their way up Lake Champlain to Whitehall, New York, stopping at every promontory and island to examine the strata. The expedition was organized under the auspices of the Vermont Geological Survey, of which the late President Edward Hitchcock, of Amherst, Massachusetts, was the responsible head. The leader of the party was C. H. Hitchcock, one of the assistants.

Two college students, who had just finished their course of study at Amherst, joined the party for the sake of learning something of practical geology. These were George S. Grosvenor and J. H. Hun-

1

tington. The latter gentleman had visited the White Mountains in 1856 and 1857, and was very enthusiastic in his descriptions of the sights and experiences of that elevated region. The question was raised by Mr. Huntington whether it would be possible to spend a winter upon the summit of Mount Washington, and he expressed his willingness to make the experiment in company with a classmate, Mr. James Collins. He subsequently addressed a letter to Professor Joseph Henry, of the Smithsonian Institution at Washington, D. C., asking whether the Institution could not advance the funds necessary for the undertaking, as his friend and himself were willing to make the attempt to remain on the summit all winter. A very kind letter was received in reply, showing a high appreciation of the subject, but declining to undertake the enterprise at that time, on account of the many obstacles in the way. In a few weeks, C. H. Hitchcock visited the White Mountains for the first time. He found a report very common among the guides and frequenters of the hotels, that the Smithsonian Institution had offered a thousand dollars to any one who would spend a winter upon the summit for the purpose of taking meteorological observations. Others said that a firm in Boston had offered five thousand dollars for the same object, with the avowed purpose of publishing the journal of the observers' experiences, expecting to be reimbursed for the large expenditure by the sale of the books. Knowing Mr. Huntington's wishes, Mr. Hitchcock addressed a letter to Professor Henry, stating the existence of the report mentioned above, and adding that two very capable young men were ready and anxious to undertake the enterprise. No answer was received, and the project shortly passed out of mind. Even to the present time, people at the mountains insist that somebody has offered a very large sum for the purpose now accomplished by the Mount Washington Expedition. In our efforts to raise funds, every such report has been carefully scrutinized, but no one could be traced to any reliable source. Whenever we were referred to any individual, that person we interrogated, but gained no additional information. The search seemed always like pursuing a phantom; the moment it is touched it vanishes. It is natural to think of what winter life upon the mountains must be, and to perceive the necessity of an expensive outfit, in case any observers could be found willing to brave the frost and storms upon the summit; hence the origin of the report.

APPLICATION FOR THE TIP-TOP HOUSE.

During the ensuing ten years, letters occasionally passed between Messrs. Hitchcock and Huntington. At length, the Legislature of New Hampshire, in the summer of 1868, authorized the establishment of a Geological Survey, and Mr. Hitchcock was appointed State Geologist. Then Mr. Huntington recalled the old conversations about the winter occupation of Mount Washington, and he applied for and received the appointment of Assistant on the Geological Survey of the State.

He commenced his work in New Hampshire in the spring of 1869, and labored chiefly in the wilds of the extreme northern part of the State. The subject of elevated winter quarters was early broached, and no time was lost in making the preliminary inquiries. In the month of July, the State Geologist went to Gorham to ask Colonel Hitchcock, of the Alpine House, and lessee of the Tip-top House, if he would allow his premises on the summit to be occupied for scientific purposes the next winter. The proposal not being favorably received, the matter was dropped for a few weeks.

Negotiations were subsequently renewed by letter, but were not successful. These long cherished plans being thus frustrated, it became evident that the winter of 1869–70 would not be known in after years as the season in which daring adventurers braved the arctic climate of Mount Washington. But in this, as in so many other cases, a higher than human foresight was preparing the way for the desired adventure.

MOOSILAUKE.

Had the expedition been attempted in 1869, it might have been a failure for the want of an experience of the peculiarities of mountain atmospheric phenomena. In a conversation with Mr. William Little, of Manchester, our disappointment was made known. Said he, " Why not spend the winter upon the top of Moosilauke? I own the house there, and the adjacent forests. You shall have the use of them without charge."

The proposal being made to Mr. Huntington, he adopted it without a moment's hesitation, even though, in consequence of bad chirography, the word " Moosilauke " was mistaken for " Monadnock." Moosilauke, in Benton, is nearly five thousand feet high, and within the arctic zone of climate. Supplies were carried to its summit, and Mr. Arthur C. Page, a recent graduate of the Chandler Department of Dartmouth College, stood ready to accompany Mr. Huntington, and preparations were made to commence arctic housekeeping the latter part of December. But an advantageous situation in Georgia was offered to Mr. Page, and by his acceptance of it, the elevated position of observer on Moosilauke was left vacant. It was shortly after filled by Mr. A. F. Clough, of Warren, a great lover of Nature, and a photographer by profession.

This expedition was carried out chiefly at the expense of Mr. Huntington, and by the exertions of both. So valuable were the experiences acquired, and so unusual were the meteorological phenomena experienced, that a full account of them is reserved for a subsequent chapter. In some respects, the Mount Washington phenomena have not equaled those upon Moosilauke.

PREPARATION FOR THE NEXT WINTER.

About two months were spent upon this summit, and the possibility of living on a mountain top during the winter was fully demonstrated. These observations were published in the newspapers, and excited great interest. We began quite early in 1870 to contrive ways and means for our Mount Washington expedition. Of course, a house was the first essential. Renewed application for the Tip-top House was courteously but firmly met by refusal in a letter dated April 23, 1870. At one time, the question of building a small house was discussed. From his elevated observatory on Moosilauke, Mr. Huntington, by letter of February 18, 1870, proposed that negotiations be commenced with the Mount Washington Railway Company, for the use of the engine-house or depot they were intending to build on the summit.

After the adverse decision in regard to the Tip-top House, a letter was addressed to Mr. Sylvester Marsh, of Littleton, president of the Railway Company, inquiring whether the house might not be used in the winter by the meteorological party. In reply, it was stated that the completion of the house before winter was uncertain; but a desire was expressed that the project might be successful. Interviews were had with Mr. Marsh, and he spoke even more favorably than we had been led to expect by his letter, but he added that he had not the authority to speak for the company. Having no reason to suppose the directors would not favor us, late in July the State Geologist issued a circular, stating the importance of establishing a meteorological observatory upon Mount Washington in the winter, and asking the friends of scientific research and mountain exploration to contribute the sum of two thousand dollars to maintain the expedition, and furnish the means of telegraphic communication between the observers and the public. The Geological Survey proposed to adopt the expedition as a part of its work, but not to furnish any funds in its behalf. The circular suggested that, with such a sum, the expedition could be made successful, and the public could daily learn the character of the arctic phenomena peculiar to the summit, and that without waiting months or years for the return of the party to civilized regions. It was promised that

the funds subscribed should not be called for before
October 1, nor then unless the whole amount had
been subscribed, and every contributor of ten dollars and upwards was to receive a pamphlet describing the history and results of the expedition. This
circular was sent to friends, and small sums were
received, but not to any promising extent. Both of
us were so occupied with necessary field work that
we had no time to beg for money. Circulars were
posted at the principal hotels among the mountains,
in full view of the guests, but they did not excite
any special interest. Great hopes were entertained
of obtaining assistance from the American Association for the Advancement of Science at its meeting
in Troy, about the middle of August. A paper
was read at Troy by Mr. Huntington, descriptive
of the previous winter's occupation of Moosilauke,
and the views of frostwork and arctic scenery there
photographed were exhibited by means of a magne-
sium light. The presentation of the subject excited
some interest, but the association declined to aid
the project, individually or collectively.

THE SIGNAL SERVICE.

It was now the first of September, and not a
hundred dollars had been promised. Our next
effort was in the direction of the Press. A prominent journal in New York was willing to give us

five hundred dollars for daily telegrams and occasional letters sent to them exclusively during the winter months. Although a telegraph line capable of use in the winter months, was beyond our expected means, our faith in ultimate success was strengthened by this proposal. About this time our attention was called to the recent establishment of the *Bureau of Telegrams and Reports for the Benefit of Commerce* in connection with the War Department at Washington. Application was made to General A. B. Myer, the Chief Signal Officer, for funds to aid us in carrying out our enterprise, while allowing the weather office to share its benefits. The answer, dated September 14, stated that the Chief Signal Officer could " hardly appropriate money for the object named; but it may be in the power of this office, with the approval of the Secretary of War, to detail an observer for the position you propose to occupy."

In answer to two additional communications from the State Geologist, dated September 21 and 22, the Chief Signal Officer states his willingness to provide an insulated telegraph wire to extend from the summit of Mount Washington to the railroad station at its base, but that he cannot sanction any special arrangement that has been made to furnish any one paper exclusively with the weather reports. He proposed himself to furnish weather reports from all the stations throughout the country to the principal newspapers, as well as to the Chambers of Commerce, and could not well omit any one. He also offered to provide the meteorological instruments required for the station. Thus the means were provided for sending daily telegrams, but it necessitated the annulling of the contract for sending the weather reports exclusively to the New York newspaper, and left us as poor as ever.

In a letter of October 7, the Chief Signal Officer announces that he has sent to the State Geologist, three miles of insulated Kerite telegraph wire, two telegraph instruments, two sections and four conductors, to the value of ten hundred and thirty-two dollars; and that an instructed observer will probably be detailed to join the expedition. These telegraph supplies were duly received and immediately transported to the mountain.

AN ABORTIVE EFFORT.

During the summer an effort had been made in still another direction, namely, application for aid to a scientific society in New York, known to be greatly interested in arctic researches. It was suggested to them, that for a comparatively small sum, which the officers of the society could easily raise by subscription, science would be greatly benefited, while the society itself would have the credit arising from encouraging so daring an adventure.

The proposal was not favorably received, — at least no reply was ever made to the communication.

MR. NELSON.

From another quarter, however, there came the required assistance. In the month of July, Mr. Durgin of the Sinclair House in Bethlehem, informed Professor Hitchcock, that a relative of his by marriage, S. A. Nelson, of Georgetown, Massachusetts, was very much interested in the meteorology of Mount Washington, and would like to join our expedition. Mr. Nelson wrote by date of July 28, presenting a request to be permitted to join the expedition, asking also for further information. It appeared that he had been led naturally to think of the great benefits to science that must accrue from the occupation of our highest mountain for meteorological purposes, and he had determined, if not able to go with some party, to attempt the enterprise " alone in the face of all hardships and dangers." His letters had the ring of the true metal in them, and an interview for the exchange of views was requested. Circumstances prevented our meeting. By further correspondence, it appeared that Mr. Nelson was ready to devote himself to raising funds for the expedition, in case he could be one of the

party. A formal invitation was soon extended to
Mr. Nelson, to cast in his lot with us. He accepted, and immediately set himself to the task of
soliciting subscriptions in eastern Massachusetts,
pledging himself to procure at least five hundred
dollars. His promise was more than realized, for
his efforts brought in more than eight hundred dollars. His labors commenced early in September,
and he did not go upon the mountain till late in
December, remaining behind after the occupation
of the summit to complete what he conceived to be
his part of the work below. Were this the place, it
would be very entertaining to present extracts from
his journal in October and November, showing how
curiously many of his applications for aid were received. Those who have been obliged to solicit
contributions for worthy, yet poorly appreciated
causes, can easily imagine his varied and amusing
experiences.

OVERCOMING DIFFICULTIES.

It became evident that the public were slowly
gaining confidence in the success of our enterprise,
and therefore, we began to purchase our supplies.
Mr. Huntington made out the list, that we might
have the needful articles at the lower mountain depot, early in October, understanding that the trains
could not transport freight for us before that time.

On the 19th of September, word was sent to Professor Hitchcock at Bethlehem, that the mountain trains would stop running on the following day, as the track was to be taken up immediately for repairs, and that no orders had been given by the officers of the company, to afford our expedition any facilities either of transportation or the use of the summit depot ; that this building had been left unfinished, there being only roof and sides without doors or windows ; that the cold weather having set in, it would soon be impossible to run the trains for want of water, etc.   To add to these difficulties the supplies had not all been purchased ; it was uncertain whether sufficient funds could be obtained, and no arrangement had then been made for the use of a telegraph cable.   Under these unpromising circumstances the party at Bethlehem, with the exception of the state geologist, came unanimously to the conclusion that the obstacles in the way were insurmountable, and the expedition must be abandoned for the next winter.   But he said the supplies should all go up the mountain, even if he turned teamster himself, and with a single horse transported them up the carriage road ; Mr. Huntington having expressed a willingness to remain upon the summit all winter even without telegraphic communication with the world below.   The next day, therefore, one of the party went to the railroad station to say that orders were coming from head-quarters to grant the needed facilities, as they must have been delayed by some misunderstanding. Another went to Littleton to borrow a few tons of coal, so that the most essential article to comfort might be sure to reach the railroad in season for transportation to the summit. Professor Hitchcock at the same time went to Boston, and obtained from the officers of the company the necessary permission to use their summit depot during the winter; and immediately transmitted it to the employees. The railway company generously gave us the use of the depot, and transported our supplies over their line to the summit without charge, and regretted that they could not have known earlier of our purpose, so that the house might have been completed. Our thanks are specially due to the engineers, Mr. Charles Aiken and Mr. Kidder, for remaining on the mountain longer than was necessary for their own purposes, to accommodate us.

Immediately after Professor Hitchcock's return, Mr. Huntington went to Boston, to purchase the necessary supplies in connection with Mr. Nelson, and to see that they were forwarded without delay. These necessaries were purchased on credit, and the amounts charged to Professor Hitchcock. They were immediately forwarded and transported to the summit.

UP THE CARRIAGE ROAD.

In spite of all our efforts the telegraphic apparatus sent from Washington, and some other necessary articles, arrived too late for the last train, and these were taken around the mountain in a buggy, partly by Professor Hitchcock and partly by Mr. Huntington, and thence to the summit on the carriage road. The distance traversed by each was nearly eighty miles, over a very muddy and hilly route. The road up the mountain had been closed for the winter, and the fifty or sixty bridges upon it taken up, so that in addition to the labor of climbing, the planks must be relaid. Several days were spent upon the summit in preparing the building for occupation — partitioning off a room, setting up the stoves, laying double-floors, etc. In this we were aided by a carpenter from Berlin Falls. On the eighteenth of October Professor Hitchcock attempted to carry up the last supplies of beef and mutton, but at the Half-way House the wind was blowing at the rate of sixty or seventy miles per hour, and it was not prudent to venture further with a horse. The load was left at the turning point, and was subsequently carried to the summit by Mr. Huntington, who remained on the mountain till the rooms were completed for occupation, the Kerite wire laid, and everything was in readiness for the incoming of the party.   He came down October 22.

A NEW CIRCULAR.

In the latter part of October Professor Hitchcock joined Mr. Nelson for a few days in the work of soliciting funds. A new circular, adapted to the changed circumstances, was prepared, and was widely distributed. In this it was briefly stated that the arrangements for the occupation of the mountain had been completed; the observers, photographers and telegrapher selected; the needful supplies purchased and transported to the summit; a Kerite telegraph wire had been laid over that portion of the route where a common wire could not withstand the wintry blasts and accumulations of ice; that the building had been secured and comfortably furnished, and furthermore that the party intended to establish themselves in their snug eyrie about the twelfth of November.

Reference was made to the approval of the expedition by the War Department, and to a special letter of recommendation signed by Professors B. Pierce, Joseph Winlock, Joseph Lovering, Asa Gray, Alpheus Hyatt, President Runkle, N. B. Shurtleff, and William Claflin.

It was also thought that commerce would be greatly benefited by our daily reports. As the farmer studies the cloud-caps upon high mountains to forecast the weather, so telegraphic reports of the condition of the atmosphere upon the highest summit in eastern America would enable ship-owners to judge of the approach of storms, and escape risk of loss to their vessels by keeping them in a harbor till the danger was past; so too, with fair weather reported from the mountain, vessels could get a day's start of any bad spell of weather, and thus escape great peril.

It was announced that these preparations had been made with the expectation that friends would contribute funds sufficient to meet the expenses. Should the public fail to appreciate the enterprise the burden would fall upon the State Geologist, who had already paid out seven hundred dollars more than the amount of the subscriptions.

This appeal proved to be efficacious, as in consequence of this and other applications, enough funds were secured to pay all the bills of the expedition. It was hoped that there might be a small balance in our favor, so that the observers might preserve some reminder of their wild experiences; but they are all well satisfied that the expedition has been able to meet its obligations without protestation.

THE PHOTOGRAPHERS OF THE EXPEDITION.

On the third of October a letter came from Howard A. Kimball, photographer, of Concord, N. H., asking to be permitted to join the mountain party and take views. Some elegant stereographs, showing what proficiency he had made in his profession, accompanied the letter. According to our original plan the artist of the expedition was Mr. A. F. Clough of Warren, N. H., hence this application was referred to him. Mr. Clough was pleased with it. The two gentlemen concluded to combine their efforts or to form a partnership, and thus go upon the mountain in company. This necessitated their spending a shorter time there, on account of the limited stock of provisions sent up. Mr. Kimball aided in the work of raising funds, adding more than a hundred dollars to our list. Both the photographers made personal pecuniary sacrifices in order to render their branch of our expedition successful. They also endured great hardships upon the mountain, as will appear further on. They have succeeded finely in taking views, as shown in their published stereographs. They have kindly permitted us to copy such as we need for illustrating this volume, the report of our doings.

OUR TELEGRAPHER.

On the third of November the Chief Signal Officer informed us that he would send an instructed operator and observer with a complete set of meteorological instruments to Mount Washington, and requested that one weather report might be forwarded to him daily by telegraph. This report would be bulletined along with those from other stations, and a copy of it be furnished to the principal daily journals in the country. After some delay Sergeant Theodore Smith, U. S. A. started from Washington, and reached the mountain early in December.

The following is an extract from the special order No. 95, brought from Washington : —

WAR DEPARTMENT.

OFFICE OF THE CHIEF SIGNAL OFFICER,
WASHINGTON, D. C., *November* 23, 1870.

*　　*　　*　　*　　*　　*　　*

Sergeant Theodore Smith, Observer, Signal Service, U. S. A., will proceed without delay to Mount Washington, New Hampshire, and report for temporary duty to Professor C. H. Hitchcock, and carry out such orders as he has received personally from this office.

The Quartermaster's Department will furnish the necessary transportation.

By order of the Chief Signal Officer of the Army.

CHARLES M. PYNE,
Captain U. S. Army, Acting Signal Officer and Assistant.
To Prof. C. H. HITCHCOCK, Mount Washington, New Hampshire.

TELEGRAPHING FROM HANOVER.

At the time appointed, November 12, Mr. Huntington promptly climbed the mountain and commenced to take and record the meteorological observations. The other members of the party were delayed by various reasons, partly because all the necessary arrangements had not been completed. One of the last arrangements perfected was the connection of the telegraph wire between Mount Washington and Hanover. In Northern New England, there are two telegraph lines running nearly parallel to each other. One starts from Groveton, New Hampshire, on the Grand Trunk Railway, and proceeds to Concord by way of Lancaster, Littleton, Wells River, Vermont, and Plymouth. At Littleton there is a branch wire extending to the mountain. The other wire alluded to follows the Passumpsic Railroad from Lennoxville, P. Q., to White River Junction. These two wires enter the same building at Wells River. Mr. C. W. Gates, the superintendent of these lines, kindly consented to arrange switches at Wells River and Littleton, so that Hanover and Mount Washington could very easily be connected in one continuous line ; and permission was given to Professor Hitchcock to use this line in the evening for an hour after the business of the company had been attended to. A few

yards of wire were added to the main line in Hanover, and thus there was direct communication from
the summit to Professor Hitchcock's office in Culver Hall, a large building in process of erection for
the mutual benefit of the New Hampshire College
of Agriculture and the Mechanic Arts and Dartmouth College. This was the only room in the
building fitted for occupation, reached by struggling
through piles of lumber, and balancing one's self
upon a single plank placed over perilous depths.
The apparatus used was one of the combination
main line instruments belonging to the Signal Service, together with a register from the Shattuck Observatory. Thus when the storms were raging, the
snow flying, the mercury freezing in the thermometer, and transportation was impossible, there could
be communication between the isolated adventurers
and their friends. The news from the mountain
was exchanged for intelligence from the papers,
almost as soon as they were received in Hanover.

We cannot forbear alluding in this connection to
the assistance rendered our cause by Mr. Field, telegraph operator and postmaster at Hanover. The
evening messages to the mountain were not sent
from Hanover by the regular employé of the telegraph company, but by members of Dartmouth
College who had learned to telegraph for their own
pleasure, or by other persons interested in the ex-

pedition. Among the latter number there was one, profoundly ignorant of the art of telegraphy, who had rashly promised Professor Hitchcock to send and receive messages for him every Monday, Wednesday, and Friday evening throughout the stay of the scientific party upon Mount Washington.

To learn to write Morse's alphabet legibly was a comparatively easy task. Then commenced the stumbling through dark halls, over piles of shavings and timbers, and climbing of broken, rickety stairs, by the light of a dim lantern, the only luminary in Culver Hall, in order to reach " S. O. ; " where, in an arctic atmosphere, corresponding as nearly as possible in temperature to that supposed to exist upon the summit at the same hour, the bewildered amateur undertook to learn how to " adjust," to " switch on," to " switch off," to " call M. W.," and all the other " ways that are dark " in this very mysterious art. At this juncture, Mr. Field came to our aid. He not only invited this telegrapher to send messages from the regular office, but made every effort to render the assumed task an easy one, and that when his time was very fully occupied with his own duties. He read our messages for us. He adjusted the instrument, and explained the various puzzling mysteries of the art. He " switched on " and " switched off " and " called " when things were " contrairy," and made inquiries for us, and, in brief, did everything that he " might, could, would, or should have done " under the circumstances, except to acknowledge the value of his time, or that the presence of comparative strangers evening after evening in his office was an inconvenience. The unskillful telegrapher whom he so kindly assisted, takes this opportunity to acknowledge both, and to thank him for the aid so cheerfully given.

MEMBERS OF THE EXPEDITION.

The complete organization of the expedition is as follows : —

C. H. HITCHCOCK, State Geologist, with office in Hanover, connected by telegraph with the summit of Mount Washington.

J. H. HUNTINGTON, in charge of the Observatory upon the mountain.

S. A. NELSON, Observer.

A. F. CLOUGH and H. A. KIMBALL, Photographers.

THEODORE SMITH, Observer and Telegrapher for the Signal Service.

CHAPTER II.

N the mountainous region parallel to the eastern coast of North America there are two culminating points, if we view the masses in a general way, and overlook some of the valleys of denudation. Commencing with the Gulf of Mexico, the country rises gradually till the highest point is reached on Clingman's Peak, 6,707 feet, in western North Carolina. Then, in going north, there is a descending slope as far as the Hudson River, or to the level of the sea. From this valley northerly the country rises till Mount Washington is reached, 6,293 feet, and there is a descent again to the Gulf of the St. Lawrence. To explain these alternating slopes we must call in the elevating agencies of past geological time. The researches of the New Hampshire Geological Survey indicate that the Mount Washington range was elevated by forces acting in different directions. After the first range with its stratigraphical curves had been formed, another force was exerted which distorted the earlier folds, piling. the strata higher, much like the waves of the ocean when disturbed by conflicting winds.

The *White Mountains* are generally understood by geographers to include all the elevated region north of Winnipiseogee Lake in New Hampshire. Territorially these may be divided into several groups, as the Moosilauke range to the southwest, the Franconia region, the Pemigewasset Mountains, the Mount Washington group, etc. It is the latter portion that claims our attention at the present time. There is an area perhaps thirty miles long and ten miles wide bounded by Israel's and Moose rivers upon the north, Peabody and Ellis rivers on the east, the Saco River on the south and west, of which Mount Washington is the culminating point. Its latitude is 44° 16′ 25″, its longitude 71° 16′ 26″ west from Greenwich, or 1° 0′ 43.99″ longitude east from Hanover.

TOPOGRAPHY OF THE MAIN RANGE.

This area shows a main range with several branches. Starting with Camel's Hump in Gorham, the land quickly rises to Mount Madison 5,365 feet high. Pursuing a course west of south, we see in order Mount Adams, 5,794 feet; Mount Jefferson, 5,714 feet; Mount Clay, 5,553 feet; Mount Washington, 6,293 feet; Mount Monroe,

5,384 feet; Mount Franklin, 4,904 feet; Mount Pleasant, 4,764 feet; Mount Clinton, 4,320 feet; Mount Jackson, 4,100 feet, and Mount Webster, 4,000 feet by estimate. The range is here crossed by the Saco River, and on the other side we have Mount Willey, 4,300 feet, and a long range running to Mount Carrigain.

Of the spurs from the main range there is one at right angles to its axis on the west side, consisting of Mounts Marsh, Dartmouth, Deception, and Cherry Mountain, extending past the White Mountain House. On the opposite side a spur points down toward the Glen House, with steep valleys upon both sides, the Great Gulf to the north and Tuckerman's Ravine on the south. Looking from the summit of Mount Washington, one can make out the outlines of an elevated plateau, from Boott's spur past the summit to Adams and Madison. South from Mount Washington there are two main spurs or mountain ranges, branching from the elevated plateau. The first lies between Dry or Mount Washington River and the Rocky Branch, and we have, beginning at the lower end, Hart's Ledge, Mount Crawford, Mount Resolution, and the Giant's Stairs as parts of the range. Iron Mountain in Jackson is the most prominent peak of the other range between Rocky Branch and Ellis River. The two valleys of Dry River and Rocky Branch are deep and very strongly marked.

MAPS OF THE WHITE MOUNTAINS.

In 1853 a most excellent map of the White Mountains was prepared by the late Professor G. P. Bond of Cambridge, Massachusetts. It was made from original triangulation, and has been the basis for everything that has subsequently appeared. In 1858 another map was published by Harvey Boardman of Griswold, Connecticut, on the scale of about two miles to the inch, somewhat larger than Bond's. Upon this the roads were laid down more accurately, the boundaries of towns were represented, and an attempt was made to show the mountain ridges and peaks by the lines known to engravers as *hashers*. It also contained views of the principal hotels.[1] Since the organization of the Geological Survey of New Hampshire, we have attempted to secure a map more perfect than any now existing. Mr. George L. Vose of Paris, Maine, contributed for this purpose a large number of trigonometrical observations verifying those of Professor Bond, and added new ones in 1869. Surveys of the Fabyan Turnpike and the Mount Washington Carriage Road were made for the Geological Survey by Walling and Gray in 1870, and the State

---

[1] The map by C. H. V. Cavis, prepared for "Eastman's Guide," is upon the scale of five miles to the inch, and covers a wider range of country than either Bond's or Boardman's.

Geologist has spent much time among the mountains in quest of corrections and improvements. As the result of these labors a new map of the White Mountains has been compiled upon the scale of two and a half miles to the inch, and it is believed to be a great improvement over all existing delineations of this interesting region. The one in this volume is a new edition of the one in the " White Hills " by Starr King.

THE MODEL.

Several years since Rev. Dr. Thomas Hill, formerly President of Harvard College, prepared an excellent model in plaster of the White Mountain region upon the basis of Bond's map. It was about eighteen inches square, and showed all the ridges and valleys between Gorham, Conway, and Littleton. In 1870, Professor Hitchcock commenced the preparation of a model of the Mount Washington range and its branches upon the horizontal scale of 139 rods to the inch, and the vertical one of three fourths of an inch to 1,000 feet. It is about five feet long and nearly three feet wide. Though mostly made without special measurements, it is thought to represent the contour of the mountains and valleys better than anything else in existence ; and therefore a sketch of it has been prepared for this report of our winter experiences. It gives a

THE WHITE MOUNTAINS.

bird's-eye view of all the elevations and depressions of the most elevated regions, and, though imperfect — as any model must be without an expense of $10,000 for accurate surveys, — it will give a very much better idea of the shapes of the several mountains than many pages of description.

VARIOUS ALTITUDES.

For the pleasure of many readers, a list of heights of many interesting points among the mountains is here presented. They have been taken mainly from Professor Arnold Guyot's memoir on the "Appalachian Mountain System." The altitudes are above mean tide water.

	Feet.
Gorham Railroad Station .	802.
Glen House .	1,632.
Peabody River, opposite Glen House	1,543.
Summit of ridge between Peabody and Ellis Rivers, in road near Glen Ellis Falls	2,018.
Hotel at Jackson	771.
Road at junction of Saco and Ellis Rivers .	576.
Mountains east of Peabody River: —	
Wildcat Mountain	4,350.
South peak of Mount Carter .	4,830.
North peak of Mount Carter, or Imp Mountain .	4,702.
Mount Moriah .	4,653.
On the main range : —	
Half-way House on Carriage Road, east side of Mount Washington .	3,840.
Limit of trees, north side of Mount Washington	4,150.
Road between Mount Madison and Camel's Hump	1,790.

	Feet.
Lowest ridge between Moose and Israel's Rivers	1,473.
Gap between Mounts Madison and Adams	4,912.
Gap between Mounts Adams and Jefferson	4,939.
Gap between Mounts Jefferson and Clay	4,979.
Gap between Mounts Clay and Washington	5,417.
Gap between Mounts Washington and Monroe	5,100.
Lake of the Clouds	5,100.
Little Monroe, south of Mount Monroe	5,204.
Gap between Mounts Franklin and Pleasant	4,400.
Gap between Mounts Pleasant and Clinton	4,050.

Other localities :—

	Feet.
Cherry Mountain, approximately	3,670.
Cherry Mountain road at summit	2,192.
Mount Deception	2,449.
White Mountain House	1,551.
Gate of Fabyan Turnpike	1,583.
Twin River on Fabyan Turnpike, about	2,083.
Marshfield, about	2,615.
Crawford House	1,920.
Gate of the Notch	1,904.
Willey House	1,335.
Mount Crawford House (Dr. Bemis)	986.
Mouth of Sawyer's River	880.
Upper Bartlett P. O.	664.
South Conway P. O.	450.
North Conway, estimated	492.
Mount Crawford	3,134.
Mount Resolution	3,400.
Giant's Stairs	3,500.
Mount Willard, about	2,570.
Bethlehem Village	1,450.
Bridge over Ammonoosuc (Bethlehem)	1,221.
Profile House, Franconia	1,974.
Carroll House	1,428.

HEIGHT OF MOUNT WASHINGTON.

There have been a great many measurements of the altitude of Mount Washington. Rev. Dr. Cutler estimated it from his first measurement in 1784, at 10,000 feet, with the presumption that the figures were too small. His second observations, in 1804, were placed in the hands of Dr. N. Bowditch, who made out the altitude from them to be 7,055 feet. In 1814 Dr. Bigelow calculated it to be 6,225 feet. . Captain Partridge's observations in 1821, gave 6,234 feet. He gave also the heights of the adjacent peaks : Adams, 5,328 ; Jefferson, 5,058 ; Madison, 4,866 ; Monroe, 4,356 ; Franklin, 4,711. The observations of Dr..C. T. Jackson, in 1840, were quite accurate for the difference in height between Mount Washington and the Notch. Correcting the error for the height of the Notch, his figures would stand 6,303, instead of 6,228, only ten feet in excess of the correct height. Prof. Arnold Guyot, in 1851, from barometrical observations, gives the figures of 6,291 feet. In his memoir on the "Appalachian Mountain System," published in 1861, he has altered these figures to 6,288. In 1853, Capt. T. J. Cram leveled to the summit under the direction of the United States Coast Survey, and reported the height to be 6,293 feet. There have been other measurements, but the last seems to be the most reliable; and we may assume it to be correct until it is proved to be erroneous.

THE ARCTIC CLIMATE.

Observation shows that the climate of any country becomes colder in proportion to the height of the land above the sea. Thus in tropical regions there may be an arctic climate at an altitude of 12,000 or 15,000 feet. Using the formulas given by the best authorities, the climate of Mount Washington corresponds with that of the middle of Greenland, about seventy degrees of north latitude, or twenty-six degrees further north than New Hampshire. The summit is thus shown to be in the arctic zone, and the animal and vegetable life corresponds with that of Labrador and Greenland. The physical character of the mountain, then, shows why it is so interesting a place for a meteorological observatory at all seasons of the year, particularly in the winter. It is an arctic island in the temperate zone, and on account of its great elevation it exhibits also the condition of the atmosphere where the mercury does not rise above twenty-four inches in the barometer. For peculiar interest, therefore, the Mount Washington station is not exceeded by any point within the arctic circle.

BOTANICAL EXPLORATIONS.

The plants of the Alpine regions of the White Mountains are of great interest. Dr. Cutler in 1784 is the first author to speak of their arrangement into zones. Dr. Bigelow in 1816 determined most of the phenogamous plants, while stating many interesting facts concerning the fauna and minerals. Other explorers were Benjamin D. Greene and Henry Little, in 1823. In 1825 William Oakes and Dr. Charles Pickering made very extensive researches among the plants, adding several species never found before. The former continued his explorations the year following and afterward. In 1829 Dr. J. W. Robbins explored the entire range, descending into the Great Gulf and visiting the eastern summits for the first time. Mr. Nuttall before this time, detected several species of great rarity, some of which have hardly been seen since. Mr. Oakes continued his botanical researches for many years, and intended to publish a full account of them.

The most painstaking botanist among the mountains has been Professor Edward Tuckerman of Amherst, Mass. He first visited the mountains in 1837, and has since that period been among them almost as many times as there have been summers. He has devoted special attention to the lichens of this region, or those plants which predominate in the alpine district. In his admirable treatise upon the " Vegetation of the White Mountains," he marks out four regions: First, the *lower forest*, in which are found the hard wood species of trees, the rock maple, the beech, the white and yellow birches. With these are often large white pines, firs, white spruces, the aspen, the witch hazel, and the mountain ash. Secondly, the *upper forest* consists mostly of black spruce and fir, with occasional yellow and canoe birches, Frazer's balsam fir, and a mountain ash. At four thousand feet of altitude these trees are dwarfed, but are very strong, and when close together form a thicket almost impenetrable. Among the plants of the third, or *sub-Alpine region*, are the mountain sandwort, the evergreen cowberry, the Labrador tea, and the mountain bilberry. This seems not to be well characterized. The fourth and highest region is called *Alpine*, and contains many plants peculiar to Labrador and Greenland. There are some fifty or sixty of these, and among them are as many more lowland species which have emigrated to the summit and manage to live there in favorable seasons, though often much dwarfed. The lichens are very conspicuous and beautiful. One, of a sulphur yellow color, is quite noticeable, and is a good indication of the visitor's arrival in the Alpine district. Another is the reindeer moss, a very common article of food for the most useful animal to man in Lapland. The best localities of these arctic plants are in the great gulfs or ravines upon the east side of Mount Washington.

CHAPTER III.

N his chapter upon the " History of the Exploration of the White Hills," published in 1859, Professor Tuckerman has given us an admirable essay eliminating the names of the earlier explorers, and their labors, from conflicting and often imperfect statements. It would appear that Darby Field of Pascataquack, an Irishman, was the first to ascend Mount Washington, accompanied by two Indians. This was in June 1642. The route lay from the Saco up Ellis River nearly to its source, thence up the projection known as Boott's Spur, between Tuckerman's Ravine and Oakes' Gulf. The summit of this spur is near "Bigelow's Lawn," upon the comparatively level tract at the southern base of Washington.

Some authors have given Walter and Robert Neal the credit of first climbing the highest summit in 1631. This statement was made by Dr. Belknap in the earlier editions of his " History of New Hampshire;" but in his edition of 1812 he states that he was in error. Field reported the existence of precious stones, and of " Muscovy glass " or mica. These reports induced him to return a month later, accompanied by others, particularly by Thomas Gorges and Mr. Vines, two magistrates of the province of Sir Fernando Gorges. Except the story of plates of mica forty feet long (!), the account of Field is reliable, and the appearance of the upper mountainous region was very much the same two hundred years since, as it is now. John Josselyn made the ascent probably about 1663 ; and has preserved the traditions of the Indians respecting the early history of the mountains. They seemed to have believed that all the human race were destroyed by a flood save a single pair, who escaped to the mountain top and got beyond the reach of the water. Other traditions represented that the highest summit was the residence of the Great Spirit, who with a motion of the hand could raise a storm and destroy the daring adventurer who should irreverently enter his abode. Hence no Indian dared approach the summit. Their names for the mountains were *Agiochook* in one dialect, and in another *Waumbek-Methna*, signifying *Mountains with snowy foreheads*.

Of later visits we have notices of " ranging " companies who climbed the northwest part of the mountains in April 29, 1728, and on a warm day in

March, 1746.   In July, 1784 the summit was reached by a party of scientific inquirers, consisting of Rev. Manasseh Cutler of Ipswich, Massachusetts, Rev. Daniel Little, of Kennebunk, Maine, and Colonel John Whipple, of Dartmouth (now Jefferson), then the most prominent inhabitant of Coös County. They attempted to measure the height from barometrical observations, but unhappily were unable to confirm their computations by a trigonometrical measurement from the plain below. They made out three zones of vegetation — "first, the woods; second, the bald mossy part; third, the part above vegetation." The small firs in the second zone, they thought, may have been " growing ever since the creation," although not more than three or four inches high. They ascended by one of the upper tributaries of the Ellis River, since called Cutler's River, though the name has become nearly obsolete. In July, 1804, Dr. Cutler climbed the mountains again, in company with Dr. W. D. Peck, and obtained better barometrical observations, as well as a collection of the peculiar Alpine plants.

It is impossible to ascertain with certainty who first proposed to call the highest of these summits Mount Washington.   Dr. Belknap in his " History of New Hampshire," published in 1792, says of it, "it has lately been distinguished by the name of Mount Washington."   He quotes from the manuscript of

Dr. Cutler in another place, the account of the zones of vegetation, where mention is made of " Mount Washington," as if it were well known. As this visit was made in 1784, it is not unlikely that the name was proposed soon after the close of the Revolutionary War, probably by Dr. Cutler's party, of which Drs. Belknap and Fisher were parties, though not to the summit. This is Professor Tuckerman's view.

With the beginning of the present century visitors to the White Mountains increased in number. In 1819 the number averaged ten or twelve annually, and the pioneer settlers began to provide means for their accommodation. In 1821 the first ladies climbed the summit. These were three in number, sisters, — the Misses Austin of Portsmouth, New Hampshire. With a firm determination to obtain a fine prospect, they remained four days near the top in a small stone cabin, until the weather became propitious. In 1840 the first ascent on horseback was made by Abel Crawford, seventy-five years old. Ethan Allen Crawford, and Dr. C. T. Jackson, State Geologist, were also of the party. With additional facilities the number of visitors increased, so that in 1858 it was estimated that five thousand persons annually ascend the various bridle paths. In 1870 the number was estimated at seven thousand. Of these five thousand registered their names at the Tip-top House, and about the same number came up the railroad.

The discovery of the "Notch," by Timothy Nash in 1771, led to the construction of a more convenient road than had before existed between the sea-coast and the extreme northern part of the State. Extensive travelling led to settlement along the route. Of the pioneers, we find first, Abel Crawford and Eleazer Rosebrook. They lived at the base of the "Giant's Grave." Rosebrook brought his family to a log hut at this locality in 1792. In 1803 he built the first public-house about the mountains. The "Willey House," was built in 1793. Abel Crawford married the daughter of Captain Rosebrook and built the house at the foot of Mount Crawford in Hart's location, about thirteen miles distant from the "Giant's Grave."

Ethan Allen Crawford succeeded Captain Rosebrook, and became one of the most noted guides to the summit. He was a giant, being nearly seven feet in height and a prodigy of strength. Many traditions are still current of his skill and strength, both as guide and hunter. The "Notch House" was built for a brother, Thomas J. Crawford, at the foot of the "Elephant's Head," just at the upper entrance to the "Notch." For many years the Mount Crawford House was kept open for the benefit of summer visitors by Mr. Davis, a son-in-law of Abel Crawford ; but in later years it passed into the hands of Dr. S. A. Bemis, who is now the Nestor of the mountains.

In consequence of the discrepancies between the early measurements of the height of Mount Washington, a party of engineers and others from Lancaster visited the whole range between the Notch and Mount Madison in July, 1820, and on a second visit measured their altitudes with a spirit level. The first party consisted of Adino N. Brackett, John W. Weeks, General John Wilson, Charles J. Stuart, Noyes S. Dennison, and Samuel A. Pearson of Lancaster, with Philip Carrigain and E. A. Crawford. Crawford was their pilot and baggage-carrier. They gave names to Mounts Pleasant, Franklin, Monroe, Jefferson, Adams, and Madison, and called the Lake of the Clouds " Blue Pond." This was probably the first party who ever spent the night upon the summit of Mount Washington.

In August, Weeks, Stuart, and Brackett, accompanied by Richard Eastman, spent seven days in leveling to the tops of all these mountains from Lancaster. For five of these days they were attended by Amos Legro, Joseph W. Brackett, and Edward B. Moore.

Of the prominent peaks, Mount Clinton received its name from some undiscoverable source, certainly before 1837. Abel Crawford called it Bald Hill.

Mounts Clay and Jackson were named by Mr. Oakes. This gentleman was with Professor Tuckerman, and sent up his guide Amasa Allen to build a fire on the top of the south spur of Clinton, and thus with a fiery baptism the mountain was christened Jackson. Mount Willard was named from Mr. Sidney Willard of Boston ; and it is probable that the name of Mount Webster was proposed by Mr. Willard for the peak known to earlier visitors as Notch Mountain. Lower down the Saco, Mounts Crawford and Resolution, as well as the Giant's Stairs, received names from Dr. S. A. Bemis. The names of Tuckerman's Ravine, Oakes's Gulf, and Bigelow's Lawn, were given in honor of three eminent botanists who had particularly distinguished themselves in the study of the White Mountain flora, to three fine localities of plants as well as marked topographical features. It is difficult to ascertain the origin of many of the names of natural objects about the mountains. Dr. Bemis has perhaps applied more appellations than any other person to these features. He has been acquainted with all the pioneers, and has for many years resided in Hart's Location. Other names have been given by chance visitors, and preserved by usage among guides.

SUMMIT OF MOUNT WASHINGTON.
(The Depot and Summit House.)

HOUSES ON THE SUMMIT.

Soon after the completion of a rude bridle-path in 1819 by Ethan Crawford, it was perceived that a house of some sort was needed upon the summit, where visitors could spend the night. Hence Mr. Crawford constructed a stone cabin near the top of Mount Washington, by the side of a spring. In this was spread an abundance of soft moss for beds, and thus travellers could be enabled to view the setting and rising of the sun. After awhile a small stove was brought up, with an iron chest and a long roll of sheet lead. The chest was the receptacle for the camping blankets, — bear and hedgehog-proof, — and the lead was the register for visitors. Every winter this house was seriously damaged. The roof would be blown away, and the stones fall down from the walls, the chest and stove remaining sadly rusted. Finally at the great storm of August 27, 1826, when the Willey family were destroyed by an avalanche, this cabin, with the iron chest and the blankets, were also swept down the steep slope and lost. A party had taken possession of the building for the night, but were terrified by the violence of the storm, and had hastened down the mountain just in time to save their lives.

In 1852, J. S. Hall and L. M. Rosebrook built the Summit House on the very top of the mountain. It is twenty-four by sixty-four feet, quite low, with very thick walls of stone firmly cemented together, and bolted down to the solid rock. Over the roof are four strong cables. This house has now stood for nearly twenty years.

A year later the Tip-top House was built by Samuel F. Spaulding & Co. It is twenty-eight by eighty-four feet, and was built in the same substantial manner as the other. It had originally a deck roof, upon which visitors could stand and secure better views than from the ground. As shown in one of our views the roof is now sharp pointed, and it is not easy for most persons to climb to the ridgepole and remain there in comfort long enough to enjoy the scenery. In the rear of the main rooms of these houses are small sleeping apartments, best compared with the state-rooms of a steamer in respect to size, and furnished with very comfortable beds. The ceiling is made of cotton cloth, and the walls covered with boards and then papered. The windows are in deep recesses on account of the great thickness of the walls.

These two houses were originally under different management. For the past twelve years they have been leased by the proprietor of the Alpine House in Gorham, and many thousand people have been entertained in them. It is probable that much more commodious quarters will soon be prepared for visitors. The depot is the latest building that has been erected upon the summit. This is shown in one of our figures in its wintry aspect.

There has been a controversy concerning the ownership of the land upon the summit of Mount Washington. In the early legislation of New Hampshire respecting the unoccupied lands of the State, little attention was paid to exact boundaries; consequently each of the two parties claiming the summit, has reason to believe it to be included within their limits. Mr. Bellows, of Exeter, owns the land upon the east side, and was the party in possession till about fifteen years ago, when his tenants were ejected by the sheriff acting for Coe & Pingry, of Bangor, Maine, and Salem, Massachusetts. Probably $25,000 have been spent already in contesting the matter of ownership before the courts.

HOUSES AT THE BASE OF THE MOUNTAIN.

The first good public house for summer visitors was built on the Giant's Grave, and came into the hands of Mr. Fabyan. This was destroyed by fire about twenty years since, and has never been rebuilt. The White Mountain House was built by Mr. Rosebrook, a descendant of the pioneer of that name, about thirty years since. The Notch House, kept by T. J. Crawford, is no longer in existence,

but its place has been more than made good by the
large and well kept establishment, a quarter of a
mile further north, known as the Crawford House.
Upon the east side, is the Glen House, at the lower
end of the Carriage Road, kept by J. M. Thompson till his sudden death in 1869, and offered for
sale in 1871 by his heirs. This is the largest house
near Mount Washington, and can easily accommodate five hundred guests at one time.

CASUALTIES UPON THE MOUNTAIN.

Several persons have lost their lives upon Mount
Washington, generally in consequence of neglecting
the advice of guides. The first was an English
baronet, named Strickland. He went up from the
Notch late in October, 1851. Disregarding the advice of his guide, he pushed on to the summit. He
seems to have fallen down precipitous places several times, and finally to have perished from exhaustion, probably in less than twelve hours after
he started.

On the 24th of September, 1855, Miss Lizzie
Bourne of Kennebunk, Maine, perished within
thirty rods of the summit. With an uncle and
cousin she climbed the mountain on foot; but after
reaching the Half-way House, the clear sky disappeared; they became enveloped in a thick cloud,
and strong winds met them in front. Not knowing

their nearness to the summit, they were compelled to shelter themselves behind a few rough stones, and Miss Bourne was not strong enough to survive the shock.

August 7, 1856, Benjamin Chandler of Wilmington, Delaware, started from the Glen House for the summit late in the afternoon. It was rainy, windy, and very cold. He was about seventy-five years of age. He seems to have wandered from the path, but no one knows how long he survived. His remains were not found for more than a year, when they were accidentally discovered about half a mile east of the summit.

DR. BALL'S EXPERIENCE.

A severer exposure was that of Dr. B. L. Ball, of Boston, the last of October, 1855. This gentleman walked from the Glen House to the Half-way House, while workmen were engaged in building the Carriage Road. The mountain was covered with clouds, and after climbing some distance above the " Ledge " he returned to the camp and spent the night with the laborers. The next morning the clouds seemed about breaking, and he started with the intention of reaching the summit if possible. The rain was changed to sleet and snow, and the temperature fell very much. Though very uncomfortable, Dr. Ball believed himself to be near the summit, and struggled on, understanding that he could find provisions and shelter in one of the houses there. His description of the storm is well appreciated by our party : —

" I could not have believed that the storm could be more violent than it had been. Yet here it was more furious than ever. It now had the full sweep of the mountain top, the highest point of the whole group, of the loftiest mountain for hundreds of miles around. If ten hurricanes had been in deadly strife with each other, it could have been no worse. The winds, as if locked in mortal embrace, tore along, twisting and whirling, and mingling their roaring with the flinty rattling of the snow grains in one confused din."

It is not clear that Dr. Ball reached the summit. Yet persons sometimes reach the summit without knowing it. An incident of this sort is related by Mr. Noyes, of Boston. One cloudy morning he was standing in the door of the Summit House, when he thought he heard the footsteps of some one approaching. He listened, and soon discerned in the fog, the form of a man. He watched him, and saw him pass the house. Thinking the man might be bewildered, Mr. Noyes followed him, and on coming up inquired : " Which way are you going, sir ? "

" *Going?* I am going to the Summit House, if I can find it."

"How far do you expect to travel, to reach it?" inquired Mr. Noyes.

"Well, I don't know. I have been tugging on for the last hour, expecting to find it. They told me it was only a few miles along; and I should think I had already been travelling fifteen!"

"But the course you are on now," said Mr. Noyes, "will take you over the other side to the Crawford House. You have already passed the Summit House." And the man was led back, astonished to find he had passed one house ten rods from the path, and the other but six.

Dr. Ball lost his way, and when night came on he crawled behind some stunted bushes, and with an umbrella contrived to shelter himself a little from the wind. All the next day he wandered about in the snow unable to find the way down, and the second night was spent in the same place. The following day he was found by a party of men very weak but in good spirits. He had been for sixty hours exposed to the severe winter weather of the mountain, and had had no sleep for eighty, yet he managed to keep himself alive without food or water. His health was somewhat injured by this exposure, but there is no case on record in the annals of Mount Washington experience, where any person has survived such a terrible exposure as Dr. B. L. Ball.

MOUNT WASHINGTON OBSERVATORY.

In 1854, Timothy Eaton of Jefferson, erected upon the summit a sort of tower about forty feet high, which was called an observatory. It was so arranged that with a rope and gearing, a party of eight persons could be elevated to its summit, and have a much better view than from the top of the mountain. This tower was very much like the derricks used in boring wells for petroleum in Pennsylvania. It cost about six hundred dollars. It did not prove to be a profitable investment, and was soon abandoned, not a trace of it remaining in three years after its erection.

EARLIER WINTER VISITS TO THE SUMMIT.

Fear of accident has prevented most people from attempting to climb Mount Washington in the winter. In the month of November, 1855, a month after Dr. Ball's experience, another party succeeded in reaching the top in safety, and in enjoying a good view. One of the most hardy men in the party that rescued Dr. Ball, said that with a friend he attempted to make the ascent in February; but when they arrived within a mile of the summit they were obliged to turn back almost frozen.

Two successful attempts to reach the summit in winter previous to 1870 are on record. The first was made by Mr. Osgood of Lancaster, December 7, 1858, with a small party of friends. He was an officer of the law, and went up to serve a legal process upon the property there. His ascent was thus described in the " Coös Republican : "

" Arrived at the summit, the view is represented as having been sublime beyond the power of description, Mr. Osgood averring that in his many trips on the mountain he never beheld so extended and yet grand and terrific a view as burst upon them on that lonely height. Measures were immediately taken to enter the houses, which, as they were covered with snow, was a labor of time. Unable to obtain ingress at the doors, they forced their way in through the windows, on which the frost had formed a foot and a half in thickness. The walls and all the furniture were draped with some four inches of frost, and the air was biting in the extreme. It was like a tomb, and a lamp was necessary in this snow cavern, to enable the party to distinguish the surrounding objects. As delay was dangerous in the extreme, and having perfected their legal duty, the two prepared to return. Upon emerging from the houses they beheld to the southwest a cloud, rapidly increasing in volume, and rolling on toward them. When first seen it was small in magnitude, but it increased in size with alarming velocity, soon spreading over the entire south.

They knew it was a frost cloud, and that to be caught in its folds would probably be fatal, and they hastened to avoid it. They had just entered the woods, at the base of the ledge, when it came upon them. So icy and penetrating was its breath, that to have encountered its blinding, freezing power on the unprotected height, would have been to have perished with it as a pall to cover them. The party reached the glen in safety, and were heartily welcomed by their friends, who, well knowing the danger attending this never before accomplished feat, awaited them with much anxiety."

The other ascent was made by a party from Lancaster, February 11, 1862. A record of their visit is preserved in a stereograph, both on a card and as a transparency, sold about the mountains. The view is of the interior of the Summit House, showing a small pile of snow upon a bedstead and other objects that had drifted in through a crack in the building. The following account of this visit was written by J. H. Spaulding, a member of the party : —

"ASCENT OF MOUNT WASHINGTON IN FEBRUARY.

" Early in the morning of February 10, 1862, F. White, C. C. Brooks, and J. H. Spaulding, all of Lancaster, N. H., started from that place for the top of Mount Washington. At eight o'clock the same evening we started up the Mountain from the Glen House.

"The moon was shining brightly, as with ample packs and provisions we slowly walked up the carriage road on snow-shoes. The night was still, and highly excited as we were by the thoughts of the adventure before us, the spring of our shoes on the glittering crust seemed music to us, while the tree-shadows thrown across our path, and the white winding road contrasting with the evergreen thickets, combined to make our night walk quite varied in incidents; and it was past midnight when we arrived at ' The Ledge.' The great barn built there last season, we found in ruins, and this, with the fire-scathed trees, boldly relieved by moonlight, the glittering ledge, and the dark old shanty in the background, combined to present a very wild picture.

"At the shanty we kindled a fire, took a lunch, and upon an old straw bed, laid on a snow-drift, drowsed until daybreak.

"At sunrise we started for the ' Tip Top,' without snow-shoes. Soon began the labor of advancing by cutting steps in the ice. When we halted to rest we noticed the stillness that reigned around us; not a breath of air, not a sound of running water, — for beneath a wintry robe every waterfall was chained.

" How like blank solitude was this death-like silence !   Yet its loneliness was pleasantly enlivened by the wonderful and wide-spread landscape beneath and around us, that afforded ample scope for admiration. Far away, and near at hand, arose glittering peaks. A thousand pyramids of smoke hung above dark objects, that were roughly set in wide white margins.

" What a host of hopes, fears, joys, and sorrows were grouped in these homes below ! But we will not speculate, for the task before us is to be accomplished slowly and carefully.

" About five miles up, we came to a wide field of ice, where we could not possibly advance without cutting deep steps.   It is not fiction to declare that, as the pieces of ice went whirling down like a heavy shower of hail, at least eight hundred feet below, a shudder, such as teaches poor mortality its weakness, came over us.

" One false step or careless motion, in such a place, would have sent us down, down, and given us a name with other victims of rashness. About six miles up, we came to a deep drift that covered many acres ; and here, not being able to follow the road, we wandered for a long way over snow thrown up and hardened in fanciful wavy shapes. At one place we climbed through the tops of a dwarf growth, that had the appearance of a buried wilderness.

" Here we took a lunch, and in a brisk south wind that had been rising for the last half hour, found the temperature 27° above zero.

" Looking towards Mount Carter, we beheld a long line of black storm-clouds with rainbow tinted borders, whirling wildly over, and filled with fear for the coming night, up we hastened, — yet gained our object slowly, for at one time, when I had slipped down, I looked, and both of my companions were down too; but remembering the old adage that ' misery loves company,' I kept silent.

" As we approached the Tip-top a heavy black cloud was whirling over; and as the wind with a roar like thunder drove the wintry mass toward us, we became enveloped in its embrace, and soon the snow and frost had so whitened, that perchance old winter was never better personated than by us.

" Words are a very imperfect medium by which to picture the scene that the Tip-top presented. The two houses stand out in bold relief, and every rock-heap and great rocks about the summit, are now to be seen through a thick covering of glittering ice. Curious leaves of snow stand out from the jagged parts on the northerly side, in all the imaginable and fanciful shapes that the frost has ever pictured on the window glass. For the last half mile below the top, we could distinctly see through the ice and snow the wheel tracks made in the carriage road last season ; and with the exception of now and then a deep drift, the whole mountain summit shows its rocks. There is a great drift at the southerly end of the two houses, and hardened snow has leveled up the irregular top so that with the exception of the *eternal* wind, it is comfortable walking on the crusted or ice-pointed snow.

" The tops of both houses are thickly coated with solid ice, — rough and pointed in all imaginary shapes. We walked up on to the drift, broke away ice from the southerly gable-end window of the 'Summit House,' and taking out a window entered the attic, where, after removing the snow, we brought up, from the darkness and icy confusion of a lower room, a stove, got some wood from the Tip-top House, kindled a fire, and piling around our little stove a barricade of mattresses, prepared to pass the night.

" The heavy wind swept by like thunder, and we slept.

" Two days' labor and excitement, with our midnight walk to the 'Ledge,' had imposed quite a tax upon our powers of endurance, and we heeded not the tempest that was gathering, till late in the morning we found our habitation in a wild, thick storm. Language cannot paint the hopes and fears that struggle in the mind at such a time. But to make the best of our condition, we prepared for a siege, and looked about.

"The interior of both houses we found much deranged by the winter storm. Snow and ice, from three inches to five feet deep, lay piled in all directions, the furniture being most curiously set in feathery white casings.

"In the bar-room we noticed a spade which was cased in clear ice ; and in one place a little cord, suspended from the roof, had assumed the appearance of a glass tube some two inches thick and two feet long. The cloth roofing and wall paper is in many rooms torn down, while fancy snow-wreaths and icicles are all around upon the walls and roof. The darkened windows, with the thick covering without, combined with the ceaseless roar of the wind, gave the whole scene a chilling air of desolation.

"To conclude without longer taxing the reader's patience. We stayed two days and two nights on the top of Mount Washington ; experienced the effect of a wild snow-storm that drove by us for thirty-six hours, had one of the most magnificent sunrise scenes that imagination can picture ; saw the sun go down in a vast snow-bank ; saw moonlight upon a hundred glittering peaks; found the most extreme cold while there indicated at 5° be-

low zero; returned to the Glen in a thick snow
storm, and now feel perfectly satisfied with our
trip.

"We were remarkably well satisfied with the
weather, and were very lucky about climbing over
the ice-clad rocks. Should others attempt to go
up among the clouds, for their own sake they
should go thoroughly prepared for the worst.

"An iron-pointed staff, with an axe, and plenty
of food and clothing, are indispensable."

Our expedition, therefore, was undertaken in the
face of all previous experience among the mountains, excepting our own the previous season on
Moosilauke. Failure was universally predicted.
Indeed, it was commonly reported in Bethlehem
and Littleton, in January and February, that one
of the party had been frozen to death, and was at
the summit embalmed in ice, waiting for the advent
of the railroad train, so that he might be taken to
some cemetery below. But we have clearly proved
to the world that it is possible for men to spend the
winter upon this frozen peak, and not to be deprived
of a weekly mail. So much finer are the winter
views from the summit than those of any other season of the year, that we anticipate shortly the occupation of one of the hotels for the benefit of visitors

in all months of the year, and should not be greatly
surprised to learn that the engine had made its way
through the drifts, in some favorable season, to the
very highest accessible point.

CHAPTER IV.

ROM a distance, the routes toward the White Mountains are quite numerous, and their respective advantages are fully set forth in the guide books. There are now three ways of ascending Mount Washington from below: two from the west and one from the east; or a railway, a carriage road, and a bridle path.

The first path to the summit was marked out by Ethan Crawford in 1819. The visitors by this time had become so numerous that a path was indispensable, at least as far as to the beginning of the Alpine region. Its construction immediately increased the number of visitors. This path commenced at the Giant's Grave, following the Ammonoosuc Valley to the base of Washington, and then passing up a ridge or spur of the mountain. At some period there was a path branching off from this to the summit of Mount Pleasant. In 1840, the bridle path was cut from the Notch over Mounts Clinton, Pleasant, Franklin, and Monroe to Washington. This is nine miles in length.

Soon afterwards a longer bridle-path was cut from the Mount Crawford House, in Hart's Location, to the summit of Mount Washington, by Mr. Davis. This passed first over Mount Crawford, and from thence along the east side of Dry- or Mount Washington River. It is now wholly disused.

Still later, the path between the Fabyan House and "Cold Spring," or the base of Washington, was enlarged, and became a carriage road. This was in use, though kept in poor repair, till it was superseded by the "Fabyan Turnpike" in 1866. The earlier road lay mostly upon the south side of the river, below what is now known as Twin River. Cold Spring is perhaps a quarter of a mile higher up the mountain than the lower depot, or what is called "Marshfield" upon the guide-board at the entrance of the turnpike.

MOUNT WASHINGTON CARRIAGE ROAD COMPANY.

In June, 1853, a company was chartered to build a carriage road from the Glen to the Tip Top House, with a capital stock of fifty thousand dollars. It was organized September 1, 1853, by the choice of president, secretary, and directors. The length of this road is a little less than eight miles. Its course is indicated upon our map. The work of its construction commenced in 1855. By its original design, the road was to be sixteen feet wide, macadamized, and to have a protection-wall three feet high in dangerous places. The road was completed as far as the "Ledge," or half way, in 1856. In 1861 it was completed to the summit. It is nearly double the length of the old bridle-path, as the grade must necessarily be much less. The average grade is twelve feet in one hundred, and the steepest is about sixteen feet in one hundred, two and one half miles from the Glen. The road was commenced under the superintendence of C. H. V. Cavis, engineer. The road is kept in excellent repair, and the rates of toll are not burdensome, considering the expense of building. There is a small house half-way up the mountain, at the point where the trees terminate and the arctic zone commences. But the greatest triumph of engineering skill is upon the west side of the mountain, and is what is sometimes fancifully called the *Sky Railway.*

MOUNT WASHINGTON RAILWAY.

During the season of summer travel, steam cars run daily (Sundays excepted) over the *Mount Washington Railway,* an iron track running up the west side of the mountain to the very summit, a distance of two miles and thirteen sixteenths, and an ascent of 3,625 feet. There is a small collection of buildings at the lower end of the railroad, seven miles from the White Mountain House, and twenty-four from Littleton.

MOUNT
WASHINGTON
RAILWAY

The first effort in the direction of ascending Mount Washington by steam power seems to have been made by Mr. Sylvester Marsh, formerly of Chicago, Illinois, and Roxbury, Massachusetts, but now residing at Littleton, New Hampshire, and the president of the railway company. He invented the special contrivances needed to adapt motive machines to a highly inclined plane.

It was found very difficult at the outset to convince mechanicians and capitalists of the feasibility of this ascending railway. Even an inspection of the working models failed to give much satisfaction. One prominent railroad manager is said to have thrown aside the early letters of Mr. Marsh as the writing of a maniac. The work was commenced, relying chiefly upon his own private resources, and little encouragement was afforded by capitalists till an engine was actually running over a portion of the route.

Application was made to the Legislature of New Hampshire in 1858 to grant a charter for a steam railway from their bases to the summits of Mounts Washington and Lafayette. A model of the invention was exhibited, and it was stated that the petitioner and his friends would assume the expense of the enterprise. The petition was received with derision. An amendment was offered by the " wit of the house," that a charter be granted for a railroad from the summit of Mount Washington to the moon! The Legislature, however, after sufficient deliberation, charitably granted a charter, allowing the cars to run for twenty years, or a longer time if not then abrogated, in accordance with the usual formulas of railroad laws in New Hampshire. It is also provided that it must keep a proper distance from the carriage road coming up from the Glen House, either the constructed or surveyed route, except by consent of the owners of the latter. The actual work of construction did not commence for a number of years.

THE FABYAN TURNPIKE.

As a preliminary operation, it was found desirable to build a new turnpike from the stage road near the White Mountains to the point where the ascent by rail should commence. Work upon it began in April, 1866. It is located along the Ammonoosuc River for six miles, starting at the old Fabyan stand, about five miles northwest of the Crawford House. The route has nearly the same objective point as the older carriage road, but at the beginning it lies along the north bank of the river. The toll-gate is upon what was formerly called the "Giant's Grave," a long mound of river gravel, deposited in past millenniums by the Ammonoosuc, though at first by some geologists fancied to have been made by the reaction of oceanic waves against the hill-side. A company has been formed to erect a commodious hotel here, but, for some reason not made known to the public, the work has been delayed. The old "Giant's Grave" has been entirely removed, much to the regret of the community, especially as the necessity for the expensive grading is not apparent. Just within the toll-gate are the graves of some of the Crawford family and others. The road passes over steep hills of gravel, and then through the woods north of the river to the "Upper Falls." These continue for about three hundred feet, the water falling about fifty feet and winding through a narrow, zigzag gorge. After further windings in the forest, the road arrives at "Twin River," so called because a tributary runs parallel to the Ammonoosuc for a considerable distance, making the stream double. The bridge is on the west border of a clearing of perhaps one hundred acres, called "Twin River Farm." This clearing is tolerably free from boulders, and is quite productive, and the next summer's visitors may be fortunate enough to taste of the early vegetables grown here. This spot is about five hundred feet above the White Mountain House, and it is spoken of as possibly the site of the future junction of the Mount Washington Railway with the extension of the Boston, Concord, and Montreal from near Littleton. The land rises more rapidly above Twin River, so that ordinary locomotives cannot pass this point. A small dwelling-house has already been erected here.

After two miles more of travelling through the woods up " Winding Hill " we reach the end of the turnpike. Here are a few buildings, consisting of a hotel, two large barns, one or two dwelling-houses, a steam saw-mill, and the various edifices necessary for the accommodation of a railroad. The village is inhabited in the winter by a party of lumbermen. The turnpike is kept in excellent repair, the tolls being sufficient to keep it in good condition. Its cost was upwards of $10,000.

THE RAILROAD.

The railroad was commenced in May, 1866. It starts from a point 2,668 feet above the level of the sea, and 3,625 below the summit. The distance traversed is two miles and thirteen sixteenths. The average grade is 1,300 feet to the mile, the maximum being 1,980 feet to the mile, or thirteen and a half inches to the yard. There are nine curves on the line, varying from 497 to 945 feet radius. The first year the road was built a distance of about a quarter of a mile. In 1867, the track was extended to " Waumbek Junction," a distance of one mile and eight rods. Work was resumed May 7, 1868, and in eighty-four working days it had advanced more than a mile, or to the top of " Jacob's Ladder." The work was continued till the cold weather set in, and the last few rods of the track were laid in July, 1869.

The road was built under the superintendence of J. J. Sanborn of Franklin, New Hampshire. The cost of the road has already exceeded $120,000, and when the depots, turn-outs, and rolling stock are fully completed, it will reach about $150,000. About 800,000 feet of sawed lumber have been used in its construction, all of which was cut at the steam mill near the depot.

The track consists of three rails, the outer four feet seven and one half inches apart, which sustain the principal weight of the rolling stock, the inner a *cog-rail*, which is the indispensable peculiarity of this railway. All three of the rails rest upon timbers laid lengthwise upon sawed ties three and a half feet apart. The lateral timbers were originally covered by a narrow strip of iron, but these are rapidly giving way to a small T rail of more modern appearance. The central rail is four inches wide, and is surmounted by two pieces of wrought angle iron, each twelve feet long, three inches wide, and three eighths of an inch thick. These strips are placed upon their edges, parallel to each other, and are connected by strong iron pins an inch and a half in diameter, and four inches apart from centre to centre. It may be likened to a ladder fastened to a wide plank. This cog-rail is held down by spikes and flanges. The teeth of the driving-wheel of the engine play into the spaces between the bolts, and as it revolves the whole engine is made to move, resting upon the outer rail. The operation is practically one cog-wheel working into another. These cog-rails have cost about two dollars per foot delivered at the foot of the mountain.

THE ENGINE.

At the first view of the engine, one is reminded of a pile-driver. The boiler is upright, tubular, and is bolted firmly to the frames. There is a covering for the engineer, and a tender is attached for storing water and fuel, as in ordinary railroad engines. The driving-shaft is connected with two cylinders, with a crank shaft geared into the centre so as to reduce the speed and multiply the power. A twenty-four inch gear works into a six-inch gear, and the engine makes four revolutions to one of the driver. Thus the contrivances in this mountain engine are adapted to develop power at the expense of the speed. Force may also be required at times to hold the train at rest upon a high grade. When moving, the engine always takes the down-hill end of the train. In ascending, a strong wrought-iron "dog" works into a wheel rolling on the cog-rail, preventing the train from falling back a single inch. The accompanying sketch will give a good idea of the engine.

The contrivances for stopping the train are also ingenious and peculiar. First is the *friction brake*, consisting of an iron band extending around each wheel, tightened at will. Second is the power of reversing the driving wheel. Next there are *atmospheric brakes* upon each side of the cars. Their application is so successful that a platform or passenger car may be detached from the engine and lowered by itself, being completely under the control of the brakeman. The mechanics who came up in 1866 and 1868 to witness the operation of the engine, satisfied themselves perfectly of the adaptedness of these atmospheric brakes to their office. These brakes enable the train to descend without the use of steam. There are in all five or six ways of stopping the trains.

Notwithstanding the perfection of these contrivances, many persons apprehend that there is a liability to serious disasters. Such may have their fears removed by recalling the occurrence of July 29, 1869. When the train was descending " Jacob's Ladder," the steepest grade upon the whole road, an unusual noise was heard beneath the engine. The engineer signaled the brakeman to stop the train, but the warning was not noticed at first.

The signal was quickly repeated, and in an instant the brake was applied, and the train stopped. It appeared that the axle of the driving wheel had broken. Such a casualty upon an ordinary locomotive is of a very serious nature, and usually involves the destruction of the train. But this mountain train was stopped in an instant, and the detached wheels scarcely changed their positions, while no very sensible jar was experienced by the passengers. This occurrence has demonstrated that the train is completely under the control of the engineer; for a more serious accident, or one in a more dangerous position could not have happened, yet no injuries were received by any one. Hence so long as the track is kept in good condition, no one need be apprehensive of danger in travelling over the Mount Washington Railway.

The first engine brought to the mountain was built by Campbell, Whittier, and Company, of Roxbury, Mass., at a cost of $3,000. It weighs about four tons, and is rated at twenty-five horse-power. Three new ones (see the figure) have been built by Walter Aiken, of Franklin, N. H., each weighing six and a half tons, and rated at about fifty horse-power; but on account of the gearing they are practically two hundred horse-power. The carriage for passengers resembles a horse-car, though longer, with a roof, side windows, and doors at the ends. There is an aisle through the centre, and seats are provided for forty-eight persons. In the first cars used, the seats were swung so as to secure for them a horizontal position upon all the grades. Walking through the car is like travelling up and down the roof of a building. Some of the cars have the sides open, and can be used only when the weather is sure to be warm, and the wind is not boisterous.

THE ROUTE.

The lower depot is upon the west bank of the Ammonoosuc, at the end of the turnpike. It is a plain wooden edifice about sixty feet long, with two stories. The stream is crossed by trestle-work about fifteen feet high, and the track commences with the grade of seventeen hundred feet to the mile, nearly as steep as upon " Jacob's Ladder." Place the end of a ladder thirty feet long upon a fence ten feet high, and an adequate idea of the inclination of the railway at its commencement will be exhibited to us. This steep incline does not continue more than three hundred feet. At three quarters of a mile is the first water station. The water comes from a spring very near the track, a little beyond " Cold Spring," which affords a delightful halting place for pedestrians. Before reaching " Waumbek Junction " the grade becomes steeper again. The " Junction " is one mile and eight rods in distance, and 1,242 feet higher than the starting point. The name is derived from the intersection here of the old Fabyan and Waumbek bridle-paths. At the Junction is a small unused building and a water-tank. Up to this point the road is nearly straight, and a wide path has been cut for it through the forest. Just beyond there are curves in the track, the trees begin to be dwarfed, and very shortly there is a cut through a ledge of andalusite gneiss, the first rock passed over in the ascent. The railway also intersects the Fabyan bridle-path just above Waumbek Junction and at the foot of " Jacob's Ladder."

This latter appellation was originally applied to a zigzag portion of the Fabyan path over a steep projection of the mountain. It now relates to a portion of the railroad in the neighborhood, a long trestle-work, at one point thirty feet high, and with an inclination of more than one in three for three hundred feet. This structure is built as strongly as any similar work upon an ordinary railroad which has to sustain a weight many times greater. Its elevation above the ground, the steep grade, the abrupt change in the vegetation from trees to lichens, the impressive views of the valleys, and commonly the first indications of the powerful winds of the upper air, forcibly arrest the attention of the passengers, especially as every upward train stops at the tank to receive an additional supply of water. This tank is 2,800 feet above the starting point and is filled from springs higher up the mountain, the water being conveyed by lead pipes several hundred feet.

Above Jacob's Ladder the inclination is not very steep, there being only about eight hundred feet of ascent, in the remaining distance of more than a mile. The main ridge between Mounts Clay and Washington is soon reached, and the traveller can look down a thousand feet into the "Gulf of Mexico," or the deep chasm out of which rises the West Branch of Peabody River, one of the tributaries of the Androscoggin. The fourth and last of the water-tanks is placed at a level of 3,132 feet above the depot. The further ascent is gradual, the broad shoulder of the mountain presenting the characteristic features of arctic desolation, — a wide expanse of large angular blocks of schist and granite, severed from the now concealed ledges by the freezing agencies of centuries. Between the fragments may be seen clumps of saxifrages, sandworts, and reindeer moss, the same species of plants which enliven the barren wastes of Labrador and Greenland. As far as the upper limit of trees, boulders that have been transported by the glacial drift from more northern summits are common. They rapidly diminish in number and size upon that point, and have not been seen far above the fourth water-tank, or above an altitude of 5,800 feet. The last landmark of interest along the railway is the " Lizzie Bourne " monument, thirty rods from the summit.

During the height of the season (Sundays excepted) double trains will run up the Mount Washington railway, from the middle of June to the first of October. The up-trains pass over the distance in ninety minutes, or at the rate of two miles per hour, stopping to take in water at each of the four tanks. The descent is accomplished in less time, as there is no occasion to stop for water on the way down. One needs to ascend two or three times before the sense of danger is entirely dissipated, so that he can appreciate and enjoy the novel conditions of the journey.

SLIDING DOWN HILL.

The employees of the company often amuse themselves by sliding down the railway upon a board. There are two ways of arranging this vehicle of conveyance. The simplest and safest is to place the board across the central rail, and the person sitting upon it checks his course with his feet, one upon each side of the rail, striking against the ties, forty inches apart. The body must lean backwards a little, else an occasional irregularity in the rail will stop the progress of the board, and the passenger will be thrown off, at the risk of breaking a limb. By the other method the board, perhaps a yard long, has two narrow strips nailed beneath, so that it cannot slip off the rail, and the experimenter can put his feet upon it, using short sticks as brakes to diminish the speed. The board does not fit so closely to the rail as in the first instance, so that there is less danger from a sudden stop ; but there is danger that the brakes may become unmanageable. By the first method a vast amount of muscular energy is demanded in the thighs, and those who try it, will have occasion to remember their journey for days afterwards, whenever attempting to walk. Persons have been known to slide the whole distance in ten minutes, but strangers are advised to avoid these " new methods." Our figure illustrating the laying of the Kerite wire shows how the slope may be easily descended.

OTHER MOUNTAIN RAILWAYS.

It is not a new idea to use a cog-wheel upon a railway, as the first road in England where steam was applied to locomotion, was constructed with notched rails. Ordinary railroads do not require them, as there is sufficient friction between the rail and the wheels for all practical purposes. There is a railway over Mount Cenis, between France and Italy, which uses a different method for climbing high grades. The power is obtained by a " V friction rail " — occupying a central position, just as on Mount Washington. The rail is shaped like two V's, $\underset{\wedge}{\vee}$, and two horizontal wheels running in the grooves give rise to sufficient friction to draw the trains. The grades are not over four hundred feet to the mile. The European method would certainly not be applicable to the inclination of the American road, while it may answer very well for so small a grade as that employed in the Alps. It is stated that a road is in process of construction in South America, up the Andes, modeled after Mr. Marsh's inventions.

RAILWAY UPON MOUNT RHIGI.

When our American railway was in process of construction it was visited by a Swiss engineer, who took away drawings, etc., of the machinery and track, and has employed them since in the construction of a railway up Mount Rhigi in Switzerland, five thousand five hundred feet high. The road is about seventeen thousand feet long, and none of the grades exceed about one foot in four. The trestle-work is of iron, sometimes over a hundred feet high, and there are cuttings in the rock for the road-bed; in one case there is a tunnel one hundred and eighty feet long. The sleepers are two feet apart, and there is a double track. The cars are like omnibuses, seating forty-five persons below, and thirty-six on top. The total cost of the road has been two hundred and fifty thousand dollars. Not less than fifty thousand people visit Rhigi annually, and there are three daily trains both ways to accommodate them. The speed is greater than on Washington, the whole route being traversed in one hour. The centre cog-rail, the peculiar feature of the American road, is in use, and thus the new world has set an example worthy of imitation to an older country. The starting point is at Vitznau on the Lake of the Four Cantons.

The officers of the Mount Washington Railroad for 1868 were Sylvester Marsh, of Littleton, President; J. E. Lyon, of Boston, Hon. Henry Keyes, of Newbury, Vermont, Judge Upham, Hon. Onslow Stearns, and Nathaniel White, of Concord, New Hampshire, Directors. These directors represent by their chief officers the B. C. & M. R. R., C. & P. R. R., C. R. R., N. R. R., of New Hampshire, and the Cheney Express Company. These are the companies whose interests are promoted by the prosperity of the mountain railway.

MR. MARSH'S PATENTS.

Some may be interested in a more particular description of the inventions pertaining to this railway and rolling stock. For such we have copied specifications from the letters patent issued by the United States to Sylvester Marsh, the inventor and patentee. The first is No. 44,965, dated November 8, 1864, and relates to the atmospheric brake :

" Most or all the brakes heretofore constructed or in use involve the principle of the application of power, directly or indirectly, to a mechanism whereby friction is produced of an intensity proportionate to the power applied. For reasons too well known to persons acquainted with this particular branch of the art, it is dangerous and expensive to use brakes of such construction on inclined planes.

" The object of this invention is the construction of a brake which on account of the absence of excessive friction on the wheels or on the rails, are less destructive to the road and material ; a brake in which power of man is applied neither directly, *i. e.*, through the intermediary of chains or levers to the wheels or to the rails, and in which power produced obtained at no inconsiderable cost is not wasted, *i. e.*, absorbed by the mechanism actuating the brake ; and, lastly, a brake the force of which may be regulated at the pleasure of the attendant. And my invention consists —

" In coupling one or more wheels of railway carriages, locomotives, or other wheeled vehicle or apparatus with a movable piston or diaphragm of a

cylinder filled with air, or other more or less elastic
fluid, in combination with valves or other equivalent means for regulating the egress from, and the
ingress to, or the displacement in the said cylinder
of the contents thereof," etc.

In letters-patent No. 101,895, dated April 12,
1870, there is described an "improvement in atmospheric brakes for railway cars." He says : "In
the practical operation of this apparatus, I have
found that although in the upward travel of the car
the valves or faucets are left open, yet it takes some
power to move the piston and small gears used in
the apparatus. For these, under my former arrangement, must move with the wheels, as it would
be dangerous to uncouple them, because they are
needed for instant use in case any accident should
happen during the ascent.

"My object in the present invention is to so
combine the coupling devices with the piston or
pistons, that the latter shall remain at rest during
the ascent of the car, and yet be ready for instan-
taneous operation, should any accident occur which
might otherwise cause the car to descend.

"To this end I combine with the car-axle and
wheels, and the piston or pistons and their coup-
lings, a ratchet and pawl, clutch or equivalent device, operating to permit the free rotation of the
wheels during the ascent without communicating

motion to the piston, and in case of the reverse movement or descent of the car, to at once throw the pistons in communication with the wheels, for the purpose of retarding or of completely arresting their movement, as may be desired."

The earliest patent was dated September 10, 1861, and was for "locomotive engines for ascending inclined planes."

"The present invention relates to that class of locomotives which is used in ascending very steep grades, and has for its objects, first, obtaining sufficient power to ascend a steep inclination with a light locomotive, instead of a heavy and cumbersome one, such as has heretofore been necessarily used ; second, preventing the possibility of the engine being thrown off, or lifted and ungeared from the track, by the interposition of any obstruction thereon, and the means employed for checking and stopping the progress of the train."

In a letter of May 4, 1871, Mr. Marsh says that he has applied for another patent for an engine. Its peculiarity consists of a driving gear at each end, with four cylinders and a horizontal boiler.

Letters-patent No. 61,221, dated January 15, 1867, relate to "improved cog-rail for railroads."

"The object of my invention is to construct a rail suitable for use on roads of steep grades. It need not, however, be limited to this use, as it may also be put to many uses for which the ordinary rack is employed in combination with gear. To accomplish my object, I take two pieces or bars of angle iron, connected by pins or rollers, which, at suitable intervals from one another, have their bearings in the upright sides of the angle iron, thus forming a rack or cog-rail with which the gear of the car truck can engage. The two bars of angle iron, which should be of wrought metal, are bolted, or otherwise secured to timber of proper size and dimensions, so as to be parallel with each other, being so placed, that their flat sides, by which they are bolted to the timber, shall be exterior to the space included between their upright sides. The rollers or cogs, which have their bearings in the upright sides, are placed at suitable distances from one another to correspond with the distances between the teeth of the truck-wheel and are preferably so constructed and arranged as to turn or revolve in their bearings. This, however, is not absolutely essential, for the pins or cogs may be rigidly connected with the uprights. But I prefer the arrangement shown in the drawings, as friction is thereby lessened, and the wear of the metal which the passage of the truck-wheels over the rail would otherwise occasion, is in a great measure prevented. An important feature of the cog-rail thus constructed, is, that its open structure will, in most cases, keep the pins or rollers from being clogged by ice or snow or dirt to such a degree as to be unfitted for use, the liability to which constitutes one of the most serious drawbacks to the employment of the ordinary rack for that purpose. The open space between, beneath, and in fact on all sides of the cogs, except at the points where they are hung in the uprights, is entirely open, so that comparatively little obstacle is offered to the passage of the wheels over the rails, even when the latter are overlaid with snow."

TRIAL TRIP.

The first public trial trip of the engines upon the Mount Washington Railway, took place August 29, 1866. A large party of railroad presidents, superintendents, etc., were present, and it was the inspection of the practical operation of the engines at this time that led the public to believe that the enterprise was feasible. The road had been completed about a quarter of a mile, and trains were kept running up and down for two hours, during which time it is supposed that every one of the assembly rode upon the train. The mechanics and engineers present managed the engine for themselves, repeatedly stopping and starting again on the way up and down. Mr. Marsh and his assistants were unremitting in their efforts to explain every part of the machinery and to answer all questions.

The party were well pleased with the road and its appurtenances, and at the White Mountain House the same day, passed the following resolutions: —

" *Resolved*, That we have witnessed with deep interest the trial trips made this day on the railroad now being constructed to the summit of Mount Washington, and would express our full confidence in the scientific principles of its construction and its practical and safe mode of operation.

" *Resolved*, That we regard the construction of this road as the commencement of a new era in the application of steam power in overcoming grades over high summits and mountain ascents, so as to open new means of business enterprise and greatly enlarge the facilities of enjoyment of the best and noblest scenery of the country.

" *Resolved*, that Sylvester Marsh, by his great skill and ingenuity in the invention of his newly constructed mode of railway for ascending high grades, and his energy and efficiency in its practical application, is entitled to the high appreciation and regard of his fellow-citizens and is richly deserving our tribute to him as a public benefactor."

OPENING OF THE RAILWAY.

The road was formally opened to the public August 14, 1868, at which time it was completed as far as Jacob's Ladder. A large party of railroad officials and others were present, rode up the mountain, walked to the summit, and returned the same afternoon. The occasion was one of great interest.

These gentlemen came by special train to Littleton, thence by stages to the White Mountain House, where they spent the night. The day for the ascent was clear and cold, the thermometer standing at 38° Fahrenheit in the morning. At eight o'clock they started for the depot. The impression had gone abroad that the trip up and down the mountain was to be a free affair for all who chose to participate therein, and therefore all the guests of the adjacent hotels and the residents of the vicinity had assembled in order to ride up the mountain. As they arrived first the cars were crowded before the invited guests made their appearance. It therefore became necessary to request those who had come uninvited — and a large number were ladies — to give up their places to the guests of the day, many of whom had journeyed hundreds of miles to be present. It was generously proposed to send the cars down again for those who were thus left behind, but it was found to be impracticable, and word to that effect was sent back by telegraph.

The two engines were used, and both trains started at twenty-two minutes past ten. The newer and more stylish turnout took the lead and transported the majority of the party, amounting to fifty or sixty. The other train carried about forty persons. For some reason the progress was slow, rather more than three hour's time having been consumed on the way to Jacob's Ladder. The party went on foot the rest of the way to the Summit, where about two hundred visitors had assembled from the Glen, Crawford, and other houses. At the Tip-top House, a bountiful dinner was provided, which was highly appreciated after the scramble up the arctic zone. The distant view was impaired by a hazy atmosphere, and the air was cool but the day was pleasant, and everything conspired to make the excursion successful. The stay at the summit was brief, and after embarkation on the trains good speed was made, the downward journey being accomplished in an hour and a half.

In 1869, General Grant with his family visited Mount Washington. They ascended upon the railway, and were much pleased with their trip. Though so many of the White Mountain peaks have received their names from the Presidents of the United States, it is not known that any one of them has ever before been honored by the presence of the Chief Executive.

About five thousand persons were carried over the Mount Washington Railway, in 1870, or a majority of those who ascended during the whole season.

CHAPTER V.

MOOSILAUKE.

NOT being able to secure a house on the summit of Mount Washington in 1869, we determined, as an experiment, to occupy the summit of Moosilauke for two months. This mountain is in the town of Benton, but it is approached from the village of Warren, from which place there is now a carriage road to the summit. It was late autumn before any preparations were made. Wood had to be hauled up a mountain bridle-path more than a mile, and this was no small task at this season of the year; a room had to be fitted up and provisions taken to the summit. On the 23d of November, having obtained men and horses, we attempted to make the ascent.

As we came where the trees were small, we perceived that it was growing cold. When a mile from the summit, we were met by such a blast of wind, with driving snow, that we were compelled to halt. The men who had gone forward soon returned, driven back by the fierceness of the blast.

They reported that the snow was in such immense
drifts that it would be impossible for the horses to
pass. Our only resource was to return to the foot
of the mountain. The contrast between our evening meal and the dinner before starting, was striking. Then all was life and animation, the conversation sparkling with wit and humor; but a chill had
been cast over the whole group; some were in
agony from frosted feet; some, if their ears were not
frozen, were suffering pain from the effects of the
cold, while others were lame from their severe
efforts in climbing the mountain. One only of the
group was jubilant and hopeful, the pioneer of this
mountain, James Clement, who will be recognized
by all that have visited Moosilauke, for they will
remember the remarkable stories by which he has
beguiled the weary hours while making the ascent
of the mountain, not unfrequently drawing upon his
imagination to make them more vivid than if related in plain language without any embellishment.
While each had something of which to complain,
he would say, " that the worst was over," and
there was probably not one besides him, who had
any idea of trying again to reach the summit before
the sun of another summer had melted the snow.
But morning came, the snow was crisp, the air
was cool, and the mountain stood out in clear, sharp
outline against the deep blue sky. Everything

now seemed propitious, and we determined to make another attempt to reach the summit, and in this we were successful. For two days the weather was charming, but on the third the mountain was enveloped in clouds, and the frozen mist adhered to everything with which it came in contact; the horses instead of being bay and iron-gray were of snowy whiteness, and the men with long hair and flowing beard seemed venerable as with age. Imagination could hardly conceive of a group more grotesque. But this day our work was completed and we descended the mountain. It was late in December before our provisions were taken up. We thought that we should be able to draw them up by hand, but we found a little too much work in this, so we fastened together two large hand-sleds and took a horse. We had to shovel some snow, but we reached the summit with our load. During the night a terrific storm arose; so fierce was it that to venture out was extremely hazardous. In the morning, however, there was no alternative, we must go down, as we had nothing for the horse to eat and the storm might continue for a week. The wind blew so fiercely that we could hardly get breath, besides the cold was intense. The horse braced himself against the wind so that he walked quite steady, but he would not move a step except as he was led. The men could not keep their foot-

ing and were several times blown nearly over the
crest of the ridge ; but we reached the woods where
it was comparatively quiet, and except ears touched
with frost we were unscathed.   On the last day of
December Mr. A. F. Clough and myself ascended
the mountain to remain for two months.   The rock
of the mountain is mica schist.   Everywhere there
are marks of the great denuding agencies that have
worn away the rocks.   The general direction of
the crest of the summit is northeast and southwest,
and it corresponds with the strike of the rocks ; the
top of the mountain is mostly covered with drift, in
which are water-worn fragments of schist and a few
erratic boulders of other rocks.   There is a space of
twenty or thirty acres on the summit comparatively
level, on which grow sedges, mosses, lichens, and
the mountain cranberry, while along the border the
spruce struggle for a scanty existence as they attain
the height of only a few inches.

THE VIEW FROM THE SUMMIT.

There is scarcely a mountain in New England
from which the view is more extensive.   We can
see nearly the whole State of New Hampshire, with
its numerous mountain peaks.   Eastward is Mount
Washington " in solemn repose," and on either side
its neighboring peaks ; all are of immaculate whiteness ; and Lafayette with its deep scarred sides

and its lines of white extending far down into the evergreen forests; and then there is Carrigain and Pequawket, and the mountain ridges along the east branch of the Pemigewasset. Southward is Lake Winnipiseogee, with its numerous isles, glittering in the sunlight like a gem of the purest water. The Uncanoonucs, Kearsarge, and Monadnock are distinct in outline. Westward is the whole State of Vermont; and Ascutney, the most pointed of its mountains, is conspicuous. As the eye follows up the Green Mountain range, the different peaks are easily distinguished, while still further to the west the sharp peaks of the Adirondacks, now snow-clad, seem to pierce the clear blue sky. Moosilauke is so much higher than the immediate neighboring peaks, that "the whole country is spread out as a grand intrusive, raised map before the beholder."

ABOVE THE CLOUDS.

On the first day of January the sun rose clear. We were above the clouds, and a grander spectacle one does not often behold. The clouds seemed to roll and surge like the billows of the ocean. They were of every dark and of every brilliant hue; here they were resplendent with golden light, and there they were of silvery brightness; here of rosy tints, there of sombre gray; here of snowy whiteness, there of murky darkness; here gorgeous with the

play of colors, and there the livid light flashes deep
down into the gulfs formed by the eddying mist,
while

> " Far overhead
> The sky, without a vapor or a stain,
> Intensely blue, even deepened into purple
> When nearer the horizon it received
> A tincture from the mist that there dissolved
> Into the viewless air. . . . The sky bent round
> The awful dome of a most mighty temple
> Built by Omnipotent hand for nothing less
> Than infinite worship.   So beautiful,
> So bright, so glorious ! . . . . Such a majesty
> In yon pure vault !   So many dazzling tints
> In yonder waste of waves."

But above all these clouds, these flashes of light,
this darkness, rise in stately grandeur the summits
of Mount Washington, " sublime in its canopy of
snow," and Lafayette, with a few peaks of lesser altitude glittering in the bright sunlight.   As the sun
rises higher the picture fades away, and the whole
country is flooded with light.   Did this grandeur,
this magnificence, this grand display of lights, of
shadows, and shades, these clouds, so resplendent,
so beautiful, portend a storm ?   In the evening the
wind changed to the southeast and increased in
velocity.

THE GREAT STORM OF THE SECOND OF JANUARY.

At daylight on the second it was snowing. This soon changed to sleet and then to rain, and at eight A. M. the velocity of the wind was seventy miles per hour. At twelve, there was a perfect tempest. Although the wind was so fearful, yet Mr. Clough was determined to know the exact rate at which it was blowing. By clinging to the rocks he succeeded in reaching a place where he could expose the anemometer and not be blown away himself. He found the velocity to be ninety-seven and a half miles per hour; the greatest velocity, until that time, ever recorded. When he reached the house he was thoroughly saturated, the wind having driven the rain through every garment, although they were of the heaviest material, as though they were made of the lightest fabric. During the afternoon the rain and the gale continued with unabated violence. The rain was driven through every crack and crevice of the house, and the floor of our room was flooded. So fierce was the draught of the stove that the wind literally took away every spark of fire, leaving only the half-charred wood in the stove, and it was with the greatest difficulty that we succeeded in rekindling it. During the evening the wind seemed to increase in fury, and although the window was somewhat protected, yet nearly every glass that was exposed was broken by the pressure of the gale. As the lights were broken, the fire was again extinguished, and even my hurricane lantern was blown out as quickly as if the flame had been unprotected. Darkness if not terror reigned, but calmness, with energy, are requisites for such an occasion, and fortunately they were not wanting now. Our necessities quickly showed us what to do. By nailing boards across the windows and by the use of blankets we stopped the openings the wind had made. After nine p. m. there were occasional lulls in the storm, and by twelve it had considerably abated, at least enough to bring on that depression that naturally succeeds a period of intense excitement; so we willingly yielded ourselves to sleep, to dream of gentle zephyrs and sunny skies.

AN OUT-LOOK.

When it was clear, there was a strong temptation, notwithstanding the cold, to be out of doors, to watch the clouds, not only when they filled the valleys, but flitted across the mountain and sailed away. At first, of almost fiery redness, then changing to gray and neutral tints, until almost black, they seemed to gather round some distant peak. Or as a dark band they lay between the Franconia and White Mountains, leaving only the snow-clad summits above the dark border; or at sunset when they lay in narrow bands, or rose-tinted clusters around the summit of Mount Washington, while elsewhere there were those of leaden hue such as are seen only in winter.

Often when the sky is partially overcast, through the intervening spaces of the clouds we see that intense blue sky which is peculiar to high altitudes. As the azure color is due to the light reflected by the air, the purer the air the more decided is this azure tint. No scene more grand and beautiful ever greeted the eye of man than when beyond the dark band of clouds just below the summits of the Franconia and White Mountains, those of rose and orange tints lie along the horizon just above the snow-capped summit of Mount Washington and against this azure sky. From Moosilauke you command the whole panorama of the White Mountain range and you may see something of the effect witnessed among the Alps. " As the day dies, the last shadows pass with strange rapidity from peak to peak. The passage is so rapid, so sudden, as the shadows vanish from one height and appear on the next, that it seems like the step of some living spirit of the mountains. Then, as the sun sinks, it sheds a brilliant glow across them, and upon that follows the strangest effect of all, — a sudden pallor, an ashy paleness on the mountains, that has a ghastly, chilly look. But this is not their last aspect; after the sun has vanished out of sight, in place of the glory of his departure and the corpse-like pallor that succeeds it, there spreads over the mountain a faint blush that dies gradually into the night. These changes — the glory, the death, the soft succeeding life — really seem like something that has a spiritual existence."

ICE COLUMNS.

Half a mile northeast of the summit is a small lake, which is the source of the Asquamchemauke, or Baker River. This stream flows half a mile, when it reaches an immense gulf, where it falls in precipitous cascades of several hundred feet. Across the head of this gulf, where it terminates so abruptly, the stream falls in a hundred stream-lets. The ice columns formed by these in winter are a grand feature in the scenery. Around an immense amphitheatre, there can be seen from below, ice in columns, in sheets, in protruding masses; and where it has poured over the edge of a precipitous rock, there is an ice cavern of wondrous beauty. Here we are surrounded by ice. On the left are columns ten, twenty, and thirty feet in height; before us is a narrow gorge, the sides of which are covered with massive ice. To the right, and almost veiled from sight by a thin film of ice, is an ice cavern, made resplendent by the bright

sunlight, and it is in striking contrast with the columns on the left, over which fall the dark shadows
of the mountain.

Besides, to-day there is frost on every bough and
every spray of the foliage; it resembles snow in its
crystals, not a perfect snow-flake, but only one of its
points magnified a hundred times. On the bridle-
path, about a mile from the summit, during a rain
in February, the trees, which are from ten to fifteen feet in height, became entirely incased in ice;
and pendent from the branches of the firs were
icicles more than a foot in length. Then came the
snow, and for two weeks we had a winter scene,
which for extraordinary brilliancy and magnificence
can probably never be surpassed. In the sunlight
the trunk of every tree was of silvery brightness,
and every spray of the evergreen foliage had its
brilliant gems, which reflected the light in dazzling
splendor.

A GRAND DISPLAY OF CLOUDS.

On the 19th of February there were two currents of air, the upper had its lowest stratum probably two thousand feet below the summit. In the
morning the upper current was northwest, with a
velocity of fifty miles per hour. About twelve the
wind changed to the north and increased in velocity,
and at five P. M. it had a velocity of seventy miles.

At the foot of the mountain there was scarcely a perceptible breeze, yet up a thousand feet there was a strong current from the southwest, and the clouds seemed to move almost as rapidly as those from the north. On account of the velocity of the wind, and the upward pressure of the currents below, the effect was remarkable. The whole country except the higher summits, was covered with clouds, and these were moving at the rate, probably, of more than sixty miles per hour, and everywhere they were broken into seathing undulating masses, for as they came near the mountains, in an instant almost, they would be lifted more than a thousand feet to be carried over the summits. As far as the eye could reach, embracing thousands of square miles, was this rolling, tumultuous mass of clouds.

A PERILOUS DESCENT.

The last of February it was extremely cold, the wind had blown fiercely from the north for several days, with a velocity from sixty to seventy miles per hour. The thermometer ranged from zero to seventeen below. Our wood was nearly exhausted, and who could tell how long the wind would blow, or the cold continue. So we loaded a sled and took it down on the southeast side of the mountain, and were thus in a great measure protected from the wind. When we came on the ridge, as long as we could keep under the firs that grow where the ridge is low, and the footing was secure, we were able to stand against the blast. But should we be able to follow the ridge where there was no protection from the wind? The only way to find out was to make the trial. When we reached the highest part of the ridge the wind swept across with irresistible fury. Clough held the sled to keep it from blowing away. When a good foothold could be secured, we were able to make some progress. When not able to brace against the wind, I was blown from the ridge, then crawling back, would make another effort, only to be blown away again, until finally, the sled, notwithstanding the most strenuous efforts were made to hold it, was blown against a projecting rock with such force that the standards were broken, and thus it was entirely disabled. Here we were, the wind blowing seventy miles per hour, and the thermometer at zero or below. What was to be done? A decision must be made at once. To remain here only for a moment, without putting forth severe physical efforts, we should become statues only too lifelike. We pulled the broken sled with its load over the side of the ridge where the wind was not quite so furious, and Clough went back to get a sled, which had been left two days before, where we first came on the ridge. It was only

after a severe struggle with Boreas, in which he
came very near being vanquished, that he was able
to secure it.   To reload here, was no easy task, but
it was accomplished, and we soon succeeded in
reaching the woods, where we were protected from
the wind.   It was with many regrets that we left
the mountain, but our brief stay gave us valuable
experience for future mountain observations.

CHAPTER VI.

THE ASCENT OF MOUNT WASHINGTON IN WINTER.

FROM the depot of Mount Washington Railway, the ascent on foot, in summer, is comparatively easy, if a person is accustomed to walking. Though the ties are three feet apart and there is a rise of one foot in three, some of the way, yet a person with muscles strong from exercise, can walk to the very summit without sitting down to rest. We would not, however, advise any one to walk merely for the exercise, as they would probably get more than they expected.

But suppose it is a fine day in early winter. The snow has already accumulated to a considerable depth, even on the ties, but then it is no great hindrance. Should we, however, attempt to ascend a second time, we shall find that the snow that was compressed beneath the feet has changed to ice, and the oval form gives a still less secure footing. If the ice is thawing, and is almost ready to slip off as we tread upon it, every one will see that upon a trestle nearly thirty feet in height, walking is *somewhat* dangerous, and to walk down is a feat from which a most expert acrobat would shrink. If at the depot, we take snow-shoes, we can walk with comparative ease up to the limit of the trees, and then the snow is so compact that they are no longer needed, and as there are few irregularities in the surface, the walking is better than in summer. Above the limit of the trees, the railway is covered with ice of every fantastic shape, and the frame-work of the Gulf tank is now so ornamented that one can hardly believe that it is the rude structure we see in summer. The Lizzie Bourne Monument, which we have been accustomed to see only as a rough pile of stones, is now an object of architectural beauty, such as no sculptor can carve from marble. The engraving represents the monument after the frost work had formed on the tablet, so that it projected two or three feet. Immediately above the monument, the timbers of the trestle are completely covered with deposits of frozen mist, extending three and four feet horizontally from the timber on which the track is laid; and every piece of timber that forms the trestle is ornamented with beautiful forms of frost-work, arranged in graceful

LIZZIE BOURNE MONUMENT.

curves where the wind sweeps through the trestle. On the summit, the buildings, the piles of rocks and stones, so rough in summer, are now completely covered with frost, while the snow fills the spaces between the jagged rocks. On the sides of the buildings toward the northwest the frost has accumulated so that now it is more than a foot in thickness. While the frost-work on the depot has everywhere the same general appearance, the points show exactly the direction of the wind as it came into every nook and corner of the building. The frost on the braces and timbers that extend outward seems one triangular mass, and on the chains it is often two or three feet in diameter.

The ascent is not always made when it is mild and calm. A person is often deceived; for although pleasant at the base of the mountain, it may be very cold, with a strong wind, on the summit. Such was the case when the photographers came.

THE ASCENT OF NOVEMBER 30.

On the 30th of November, 1870, we started from the White Mountain House for the summit of Mount Washington. Our party consisted of Charles B. Cheney, of Orford; A. F. Clough, of Warren; C. F. Bracy, of Warren; and Howard A. Kimball, of Concord. Our team, a sturdy span,

and our vehicle, a stout *pung*, we were speedily
aboard with our luggage and traps, and moving
onward with buoyant hearts, with the untrodden
snow to test the mettle of our team. November
was making its exit in what might be termed a
lovely winter day ; and the prospect of so choice
a time to make our ascent — toilsome, at best, at
this season, and very hazardous except at special
times of good weather — inspired us with enthusiasm, more and more increased as we approached
the final reach that stood in defiance of any aid
which could be rendered by the panting steeds
that now bore us forward. Plodding on amid increasing depths of snow, the keen outlook of our
driver discovered trouble ahead ; when, calling out,
" O, how stupid not to bring an axe !" we looked
before us to behold our way blocked with trees
which the wind had hurled directly across the road.
Falling to work as best we could, we succeeded
in breaking away limbs underneath the reclining
trunks, till we had opened a passage, through which,
after detaching horses, we dragged the pung, and
then led the team. Our advance found the snow
deeper and deeper ; yet there seemed no occasion
to indulge misgivings, for the weather was still all
we could desire, and there appeared to be sufficient
time. But at last we came to a new fence of wind-

falls that positively barred our progress. It was found impossible to go on without *cutting* through, and we had nothing to cut with.

We were now within about a mile and a half of Marshfield Depot, the terminus of our convoy. Mr. Clough volunteered to walk the rest of the way, rally a "chopper," and return and chop us out. This was all duly accomplished; but it consumed some two hours of precious time; and, with the previous delay, made our arrival at the depot two o'clock in the afternoon, instead of eleven or twelve in the forenoon, as it should have been.

At Marshfield we are three miles from the summit, and, at present, all travel over this distance must depend solely upon human muscle and energy to achieve; though Mr. Marsh, the president of the railway company, says he will yet see it run at all seasons of the year.

"Jim," the wood-choppers' cook, prepared us a lunch; and, after duly disposing of this, we held "a council of war," and decided to make the ascent at once, though there were serious misgivings on the part of some of us in view of the near approach of night, when, at this season, half-past two o'clock leaves a small margin of the day, at best, for such a task as stood before us. However, the weather was fine, and we were fired with the promise of an adventure, amid scenery new and grand, from which we had been unwillingly detained several days beyond our previous designs.

THE ASCENT.

In ascending from this point, we followed the railroad track. We were compelled to walk upon the ties, for the snow was several feet deep. With a sharp upward grade, in some places rising one foot in three; with the ties three feet apart and loaded with ice and snow, and built on trestle-work over gorges of some twenty-five to thirty feet in depth, the careless, eager steps of unbaffled enthusiasm are soon compelled to give place to great caution and the constant stress of nerve and muscle. It is found impossible to make every foothold sure; hence there come occasional slips and bruises; and, unless one is robust and hardy, the ascent thus soon becomes decidedly wearisome and even exhaustive.

The end of the first mile — carrying us up to within one half mile of the limit of wood-growth — found us in tolerable condition; when a halt for breath and observations discovered to us an approaching storm lying on the Green Mountains of Vermont. It would undoubtedly strike us, but we still hoped we might press on and reach the summit first. The thought of being overtaken by a furious storm on the wintry, shelterless cliffs of Mount

Washington, with the night about to enshroud us, was fearfully impressive, and prompted us to our best endeavors. With all the effort we could well muster, we had only advanced a half mile more, carrying us fairly above the wooded region to the foot of "Jacob's Ladder," when the storm struck us. There were suddenly wrapped around us dense clouds of frozen vapor, driven so furiously into our faces by the raging winds as to threaten suffocation. The cheering repose of the elements but a moment before had now given place to what might well be felt as the power and hoarse rage of a thousand furies; and the shroud of darkness that was in a moment thrown over us was nearly equal to that of the moonless night. Compelled to redoubled efforts to keep our feet and make proper advance, we struggled with the tempest, though with such odds against us that we were repeatedly slipping and getting painful bruises. Mr. Kimball finding himself too much exhausted to continue this struggle on the track, we all halted in brief consultation. It was suggested that we return to Waumbek Station, an old building a half mile below us, and there try to keep ourselves from freezing by brisk exercise. Mr. Clough emphatically vetoed this as a most dangerous and impracticable proposition, saying that our only hope consisted in pushing upward with all our might.

Here we became separated, three of our party left the track, and Mr. Kimball willingly left behind his luggage in order to continue the ascent. By thus leaving the track we escaped liability to falls and bruises, but found ourselves often getting buried to our waists in snow, and forced to exert our utmost strength to drag ourselves out and advance. We repeatedly called to Mr. Bracy, who had kept on the track, as we supposed, but could get no answer. The roar of the tempest overcame our utmost vocal efforts; and the cloud of frozen vapor, that lashed us so furiously as it hugged us in its chilling embrace, was so dense that no object could be seen at a distance of ten paces.

Against such remorseless blasts no human being could keep integrity of muscle and remain erect. We could only go on together a little way and then throw ourselves down for a few moments, to recover breath and strength. We had many times repeated this, when Mr. Kimball became so utterly exhausted as to make it impossible to take another step. He called to the others to leave him and save themselves if possible. The noble and emphatic " *Never* " uttered by the manly Clough, whose sturdy muscle was found ample to back his will, aroused him to another effort.

The two stronger gentlemen, whose habits of life and superior physical powers gave hope of deliverance for themselves, were both immovable in the determination that our fate should be one, let that be what it must.

The situation was one of most momentous peril, especially as to Mr. Kimball, whose exhaustion was now so extreme that he was wholly indifferent to the fate that seemed to impend ; only begging that he might be left to that sleep from whose embrace there was felt no power of resistance. Still there was forced a listless drag onward, mostly in the interests of his companions and in obedience to their potent wills. After this sort we struggled on, a few rods at a time, falling together, between each effort, to rest and gain new strength. At each halt Messrs. Clough and Cheney used their best endeavors by pounding and rubbing Mr. Kimball's feet and limbs, and in various other ways endeavored to promote circulation and prevent freezing.

The last saving device was supplied by a cord which we chanced to have. At one end of this was made a noose, which was placed in Mr. Kimball's hand, while the other end was passed over the shoulder of Mr. Clough who tugged along in advance, while Mr. Cheney helped at his side. Most of the last mile was accomplished in this manner.

With the wind at seventy miles per hour, and the thermometer down to 7°, as was found after arriving at the Observatory, we came at length to

"Lizzie Bourne's Monument," only thirty rods from the Observatory. One of our party shouted an exultant hurrah at the glad sight of this rude pile which was erected to commemorate the sad fate of one who was overtaken by the darkness and bewildering fogs and chills of a rude October night. "Then," in the words of the eloquent Starr King, "was the time to feel the meaning of that pile of stones, which tells where Miss Bourne, overtaken by night and fog and exhausted by cold, breathed out her life into the bleak cloud."

It took more than a half hour's time to make this last thirty rods. Even the stronger ones had become wearied by their unusual exertions, and had this not been the case, their progress would have been slow, for it was found absolutely impossible to force on the one who had now become unable to regard his own peril, more than a few feet at a time. He would then sink down into a deep sleep, while the others would employ the time in chafing his hands and feet, and after a few moments manage to arouse him and make another struggle onward.[1]

[1] So utterly exhausted was our friend that his reason tottered, and he speculated as to the methods by which his dead body should be carried down to his friends, and seemed to be anxious to make the necessary arrangements beforehand; and the prospect of another monument was certainly very promising. This idea also furnished him with words, as he insisted that his untimely end would attract many

From Lizzie Bourne's Monument to the summit Mr. Kimball was mostly insensible to passing events, and only awoke to clear consciousness, as from a dream, to find himself in bed in a comfortable room in the Observatory building, safe from the dreadful tempest, and owing his life to the unyielding devotion of these brave men who scorned to save themselves at the expense of a comrade left to perish.

We were very glad to find on our arrival that Mr. Bracy, who had got separated from us during our earlier struggles, had got in about seven o'clock; our own arrival being at half past seven; he having kept on the track.

Thus at least three hours of this ascent were made amid the darkness of a moonless night, in the howling tempest, the horrors of which will be more readily appreciated when it is remembered that a wind of forty-five miles per hour blew down buildings and uprooted trees in New York city. Twenty-five miles added, make a most fearful hurricane. We were abundantly supplied with nourishment on our ascent, chiefly in the form of a strong decoction of tea, of which we occasionally partook. This is found to be by far the most

visitors to the lonely spot, and be the means of enriching the hotel and the railroad the following summer. Also when being carried through the entrance to the Observatory, he thought himself falling down some steep place, and begged the others to save him. C. H. H.

potent and effective stimulant that can be used in such conditions of extreme exposure.

Mr. Bracy, too, had a narrow escape. Losing his foothold on the track, he at one time fell through, into a gorge beneath the trestle-work. Exhausted, bruised, and discouraged, he crawled beneath the ruins of the old "Gulf House," which were found to be at hand, thinking he would try to weather the storm there; but finding himself, in spite of every effort, getting numb and dozy, he rallied to a new struggle, and thus saved himself.

Mr. Huntington, aroused by the arrival of Mr. Bracy, sallied out with a lantern in search of us, but found his best exertions of little avail, the storm being so fierce and thick he could neither make himself seen nor heard beyond a few paces; and they were regarding us as probably lost, though preparing for another effort in our behalf, when we arrived.

A sleepless night gave place, at length, to a day thick and stormy. And for several days the clouds gathered densely around us and the storm continued its rage; during which we were recovering from "the wear and tear" of our adventures and recruiting for the work in store for us.

THE ASCENT OF FEBRUARY EIGHTH.

An ascent without great difficulty was made on the 8th of February, by Mr. Luther L. Holden, of

the " Boston Daily Journal," and Mr. P. B. Cogswell, of the " Concord Daily Monitor." As they
were the first newspaper men ever upon the summit of Mount Washington, in mid winter, an account of their *tour*, will not fail to be interesting : —

" Mr. Huntington informed us that it was magnificent
weather that morning at the summit, and that we could
not have selected, apparently, a better day for the trip.
He knew better than to promise us good weather all the
way through, however, for the changes about the mountains, and especially at the summit, are sometimes very
sudden and unexpected. In a few minutes our preparations for the upward journey were completed, for they
comprised nothing more than the buckling on of knapsacks, the putting on of buffalo overshoes and the grasping of Alpen-stocks. The latter is an almost indispensable assistant in mountain climbing in the winter. We
had brought snow-shoes for use through the woods if
necessary, but we found they could as well be left behind. As for overcoats, we strapped them upon our
knapsacks or disposed of them as best we could, for the
exertion of the walk was likely to keep us warm enough
until we got near the top, and so it certainly proved.
Our party, four in number, left the base of the mountain at a quarter past ten o'clock. No travellers ever
had safer, surer, more experienced, or more intelligent
guides than we two newspaper men could boast of.
We had received ample directions in regard to the ascent in case we undertook it alone, but with two such

8

able guides as Mr. Huntington and Mr. Clough, we certainly could not go amiss. Here let me add that no person ought attempt the ascent of Mount Washington in winter unless he is blessed with more than common physical strength and hardihood, for although under favorable circumstances and with good weather (which means the absence of adverse winds more than anything else), the trip may be accomplished safely enough, and, in truth, with greater ease than in summer, yet the sudden and severe changes liable to occur are in themselves dangerous, while physical exhaustion in any case might lead to serious results. There have been two instances, at least, the present season, where persons have become so exhausted in climbing the mountain that they could not have proceeded without aid from others, while death would have ensued had they been abandoned. On one occasion a young man became so fatigued and so benumbed with cold, that his companions were compelled to carry him a considerable part of the way. The sad deaths of poor Lizzie Bourne and Benjamin Chandler, one of whom perished on the mountain side in September, 1855, and the other in August, 1856, and the terrible adventure of Dr. Benjamin L. Ball, who narrowly escaped death from exposure in October, 1855, are solemn reminders of the dangers of mountain climbing.

" As we were sure to occupy several hours in the ascent, we took a light lunch to refresh us on the way, and proper restoratives, the chief of which was a plentiful supply of the beverage " that cheers but not inebriates " — cold tea. A flask of strong tea is more efficacious than a flask of brandy in reviving and refreshing exhausted nature upon a mountain tramp, although it is well enough to take along the latter for emergencies. For a little way up the mountain we took a winding path through which timber is hauled, but soon struck the railway, alongside or upon which we kept the remainder of the distance. The snow in the woods was from two to three feet in depth, and the crust was sufficiently hard to bear our weight, except in places where we might sink through at the side of a log or in the bushes. In most places we could easily walk over the low bushes, and also upon getting above the line of tall trees it was found an easy matter to travel over the belt of stunted, scrubby trees, which surrounds the mountain and marks the limit of arborescent growth. These trees are so thick that in summer they form impenetrable barriers, compelling the pedestrian to keep to the railway track, or to the old Fabyan bridle-path. Farther on, the rocks are for the most part covered with snow, the crevices being filled so completely that there are few irregularities in the surface. In short, the rough places are made smooth, — in not a few instances a trifle too smooth, — for the way is, at some points, very steep. In a few places the snow lies drifted over the railway, but along the line of high trestle work at Jacob's Ladder, and for the most part above, the snow had blown from the top, so that easy locomotion was found for some of us over the sleepers. Before we had reached the Waumbek Junction, a slight snow squall struck us, and we could see that there was a storm in the neighborhood of the Notch. This, however, was no impediment to our onward progress. As we had occasion to rest quite frequently, we had ample opportunity to stop and admire the glorious panorama which was gradually unfolded behind us. After getting above Jacob's Ladder we found that the wind, which was blowing from the south or southwest, was quite strong, and by the time we reached the Great Gulf we were in the midst of a furious snow-storm. As we entered the snow cloud the country below was shut out from our view, and we could not see a great distance in any direction, although the cloud was not very dense. The frost work on the Lizzie Bourne monument, which had been very beautiful at times, had for the most part disappeared in the recent thaws and furious wind-storms."

"We arrived at the summit at 2.45 p. m., having occupied four and a half hours in the ascent. By 'taking it easy' *en route,* we reached the end of our journey very slightly fatigued. Sergeant Smith and Mr. Nelson, Mr. Huntington's companions in exile, gave us a warm welcome, and we were soon snugly ensconced under the depot roof. Upon our arrival it was ascertained that the wind was blowing at the rate of forty-five miles an hour, while the thermometer indicated 13° above zero."

Since we began our preparations for the winter, over fifty persons, including members of the party, have been on the mountain, and the number of ascents made amount to more than a hundred, seventeen having been made by myself, and not a single accident that has proved serious has happened to any one, although before we began to go up and down, there was probably scarcely one person in a hundred but that would have considered a trip to the summit of Mount Washington in mid-winter, even in the most favorable weather, a perilous undertaking.

CHAPTER VII.

OF all the valleys that radiate from this group of mountains, that of Israel's River is the broadest. By following a line a little west of north we look directly down upon this valley with its broad, open fields, now covered with a white mantle of snow. Where a point of woods penetrates this open area, it looks like a headland jutting into a frozen lake; but the deception is not perfect, for we can see a road running through the entire length of this open space, and it crosses some of these points; besides, houses are distinctly visible along the entire length of the valley. A little to the left of this valley, and westward, are the hills of Whitefield, and beyond is Dalton Mountain, from which there is such a fine view of the whole White Mountain range. In Lancaster we see Mount Prospect and Mount Pleasant; along the base of these is a line of snow, which is now brilliant from reflected light. Westward still, and stretching northward along the Connecticut, are the

Lunenburg Hills, so famous as a point from which to view the mountains; and beyond, so far away are the hills, when there is the least haze in the atmosphere we can hardly distinguish their outline, and the snow which covers them " wells into the atmosphere, as it were, and dies away in the heavens like the indistinct outline of a bright but partially remembered dream."

TOWARDS PERCY PEAKS AND NORTHWARD TO QUEBEC PROVINCE.

North of Jefferson is the Pilot Range, with its wooded summits. Looking down upon it, every ridge is sharply defined; and there are Percy Peaks, now so purely white, and almost as distinct as they appear from the road along the upper Ammonoosuc; and beyond are the mountains in Stratford; that sharp point rising above the other peaks is Sugarloaf Mountain. But we can look far, far beyond, for we can see Owl's Head in Canada; and although so far away its outline is sharply defined as it stands solitary and alone.

A LOOK INTO THE GREAT GULF.

Looking almost directly north, we look down into the Great Gulf between Mount Washington and Mount Adams. We cannot see far down, as we stand here; suppose we walk down as far as the Gulf House, and then just a step will bring us to the very border of this immense gulf. Just above the point where we stand, the whole side of the mountain is one sheet of ice, and there is some where we stand, so we have to be very cautious in our movements, for we are upon the very brink of a precipice hundreds of feet in height. The snow which has blown over into the gulf covers now in part the ragged, jutting rocks that form the abrupt precipice at the head of this great chasm, yet still enough protrude to give to it a picturesque grandeur, especially when the rays of the sun fall aslant its rugged slope. The peaks of Jefferson and Adams seem mountains of themselves, even above the point where we stand, for they are between two and three hundred feet higher than the gap south of Mount Clay. Adding to this the depths below, and remembering that Mount Washington is nearly five hundred feet higher than Mount Adams, and you have some conception of the awful grandeur of the scene, and you will no longer wonder why we run some risk by standing here. The depths below with their dark shadows, and the heights above gleaming in the bright sunlight, are enchantment enough to draw one to the very verge of these precipitous heights. If in summer it is one of the grandest spectacles Mount Washington affords, words certainly fail to give an adequate

description of it in winter, whether we see it when
the morning sun shines into it from the east, — at
noon, when the sun scarcely reaches its lowest
depths, — or late in the afternoon when far down it
seems almost night, although the mountain-peaks
are all aglow with light, — or watch the clouds as
they pour over into it from the west.

UP THE ANDROSCOGGIN AND MAGALLOWAY.

Returning to the summit of Mount Washington,
we follow up the valley of the Androscoggin, and
look down upon the breadth of sombre forests stretching northward towards Lake Umbagog, which is
now so distinct, though thirty or forty miles away.
West of Umbagog is Mount Dustan, and north is the
rounded summit of Escalios, with its breadth of
snow. Beyond is the wilderness along the Magal-
loway; and that mountain so precipitous on its
eastern slope is Mount Carmel, on the line between
New Hampshire and Maine; and northward still is
the blue outline of the mountains in Quebec Province. To the east of the line just indicated we
look down the Peabody River to the valley of the
Androscoggin, and when we feel as though we were
out of the world we take our glass and watch the
trains on the Grand Trunk Railway. Beyond
Gorham and Shelburne we see the hills and mountains of Maine, and conspicuous among them is
Katahdin, which stands " regal and alone."

EASTWARD.

The guide books tell you that from the summit of Mount Washington, not only the lakes in Maine, but that also the ocean can be seen. As most persons who visit the mountain are here only for a short time, and then at mid-day in summer, and as they look through the hazy atmosphere they conclude that what they say is a myth, and that it is told to allure people here; but suppose you go out with me, and we will take a look eastward to-day; a chill may run through you at the thought of standing out in an atmosphere where the thermometer is at zero; but we can find a place by the side of the building where we are protected from the wind, and as you look you will forget that it is cold. In some respects the view is the most remarkable outlook from the summit of Mount Washington; in every other direction in the distance lofty mountains greet the eye; in this, except the Carter Range looking a little south of east, the broad expanse that stretches out before you is comparatively level; the first time we looked in this direction through the rifts in the clouds, as a storm was clearing away on one of those days in late autumn, when the air has a remarkable transparency, we could hardly believe that what we saw was something real; it seemed rather like a picture conceived by a vivid imagination, excited perchance by this pure and rarefied atmosphere ; but the scene must be real, for there is the Carter Range, now apparently so near that we can forgive Leavitt for representing old Abel Crawford in the act of shooting a bear, which is at least a mile away. To-day we can see not only the trees that grow upon its western slope, but their very branches. Beyond the Carter Range are the numerous lakes in Maine, and we can see distinctly the valleys, hills, and mountain ridges, as they stretch onward seventy, eighty, and ninety miles. That bright line extending so far along the coast is the ocean ; but we can rarely see it with the unaided eye, except when the waters reflect the sunlight; and then, with Tolles' telescope, having an object-glass of one inch and a focal length of four inches, we can see not only vessels as they sail along the coast, but can distinguish their rig. We have however seen the ocean once or twice on a moonlight night. These vast stretches of vision, transferred to the mind, are a "mute material warning against all moral narrowness and bigotry. Liberty and law, magnanimity and humility, inflexible sincerity and inexhaustible bounty, are their lessons."

OFF AN HOUR TO TUCKERMAN'S RAVINE.

From the point where we stand we can look down into the Pinkham Notch. The point where we see the road is nearly five thousand feet below us, and we see also the immense gorge of Tuckerman's Ravine; but we cannot see far into its depths, so we will walk down to its very border, for we are sure of being repaid for all our toil. We will go to the point of rocks on the north side, a mile below the head of the ravine; we have stood here before; then there was only one bright spot of snow, and above it the thousand streams glittered in the bright sunlight; but now winter reigns supreme. The whiteness along the bottom of the ravine is relieved by the tree-tops, protruding above the snow, besides the jutting rocks and crags are brown and bare, and the shadows fall over the cliffs opposite. But there is a gleam of light from the Thousand Streams; for where they have poured over the head of the ravine they are fixed in ice columns of gigantic proportions, and they are of wondrous beauty; they extend almost entirely across the ravine, and we can hardly believe that they have been formed from a few trickling streams, for one might suppose that a mighty cataract had there been suddenly congealed. Later in the season we shall find that the snow extends almost up to the point where the streams first leap over the precipitous rocks. We have hardly time to-day to look down on Hermit Lake, only a white spot now among the trees, or to follow the valley below; and much less to walk down so that we can see the path the avalanche has made; for there was at some time not very remote an avalanche just north of the ravine, which bent or broke off the trees along a path many rods in width. We should like to walk north along this plateau, and to look into the deep ravines along its border, but we must return to the summit. Here half way up we will sit down and rest. As we view the grandeur of the scene, we almost forget our weariness. Just there, fashioned in beautiful symmetry, is Pequawket, now a snowy cone, tinged with opalescent light. Beyond, in Maine, is Mount Pleasant, with its triangular area of mountains; and there is Sebago Lake, and beyond the harbor of Portland, and the point of land running out into the sea on which stands Fort Preble. This grand panorama need only once be seen to remain ever after "a new and glorious furniture of the mind."

CHAPTER VIII.

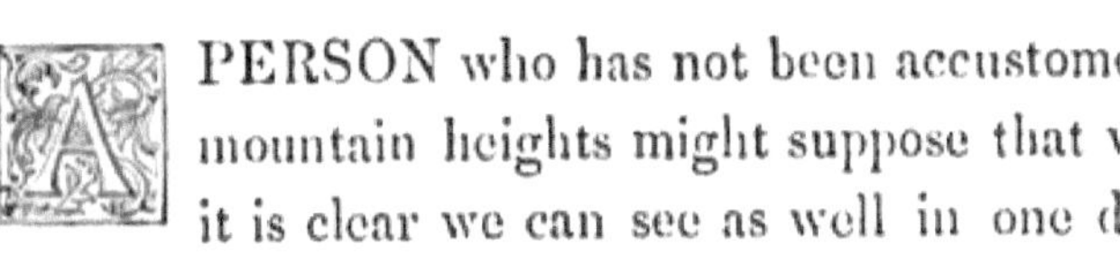

PERSON who has not been accustomed to mountain heights might suppose that when it is clear we can see as well in one direction as another. But to-day it may be remarkably clear in the north, and yet quite hazy in the south ; or clear in the west, and yet in the east everything may be indistinct. So it may be many days before the best views, embracing the whole horizon, can be obtained. It is very rare that the atmosphere is as clear southward as in other directions, especially in the distance ; but sometimes within a range of sixty miles every lake and mountain is remarkably distinct, and the picturesque beauty of the scene compensates for distance. Look down the valley of Ellis River, its wooded sides slope almost down to the stream. Below is the valley of the Saco, with its broad intervales, and there is Conway, guarded by noble mountains. To the west is Mote Mountain, with its sweeping outline, and Chocorua with its sharp, snowy peaks surrounded by forests of fir. When at evening it glows with light rose tints, crimson and gold, it has a beauty peculiar to itself, and with eager eyes we watch the lingering light until it fades into the night.

TOWARDS LAKE WINNIPISEOGEE.

But for another day there is still reserved a vision of beauty that cannot fail to fascinate, even those who are insensible to the ordinary charms of nature. It is the view embracing Lake Winnipiseogee and its immediate surroundings. Now that the lake is covered with ice, how it gleams in the bright sunlight; how distinct its islands and jutting headlands; and then the light on the hills, so rich in purple tints. The whole scene is of such minuteness, yet so vast, that we stand in wonder, attracted as though by some great enchantment.

> "Ah! that such beauty, varying in the light
> Of living nature, cannot be portrayed
> By words, nor by the pencil's silent skill;
> But it is the property of Him alone
> Who hath beheld it."

Southward still is Mount Belknap with its double peak; and Copple Crown is distinct, but beyond the haze gives only dim outlines. So long has our attention been directed southward, we had almost forgotten that we are standing on the summit of Mount

Washington, and that we are isolated from the world below on which we have been looking so intently.

WESTWARD DOWN THE VALLEY OF THE AMMONOOSUC.

One who has viewed the grand panorama that is spread out before the beholder who stands on the summit of Mount Washington, only through the haze of a summer's day, can hardly imagine the grandeur of the scene as it appears on a clear day in mid winter. Would you not like to see it? Then go with me, for to-day it is so mild and pleasant that we cannot stay within doors. The sun shines brightly; above, the sky is intensely blue, and in the zenith it deepens even into purple. Such a sky is seen only at high altitude, and there only when the atmosphere is free from all impurities. We will stand upon the highest point of the mountain, — no, this will not do, we cannot see westward. On the Tip-top House the view is better, but the roof is steep. Can we walk up? Certainly, for the frost adheres to the roof, so we have a secure footing. Now we can go no higher; but this is all we could wish. To-day, so clear and transparent is the atmosphere, that space seems half annihilated. Instead of one vast mantle of white, as we might have expected, the variety of colors is greater even than in summer; and the shadows, — could any artist desire anything more grand? Before us is the valley of the Ammonoosuc, with its gray forests of deciduous trees, and we can follow the line which runs along the range that ends in Mount Deception, which separates this forest from that of the evergreen which crowns the summit of the ridge. There in the valley is a white spot, it is the Twin River Farm; and below is another, that is the intervale, where stood the Fabyan House.

LAFAYETTE, WITH ITS RIDGES AND NEIGHBORING PEAKS.

But look beyond; how sharp in outline is each ridge, as the sun strikes upon them and throws the shadows westward; but above all these ridges rises Lafayette, grand in its canopy of snow; but now its sterner features are softened by a glow of rose-tinted, amber light. South rises a peak symmetrical in outline, its pointed summit so pure, that for anything to touch it, except those beautiful rays of sunlight, would destroy the charm with which it is now invested. Has it a name? Certainly; they call it Haystack. What a name for a mountain of such grand and noble proportions! How poetical! Can the name be found in any book on rhythm? If Indian names are exhausted, let us at least have a respectable English name for peaks that are so prominent. Beyond, and a little to the south, is Moosilauke. Here we have, thanks to Mr. William Little of Manchester, an Indian name substituted for a most inappropriate English name Mooschillock; for hillock is a small hill; and moose are not apt to climb bare summits. A mountain nearly five thousand feet high deserves something better than to be called a small hill. "Broad-shouldered" it is, its crest having been rounded by the glaciers that came from the north; and grand is the panorama seen from its summit. Westward, in Vermont, is the whole line of the Green Mountains, Camel's Hump and the long line of Mount Mansfield being white with snow.

TOWARDS THE NOTCH.

Looking a little south of the line above indicated, we follow the range that runs towards the Notch. How the peaks glitter in the bright sunlight; for the light snow has all blown over into the ravines, and the Notch seems so near that we feel almost like taking a walk to view there the winter scene. Beyond is Mount Willey, and a ridge from thence stretches southward to Carragain, a noble mountain, with precipitous cliffs and deep gorges on either side, and so far from the haunts of men that its summit is rarely pressed by human footsteps, and grand on account of its very solitude. To the west is the valley of the east branch of the Pemigewasset; we can see to-day the ridges on the south, that reach down to the stream itself, each one almost as sharp and distinct in outline as if we were at their very base. Southward from Carrigain, peak follows peak until the range ends in a point south of Osceola. To follow round the whole horizon and study the scene that is spread out before us would take several days. One feature more of the scene that is particularly striking we will notice here, namely, the shadows as they fall aslant the sides of the mountains or across the deep valleys. On account of the snow and the transparency of the atmosphere, not to say anything of the lengthened shadows of winter, they are much more noticeable than in summer. On Monroe, Franklin, and Pleasant, there is the most beautiful rose-tint, just over the border; the dark shadows of the mountains fall on the snow where the light streams through the deep ravines, and, as the sun climbs higher, we watch the shadows until the sunlight flashes down the sides of the mountains.

<h1 style="text-align:center">CHAPTER IX.</h1>

PHOTOGRAPHING UPON MOUNT WASHINGTON.

AS photography has got to be so common in every-day life, and so necessary to the full success of every expedition of importance, its omission on the present occasion would have been a great oversight, and have left the practical results of the expedition but half complete. It is the province of the photographer to bring to the eyes of the public that which is not of a readily accessible. character; thus to give those who cannot visit such places a chance to see wonders and beauties, while they enjoy the comforts of home, enduring none of the perils, dangers, or hardships, which are necessary to get at the real.

Though the pictures can convey to the mind but a small portion of the real grandeur of the scenes as beheld by the eye, they nevertheless have a fascinating beauty that charms and gives a sense of sublimity to the lover of nature, in her varied forms.

The photographer who makes nature his study,

with a view to reproduce her various charms, soon becomes an enthusiast, and is ready to brave almost any hardship or danger in order to secure the likeness of a gem or " bit." A musical waterfall, or thundering cataract, a peaceful vale where the flocks graze in quiet security, the wild mountain crag where the eagle screams its shrill notes, a tropical bower where perpetual summer brings forth rich and continuous verdure, and the barren, desolate mountain peaks of snow and frost towering far above the clouds; they will all afford some subject for the Knight of the Camera to " bang away at," and from which to bear off a trophy that shall delight " the millions," and fittingly reward the enthusiam of the true artist, and also line his pocket with " greenbacks."

October of 1864 was the first time I ever beheld the beauty of the frost-work upon the mountains. It was on the occasion of a visit to Moosilauke ; and my attempts to photograph it were frustrated by the storm, as I was not prepared for any lengthy stay or proper effort. I visited it again the next year, but failed from the same cause ; and not until the year of 1869, when Mr. Huntington and myself made arrangements to spend the winter up amongst storms and clouds, did I meet with anything like success.

When we first proposed to make that mountain

our home for the winter, it had become late in the season, and the mountains were already covered with snow. Provisions and fuel had to be got up, which was no easy task, where but few had any sympathy for us, and fewer still were willing to help, while a larger share were ready to raise all sorts of " bugbears " not calculated to inspire us with confidence in anything like success. The idea of photographing under such adverse circumstances wanted something of the proper stimulus; but still I determined to try it, believing the more obstacles overcome the greater the satisfaction, so long as it proposed only a bloodless offering.

When so many of the craft fail, with every convenience at hand, and with every requisite for producing good work, it should not be expected that uniform success could be met with where every convenience is wanting, in the matter of materials, and where nature has opposed serious obstacles; but, with a full appreciation of the troubles to be met and overcome, I was determined to try until my chemicals or myself froze up; so with my traps lashed on a hand-sled, we toiled up the mountain of 5,000 feet, walking on snow-shoes. It was a hard task, but was accomplished in good time; and though my success was not always complete, it served to show what might be done with proper will and perseverance, even in extremities.

This experience was of value, and many of the views taken were of interest; and I may say that some of them have never been surpassed for beauty.

When on a clear day we could see the glistening summit of Mount Washington, we often asked ourselves the question, "Shall we next winter occupy the top of that mountain?" And I think that it was as fully settled in our minds then as at any time after, if the necessary funds could be raised. In this expedition we paid our own expenses, excepting what a few of the citizens of the town of Warren gave by assisting us to get up wood, and one other man who gave some money. So we had most of the glory to ourselves.

When it was determined to make the effort to occupy Mount Washington, I felt that it was to be a hazardous job; but was ready and willing to do the best I could, and made all necessary preparations; had all chemicals, apparatus, etc., that could be forwarded, packed and sent up by the railroad; yet there were many things that could not be safely sent up in that way, as there was to be some lapse of time between the arrival of them and the time of the commencement of the occupation. As it is winter weather there in October, many things that would spoil must be taken up at the time of the final ascent.

In the interim Mr. Kimball, of Concord, N. H., proposed to the Head of the expedition, to go as photographer, not knowing that I was to occupy that place. He was referred to me, when we soon made satisfactory arrangements to have him accompany me; and from his Diary kept while on the mountain, a part of which will complete this chapter, will be found some of the more minute details of our work while there.

We made the ascent on the afternoon of November 30; a time that will not be soon forgotten by the parties. Mr. Kimball's narrow escape from death on that night, will ever be a thrilling epoch in his life, as well as in that of some friends who accompanied us. Shut in the folds of a dense cloud, the wind sweeping across the barren frozen waste at a hurricane speed, and the darkness of night gathering fast around us while we were a long way from the top, and our friend sinking down *exhausted*, begging to have us leave him and save ourselves, and when told it was sure death, firmly accepting what he deemed inevitable, all made it a time that would try the nerves of the most resolute; but to leave him was as remote from our thoughts as anything could be; so we abandoned everything to save him; and, by taking him almost by main force, we could get him up a few steps at a time, when we were obliged to let him rest, and we ourselves were glad to take a respite. By two hours hard and unremitting toil, we got to the top, and brought our man in safety; though he says he has no distinct recollection of the last part of the journey.

He was not frozen, but completely exhausted. We were all pretty well exhausted, but soon recovered. With the wind blowing at the rate of seventy miles an hour, and the thermometer nearly at zero, there can be but a small amount of pleasure in climbing a mountain at night in a storm cloud. There is truly nothing but extreme hardship and hazard.

Herewith is a part of Mr. Kimball's Diary, kept while on the mountain; and as it was written at the time when the events were fresh in the mind, it will be more interesting than anything I can write regarding our work.   A. F. CLOUGH.

MONDAY, DECEMBER 5, 1871.

FIRST DAY'S WORK AT PHOTOGRAPHING ON MOUNT WASHINGTON.

Mr. Huntington called us early this morning to see the sun rise out of the ocean. It was a grand sight, not soon to be forgotten. It was several minutes after he came in sight before he was, as it seemed, out of the ocean, and he looked much larger to me than ever before, and did not dazzle the eyes as he usually does. We concluded to avail ourselves of the fair weather, and commence our series of views at once ; so we regulated chemicals and instruments as soon as possible, and commenced operations immediately. After breakfast, Mr. Huntington started down the mountain on his way to Littleton, for the purpose of repairing the telegraph wire, which we hoped soon to have in working order. An extract from my Diary reads : " The day is beautiful, we are perfectly comfortable outside without overcoats, and on the east side of the Observatory the frost is thawing quite rapidly. Thermometer 22°."

We have succeeded in making some very good views, but not as large a variety as we intend to have before we complete our winter's work. Our first was looking east, with the Glen stable in the foreground. It is a pretty cloud view, showing as it does, grand masses of silvery, cumulus clouds, as they pour down over mounts Monroe and Franklin, over Tuckerman's Ravine, and down through the Glen. Another gives a fine view of the Carter Range of mountains, and in the foreground the Glen and Alpine stables, two buildings a few rods below the summit of the mountain, which are now covered with beautiful frost-work several feet thick, as is everything on the top of the mountain. We have also made three negatives of clouds, which were at least half a mile below us. They resemble the waves on the ocean, only the cloud waves are in some places twenty or thirty miles long. They pass over a range of mountains, and take a long sweep across the valleys, and then rise over the mountains on the opposite side ; and, as a general thing, after passing over and coming down on the other side, they break up in small clusters, resembling, on a grand scale, the surf from breaking waves. We have made some photographs of this, but they give only a limited idea of the grandeur of the captivating view thus spread out beneath us. All these clouds move rapidly from the southwest, probably at a velocity of forty miles an hour, while on this summit it blows generally from the north- west. We have made a view which shows a small portion of a remarkable cloud effect, or phenome- non. It was like a parallel belt on the distant hor- izon, whose circuit must have been more than a thousand miles. It resembled the tire to an im- mense cart-wheel (we occupying the place for the hub), which was beyond, and encircled all the lakes, mountains, etc. It was even beyond Mount Katah- din. At the south its upper edge was parallel with the point farthest north. At noon it appears to be approaching us as a centre, and as it nears us it breaks up in magnificent great thunder heads, minus the thunder. All this time our view is becoming more limited. Now we look over to Mount Washington's younger brother, Mount Adams, covered with clouds, with the exception of the top, which looms up like a mighty Titan, scorning to have a cloud-veil thrown so soon over his majestic head. The sun responds to the royal endeavor, and sends a shower of his warm beams down on the bleak summit, standing up alone to our view, a bright little island white with snow, as pure as the purest velvet, in a rough silvery ocean of clouds. All this time it was snowing below, but we knew nothing of it until to-night. Our view of the surrounding mountains lasts only a short time longer, for we see to the west thick, heavy clouds, marching upon us, and by four o'clock we become densely shrouded. We cannot see the Tip-top House from the observatory, not many feet distant.

Sergeant Smith made his connections with batteries and cables, and we hope soon to be in communication with the world below.

Last night we discovered a new boarder, in the form of a sable. He must like well, for we make liberal waste for his sake. I suppose in passing over the mountain he scented our larder, and was attracted by the prospect of a nice dinner. We hope to see more of the sly little fellow. We shall feed him like a prince. I hope he won't kill our mice, for it is pleasant to know there is animal life near us, if nothing more than a poor little " varmint " of a mouse.

While making a negative to-day, a crow flew past me. He seemed in haste, and so did not stop to sit for his picture, which I would gladly have made.

Thursday, December 29, 1870. This morning I went out to see if we could make some negatives during the day. I had barely got out, when the wind swept me, with resistless force, away from our entrance or door, and I only saved myself from the rude handling and probable bruising, by catching the chain which passed over the building. It hurled me with such power as to swing me in toward the depot into a snow drift, which was much better than to have been swept upon the rocks covered with the frost feathers. How was I to face such a wind and get back? I tried several times, each time carried back by the force of the wind, the velocity of which, at times, must have been as high as seventy miles an hour, but not steadily thus. There were lulls when it did not reach more than forty miles an hour, and in one of these I crawled back on " all fours," and got into the Observatory, determined to stay there as long as the wind blew so furiously; and we have decided, without much question, that it will be impossible to make a photograph to-day.

The day is clear and cold. To look out of the window it seems very inviting, but it is like the apples of Sodom, fair to look upon but " bad to take." The wind has been increasing all day. At seven A. M., observations: velocity of wind forty-six miles an hour; two P. M., fifty-seven miles; four P. M., seventy-two miles; at seven P. M., forty-six miles, and at nine P. M., nearly calm. A great change in fourteen hours, especially in the last two hours. Barometer has fallen rapidly all day.

Friday, December 30, 1870. The morning is calm, clear, and beautiful. It is what we have waited a month for. We commenced work on our chemicals at daylight, warming and filtering our baths, suitably tempering developer, etc., and heating all our instruments, to drive the moisture from them; putting our dark room in order, and melting ice for water to use in washing negatives. We commenced making negatives at sunrise. Experienced great difficulty, in exposing the sensitized plate, to avoid the destruction of the film by freezing. We carried the plate in a warm woollen blanket, but this could only serve in carrying. As soon as the plate was put in the camera from the warm blanket, it would raise a cloud of vapor from the moisture inside, which would congeal on the plate and inside of the camera, and give the inside lenses of the tubes the appearance of ground glass,

which of course would prevent the landscapes being imaged upon the plate. Our only resort was
to keep the plate and holder only a few degrees
warmer than the camera. Then putting our plate
into the camera, exposing, taking it from the camera, and carrying it under protection of the heat of
the body and coat, developing as soon as possible,
success crowned our efforts. We were from two
to five seconds in taking the plate-holder from its
shelter under our coats, fixing it in the camera, lift-
ing slide, exposing and returning plate to shelter.
If we delayed in the least, the negative would be
frozen and thus spoiled.

In the morning we made a few eight by ten
negatives ; but as we were making the last of them,
the wind freshened up, and we could not make as
many as we wished. The camera presented a large
surface to the wind, and was very decidedly shaken.
We could not have had a much better day for our
work. In the morning there was not a cloud to be
seen in any direction, so to-day we finish all we
intend to do before spring. And now we are ready
to bid " good bye " to our pleasant winter home
above the clouds, and seek a more comfortable place
" down on the earth," as we say. We have been
here a little more than a month, but have been
obliged to keep housed so much of the time that it
seems much longer. Employments and associations

here have been full of interest and extremely pleasant, and it will be with many regrets that I leave
friends and comrades, hoping no accident will befall
them, and that the completest success will crown
their toilsome and hazardous efforts.

Before I close to-day's memoranda, I must speak
of the splendid view which we had, after the wind,
by blowing so fiercely, obliged us to quit work.
We could see distinctly hundreds of mountains,
lakes, ponds, etc.   Off to the northeast in the
distance — one hundred and fifty miles distant —
we see Mount Katahdin, the highest mountain in
Maine; and a little to the north we see mountains
which apparently are much farther away than
Mount Katahdin, and must be in the upper part
of Maine, near Canada.   We never before saw the
ocean nearly as plain as to-day.   We could see a
great distance " to sea."   Off to the southwest we
could see Kearsarge Mountain and Monadnock, and
over the Green Mountains the Adirondacks and
Lake Champlain, in northern New York, were distinctly visible.   About two o'clock P. M. I noticed
a long hazy line over the ocean.   Soon it grew
larger, and then I could see it was nearing us, and
in an hour it was within forty miles; and we could
see it as a vast sea of cumulus clouds.   The wind
was increasing, and had changed from the east to
the south, and it carried the approaching clouds and

storm to the north of us. We were thankful to see it go by without striking us, for it is grand to behold, but not desirable for a covering. To-night we have some of the effects of it in the wind, which, as I write, is blowing a 'most violent hurricane,' making the Observatory creak. A rew hours ago the wind was scarcely noticeable; now, its velocity is over eighty miles an hour. And for a wonder, it comes from the south, instead of northwest, as usual, and, as a natural consequence, it tears off all the loose ice and frost from the Observatory. It seems as if we were at sea in a severe gale, and broken ice and timbers were beating against our ship, and at times our building shakes like a vessel in storm. We don't sleep much on such a *stirring* occasion. H. A. KIMBALL.

10

CHAPTER X.

THE TELEGRAPH WIRE, HOW OBTAINED, HOW LAID, AND HOW WORKED.

IT was found early in the history of the White Mountain Expedition that a telegraph was essential to success. The common wire could not be used in winter, as the ice collecting on it would break it, and the wet snow covering the wire on the lower part of the mountain would cause a constant escape of electricity; so we must have an insulated wire. The cost of such a wire was about a thousand dollars, but fortunately, the Bureau of Telegrams and Reports for the Benefits of Commerce, decided to make Mount Washington one of their stations for the winter, and from this Bureau we obtained an insulated wire and telegraph supplies. It was planned to take the wire to the summit by the railroad, but it did not reach the mountain before the engines were laid up for the winter. The only alternatives were to get men to carry the wire up the west side, or else transport it by a long and tedious route around the mountain and haul it up the carriage road, rebuilding the hundred bridges which had been taken up for the winter. We decided upon the last method.

After the wire had been taken around to the east side of the mountain, we found that the instruments, batteries, etc., were still at Littleton, and another journey had to be made. So important was it that there should be the least possible delay, we started from the east side of the mountain after the sun had disappeared behind the mountain summits. As it was the evening of the grand auroral display in October, the night ride gave us an opportunity of observing a scene of unusual magnificence. Through Randolph, the grand peaks of Madison, Adams, and Jefferson, tower high and seem to touch the streamers as they shoot upward towards the zenith and form a beautiful corona. Now it fades, but reappears in red and crimson lights; even in the dark woods of Jefferson the glow of light illuminates the dark forests. When we reach the hills of Whitefield, the aurora has entirely disappeared, and the full autumn moon shines in all its wonted splendor. Having obtained the supplies, the next day we returned, and the day following they were taken up the carriage road to the summit of the mountain.

THE WIRE HOW LAID.

Though the wire was now upon the summit, it was still a serious question how it was to be laid along the railway. A sled seven feet long was constructed, the coils were placed upon it, one being mounted on a reel. One of us sat upon a board in front to guide the sled and the other was behind, sliding down hill, as explained on page 75, and illustrated in the accompanying sketch. The sled upon the railway glides smoothly down the steep grade, and the wire uncoils beautifully and is laid just where it is wanted. It was something fearful to pass over the high trestle below the Gulf Tank and on Jacob's Ladder, and even now it almost makes one shudder to think of those dizzy heights, the load we had, and the steep grade. But we reach Marshfield in three hours from the time of starting, and the wire has been successfully laid. On our return the wire is fastened down with eyelets close to the outer rail, and the summit is reached just at dark. We put it on the ties, because if placed on the ground where there was little snow, it would be constantly moved by the wind and soon worn off; and should it be broken in the snow and ice there would not be the least possibility of finding where it was broken, as we should not know where to look for the wire. On the railway we always know

LAYING THE CABLE ON JACOB'S LADDER.

where the wire is, and more than half the way to Marshfield it has been most of the time out of the snow.

PUTTING THE LINE IN WORKING ORDER.

Sergeant Smith, on his way to the mountain, found the line between Littleton and Marshfield broken, and in several places the wind had blown the wire from off the insulators. The inclement weather in the first part of December prevented all attempts to repair it. One of the party went to Littleton on the 10th, repairing the line on his way there. No breaks had been detected in the cable so far, as it was almost throughout its entire length covered with snow and frost.

On the 12th we descended the mountain, and putting an instrument into the circuit at Marshfield we had communication with Littleton, N. H., showing that the main line of the Western Union Company was in working order and that the breaks were in the cable. The chances of finding them were very small, the snow being in some places over twelve feet deep, but we had determined to make the cable a success. Digging out the wire as we ascended the mountain, and testing the current by connecting the cable from time to time with the main wire to the summit, which we used for a ground connection by running it into the brook at

Marshfield, we ascertained that the cable was all right as far as Jacob's Ladder. Here after a diligent search, we not only found the cable broken, but also the main line or the ground wire. We were convinced that it would be necessary to detach the cable here from the railway, as the trestlework is from twenty-five to thirty feet high, exposing the small cable, which is merely a No. 16 copper wire, covered with gutta percha, to the force of the wind. So a new piece was put in and buried in the snow along the railway to the upper end of Jacob's Ladder. We proceeded on our weary trip up the mountain, still testing the current as we went along, until we reached Lizzie Bourne's monument. Here, after removing some six feet of snow, we found another break ; but, as night set in, we were unable to mend it.

The following day found us early at work mending the last break, although the weather was fearful. A dense cloud rested upon the mountain, and the drifting masses of frozen mist soon covered us with a coat of snow and ice. Returning to the Observatory we found the instrument working and Littleton calling. We all were overjoyed, as our arrangements were now completed, and the cable a success. Although the line was worked with a powerful battery, the current remained rather feeble, a circumstance which we attributed to the great number of naked joints in the cable. The difficulties that were to be overcome in transmitting and receiving messages may easily be imagined. As a matter of course, our telegraphic connection with the "world below" is looked upon by us as the most important outfit of our Observatory, as we can thus transmit meteorological observations, and in return hear of all news of importance as soon if not sooner than many a person "down on earth." For the latter we are under many obligations to the obliging operator (Mr. A. H. Currier) at Littleton, N. H.

The length of the cable is nearly three miles, and the distance from Marshfield, where it connects with the Western Union Company's line, to Littleton, is twenty-three miles. The instrument used here is a box-sounder, a combination of relay and sounder with key attached, manufactured by L. G. Tillotson and Co., in New York, and it belongs to the Signal Department U. S. A. These instruments are used in the army field-telegraph-trains, and dispense, up to circuits of over a hundred miles in length, by fair insulation, with the use of local batteries and sounders.

The line has frequently been charged with atmospheric electricity, especially in the afternoon of the 7th of January, when on account of the high tension of these currents it became utterly unmanageable. When the key was opened, the flow of

the current still continued, exhibiting bright sparks
leaping from one platinum point to the other.
After dark no auroral display could be seen.
There is a wire connecting the summit with the
Glen House, which is detached from the poles and
laid upon the ground during the winter to protect
it from the violent winds prevailing at this season.
We had it attached to an instrument, and although
no battery was used, we discovered that it was
sometimes charged with electric currents, which
deflected the needle considerably. The Glen wire
was broken about a mile and a half from the summit, and the one down the railway had parted at
about the same distance, thus making the phenomenon quite remarkable.

REPAIRING THE LINE UNDER DIFFICULTIES.

The first interruption occurred on the morning
of January 14, but the break was soon found and
repaired. Eight days later the cable broke again,
and Sergeant Smith, while searching for the break
near Jacob's Ladder, slipped on the ice and slid a
considerable distance, and only saved himself from
being dashed to pieces on the rocks by catching in
the trestle-work of the railway. The return to the
summit was a feat which took him some four hours
to perform, he being deprived of the use of his left
foot. Another break occurred early in February,

but fortunately it was near the summit. Six trips had to be made before the damage was repaired, the wind blowing at the time seventy-six miles an hour and the temperature being 16°.

During the tremendous storm of February 17 the cable was considerably damaged near the Great Gulf, and the extreme cold and stormy weather during the subsequent three days prevented repairs, although Sergeant Smith made several attempts, returning once with the tips of his fingers frozen. Communication was finally reëstablished on the afternoon of February 22.

Only a few days later, the cable ceased to work again, and it was found that the ground wire was broken. The operator then tried one of the iron strap rails of the railway for a ground and it worked all right, although not as satisfactory as the wire, for the wet snow covering the railway near the base of the mountain formed the only medium of escape. Through some unknown cause this ground connection failed to work in April, and the break in the main wire not having been found yet, we tried the water pipes running from the upper springs to the tank at Jacob's Ladder, and this worked excellently, especially after a long iron spike had been driven into the soil near the upper line of vegetation and the pipe connected with it.

Ever since then the line has worked finely, and we consider ourselves fortunate that no more serious troubles have interfered with the sending of messages. The main line to Littleton remained in good order throughout the winter, while during the previous season it had been severely damaged by the falling of decayed trees, etc. As the greater part of the messages transmitted over our line were for places quite distant, the Western Union Telegraph Company has derived a handsome income from that source.

CHAPTER XI.

LIFE ON THE SUMMIT.

OST persons suppose that life on Mount Washington in winter must be gloomy, and gloomy enough it would be, at times, when the summit is enveloped in dense clouds for weeks, if it were not for the cheering click of the telegraph instrument. They might suppose also that time would be extended indefinitely; that at night we should wish it was morning, and that in the morning we should long for night to come, and thus drag out a weary existence. If the time of any persons in excellent health is wholly occupied in a pursuit that is congenial they are rarely gloomy, and are almost unconscious of the flight of time. But here, besides good health and time occupied, there is an excitement found nowhere else.

THE EXCITEMENT OF LIVING ON A MOUNTAIN SUMMIT.

One gorgeous sunrise throwing a flood of light across a sea of clouds, one glorious sunset tingeing the clouds with crimson and gold, and as the sun descends leaving the blush of day upon these snowy summits, or a storm unprecedented at lower elevations, infuse into our life enough that is grand and sublime to occupy the thoughts for weeks. With such surroundings, a person, on account of the intense excitement, may live too fast to have life extended to full threescore years and ten ; but there is a pleasure in it that would fully compensate for a few days cut off from the number to which life might be lengthened if passed in some quiet retreat, undisturbed by anything that arouses the whole being, and carries the mind into ecstasies of delight. So days and weeks pass, and we are almost unconscious of the lapse of time.

OUR ARRANGEMENTS FOR COMFORT AND CONVENIENCE.

But this record would not be complete without something specific being said of our habitation and our daily life, and it cannot be told better than in the language of " Ranger," the excellent correspondent of the " Boston Journal."

" As the lessee of the Tip-top and Summit houses raised objections to the occupancy of either of those buildings, Mr. Huntington and his companions obtained permission from the Railway Company to set up their lonely habitation in the

THE HOME OF THE EXPEDITION.

This illustration is from a photograph of the building, taken the middle of December, when the frostwork was nearly three feet thick over almost the entire structure

newly erected depot. The depot was built last summer, and occupies a site of the same elevation as the Tip-top and Summit houses, northeasterly of those structures, upon the verge of the little plateau forming the summit of the mountain. The building, unlike the two diminutive public houses, whose sides are of stone, is constructed wholly of wood. It is sixty feet long by twenty-two feet wide, and stands nearly north and south. It has eleven-feet posts, and the elevation of the ridge-pole is twenty-five feet, the roof being of the same form as the roofs of ordinary buildings. The apartment inhabited by the party is situated in the southwest corner of this edifice. It is a room about twenty feet long, eleven feet wide, and eight feet high. The larger portion of the depot forms a sort of vestibule to this room and is wholly inclosed except at the easterly end of the northern face, where the outer door is situated. The little room was formed in the following manner: 1st, there was the thick plank floor of the depot itself, which constituted a good foundation to build upon; 2d, a course of sheathing paper was laid over the original floor; 3d, an additional floor of close-fitting boards was then laid down; 4th, two thicknesses of sheathing paper were placed on the top of the second floor; 5th, a layer of carpet lining was added; and 6th, a thick woolen carpet was made the uppermost layer of all. The inside of the outer walls was covered first with tarred paper, then with boards, a layer of sheathing paper was added, and wall paper was spread upon this. The ceiling is formed of two thicknesses of boards with sheathing paper between, and the inner walls consist of single thicknesses of boards, sheathing paper, and wall paper. There are two double windows — or rather half windows — on the westerly side of the room, and these are protected by strips of board without. The door of the room is of ordinary size, but the outer door is nothing but a little opening two feet square, some two feet from the floor. After the last observation is taken at ten o'clock P. M., the little aperture is closed by means of two sliding boards, but at all other times is left open. Very little additional cold finds its way into the building through this aperture, and its elevation from the floor prevents the snow from blowing in to any great extent. More snow finds its way through the crevices between the boards upon the sides of the building than through this hole. Contrary to what ordinary experience would seem to teach, the north side of the building is less exposed to the fury of the elements than any other.

"We have thus far described none of the precaution taken to prevent the building from being torn to pieces by the terrible winter tempests, or from being blown away altogether. The frame-work is of the strongest possible kind, and is fitted together in the best manner. The sills extend beyond the walls eight or ten feet, and every means are taken to fasten the whole structure down to its rocky base. Within, bolts, iron rods, and wooden braces add strength to the walls, and three strong iron chains, securely fastened to the rocks, pass over the roof. Notwithstanding all these provisions the building rocks and bends before a furious wind-storm in a manner well calculated to create consternation and dismay. An ordinary house would stand no longer before such terrific blasts than would a house of cards before an ordinary wind. The great gale in December awakened the fears of the party for the safety of the depot, but as the structure stood that frightful assault it was thought no further danger on that score need be apprehended. It was nevertheless thought best to strengthen the walls with additional braces and supports.

" Young couples about to enter upon the responsibilities of housekeeping might learn some useful hints from these dwellers of the clouds. The little snuggery is made to serve not only as a kitchen, dining-room, sleeping-room, sitting-room, parlor, library, and study, but also as an observatory and telegraph office. Every inch of space is utilized. The telegraph instrument, battery, and other appur-

tenances of lightning communication with the outside world, are in one corner of the cozy apartment,
beneath one of the windows.   At the same end of
the room is a bedstead, while above it is a wide
bunk, arranged after the manner of an upper berth
in a steamboat.   The most prominent objects that
greet one upon entering the door are two stoves,
which occupy the middle of the floor.   One is an
ordinary cook-stove, and the other is a Magee parlor stove.   The latter is prized very highly on account of its marvelous heating properties.   A story
was published not long since to the effect that it
required seven dampers to regulate the draft, and
also that considerably more than one half of the coal
was already consumed.   Neither of these statements
are true.   The stoves are easily enough governed
by single dampers, and as for fuel, Mr. Huntington
has enough on hand to last until next summer.
The dining-table, which is generally covered with
books, papers, and writing materials when not otherwise in use, occupies one corner of the room, while
between it and the telegraph instrument is a well-
filled book-case and several shelves.   Shelves, in
fact, appear everywhere, and they contain a general
assortment of everything, while clothing, and at
least an hundred articles of utility, hang suspended
from pegs and nails. A writing tablet is hung upon
the wall near the head of the bed, and upon this

VIEW OF INTERIOR OF THE OBSERVATORY

the observations are bulletined until they can be telegraphed, copied into the record books, or placed in the blank forms provided by the Smithsonian Institution. Beside it are two barometers, from one of which observations are made, and further on is a formidable row of smoking pipes. Some waggish member of the party has hung the tin sign of the old telegraph office over Sergeant Smith's seat, and also inscribed something of similar import on the door without. During the early part of the winter the corner of the room now occupied in part by the telegraph was used by Messrs. Clough and Kimball as a ' dark room ' in their photographic operations. The anemometer — the curious little instrument for measuring the velocity of the wind — is in a state of quietude on a shelf over the table. Beside the book-case, upon a projecting beam, is a coffee-mill, affording a striking exhibition of the combination of the scientific and practical. Among the other wall ornaments are a pair of snow-shoes, a hand-saw and other mechanical implements, an infinitude of tin dishes, a map of Paris and its fortifications, the photograph of a young lady, etc. The floor is made the receptacle of numberless articles which cannot be put anywhere else. There seems to be, in short, ' a place for everything,' but it not always happens, I believe, that everything is found in its place. In the absence of the female element of a well-regulated household, the scientific gentlemen content themselves with following out one half of the apothegm. They all complain that it is the easiest place to lose anything in they ever saw. In justice, however, it should be said that the apartment in general is in a very neat and tidy condition. A rocking-chair and three or four common chairs and stools, together with the table and beds, comprise all the movable furniture, while an ingenious member of the party has constructed a reclining seat upon one of the wooden braces. Most of the provisions are kept in the open part of the depot without,—about all, in fact, that freezing does not affect. Frozen pieces of fresh meat and of salt pork are suspended from the roof of this commodious refrigerator."

CHAPTER XII.

October 8th.

STARTED for the summit of Mount Washington with Mr. Cole of Berlin Falls; passed the Glen House at 4.30 P. M. Stopped just above the first mile-post and ate our supper. We intended to camp, but it was so mild and pleasant that we concluded to keep on. When near the Half-way House we had a grand view of Mount Adams. How high it seemed as it lifted its huge form up into the night. When between the fourth and fifth mile-posts, the moon just on the wane rose over the Carter Range. What a charm there is in looking out upon these mountains, when the moon throws her gentle light across them. How mysterious those deep gorges as we look down into their depths, or rather try to look, for their lowest depths are veiled in impenetrable darkness. The ascent, which on a warm day in summer is so fatiguing, now seems like a dream, for we scarcely know that we have put forth any effort to reach the summit. Found Professor Hitchcock, Mr. Phelps, and two men from Brooklyn, N. Y. It looks rather dreary here, no room finished in this immense building; they were trying to get fire enough to serve some tea for supper, but I think we had better sleep awhile, perhaps the coal will get up heat enough before morning, and we shall have tea instead of coffee for breakfast.

October 10. To-day we worked fitting up our room. We put in double windows, laid a double floor above and below with felt between the boards. Around the room we put felt, then boards, and on these we put sheathing paper; on the floor a lined carpet. We then put our two stoves in place. I think we shall be able to keep warm. Having some calcined plaster, I suggested to Cole that we might have hard finish overhead, but looking up to the rough joist and boards, he said he thought it was "*hard* finished" already.

October 13. How clear it is to-day; can it be that what I see is something real ? Are those certainly hills, mountains, and lakes, and can that bright line be the ocean, or does an excited imagination form this picture in the mind ? It is clear northward as well, and I recognize many places, so the scene must be real ; but I would not have believed, that I could see with such distinctness so far away.

October 18. Went down as far as the Gulf House,

and returning put the wire of Western Union Company on the trestle to be used as a ground. When we reached the summit it was raining, and the wind was blowing fiercely. Cole lay on the bed, and covered up his head so that he should not hear the wind. Going out I saw that our door was giving a little, and thinking it might possibly blow in I told him I thought he had better make it more secure. He went out and put on additional fastenings, but in half an hour in it came. The boards and planks lying about in the building, were thrown in every direction. I never saw boards move about so lively, they seemed to have lost their weight. I know they were heavy enough the other day, when I put them in the building. We tried to put the door in place, but with all our efforts we could not get it near the doorway; we found ourselves almost powerless, for several times we were thrown down as though we had no strength. We put the door against the side of the building and tried to push it along, but when about six inches of it became exposed, in it came again. As a last resort we nailed a piece of plank on the floor, put the door against the side of the house, then took a piece of scantling, put one end against the plank, the other against the centre of the door. One held the scantling while the other pushed the door, and in this way we got it into place and nailed it so securely, that I do not think we shall open it again soon. We were not out more than half the time I have been writing these lines, yet my fingers were nearly frozen.

October 22. There is a little snow but considerable frost-work on the mountain. Went down to-day and took up the bridges.

November 12. Started from Marshfield at seven A. M., arrived at the summit of Mount Washington at 9.30. It rained until I got within three fourths of a mile of the summit, then there was a frozen mist. The snow was six inches deep at Marshfield, at Waumbek Junction a foot. At the second tank the snow was drifted, none on the ties above. On the summit it was drifted so that neither at the Summit or Tip-top House could the doors be seen; there was very little about the depot. I am here alone, but should have come if I had known that I had to stay alone all winter.

November 15. Have been above the clouds all day long, some of the time not a single mountain top could be seen, occasionally Mounts Adams and Jefferson would appear, but most of the day in every direction was this illimitable sea of clouds. Being here alone, one has nothing to do but to contemplate this immensity of space bounded only by the sky.

November 24. The barometer lower this morning than it has been before. Wind blowing fiercely from the northwest, not steadily but in gusts. The house creaks in every joint. It is something fearful to sit here alone and hear the wind howl while showers of ice are blown against the side of the building and along the roof. But there was something still more to be dreaded. In the afternoon, as it was growing cold in my room, I put some wood in the large stove, thinking I would have a fire, but instead of the smoke going up the pipe, it all came out in the room. I was nearly suffocated, but the smoke cleared away; then the gas began to come out of the other stove. If the smoke was bad, the gas was still worse. All the calamities that people had predicted would befall us, stood before me as so many grim demons ready for their victim. I suspected the cause : the frost-work had formed on the cap over the pipe, and had left on the opposite side a place for the smoke to escape, but a change in the wind was driving the gas out in the room. I could not go upon the roof to get the ice off, that was impossible. I tried to unjoint the pipe, but it was put up to withstand the storms, and besides on account of the rust the joints adhered so firmly that it seemed impossible to get them apart. Finally it came off near the stove, then it was taken off joint by joint, but when near the roof I thrust a stick up the pipe and knocked off the frost. The pipe was replaced and the fire burned all right. I think I shall take the cap off the first pleasant day.

November 30.   Clear until two P. M., when light clouds began to pass over the mountain, but became dense toward night. Was surprised by the arrival of Clough, Kimball, Cheney, and Bracy. I am not likely to be alone again this winter.

December 4. Sergeant Smith arrived to day.

December 12.   Clough and Smith went down to the base of the mountain, and as they returned they found that the wire would work to the second tank, but could get no current on the summit. In the morning the wind was south, but changed to northwest in the afternoon.   At ten A. M. there was a bow on the clouds, and at twelve P. M. there were in addition three supernumerary bows which remained for an hour and a half, and some of the time they were remarkably distinct. Late in the afternoon the sky was intensely blue.

December 13.   The telegraph worked to-day for the first time ; now we are in the world again.

TIP-TOP HOUSE.

CHAPTER XIII.

JOURNAL CONTINUED.

December 21.

FOREFATHERS' DAY was celebrated by the arrival of Prof. Hitchcock, L. B. Newell, E. Thompson, F. Woodbridge, and the writer. We ascended in a rough southwest snowstorm, with the velocity of the wind at 59 miles per hour. It is pleasant to be located at last and settled down for the coming six months. It is quite a change in one short week from busy Boston to this out-of-the-world-up-in-the-clouds Observatory. In the face of a gale blowing sixty miles per hour, Messrs. Kimball and Thompson took an observation, — nothing very remarkable in itself, — but as it was from the roof of the Tip-top House, the feat is worthy of record. They were out but five minutes, yet their coats, caps, and hair were covered with frost, and Mr. Thompson had slightly frozen a finger. Later the wind had fallen to thirty miles, and now (eleven P. M.) it is moderate for Mount

Washington. There are no signs of animal life outside. Mice are plenty in the house, and it is thought that a sable has taken up winter quarters under the building.

December 23. Kimball was up first this morning, and had the first sight of as beautiful a sunrise as one could wish. Unwilling that we sleepy fellows should lose it, he called us out. All were on their feet instantly, quickly washed and dressed. The wash-stand is a discarded butter-tub. It was a cold morning, the thermometer indicating $0°$, but we don't feel the cold as sensibly as in the lower regions. C. and K. took some fine views to-day, among them one of the Observatory with C., S., and N. standing by the door. Later in the day they took one from the roof of the hotel. They have been successful against odds, having had but three days so far suitable for work during a month's residence. To return to the morning: after breakfast we all took hold of the forenoon's work. Mr. Woodbridge and myself washed the dishes, the others clearing the room; for though this party are shut out from society, they seem to stick to the ways they have learned " down in the world," and keep house in the most approved style.

December 24. Yesterday afternoon and late at night a " snow-bank " lay along the south ; this forenoon snow was falling with a temperature of —13°. At times during the day the wind was as high as seventy miles an hour, consequently we were confined to the house. Mr. S. has much to do, many messages being sent to and from the " lower regions." He sends his first regular report to Washington to-night. So it seems that the government consider this station of importance, if the public do not. In working this line, Mr. S. has had many obstacles to overcome ; but he seems to be determined to have it work all right ere long. Canned beef, tomato sauce, coffee, and pilot bread constituted our dinner. Find no vegetables but onions, — bad for us. It is cold to-night (now, nine P. M., —15°), and only 42° in the room, although we have two fires. Mr. K. received a telegram from home to-night. We sent a press dispatch of " A merry Christmas to all the world below." Christmas! And what a contrast to some former ones! — in situation at least. But I would not exchange places with the most favored of fortune this night, nor do I esteem any preceding Christmas Eve above this one. A jolly party we are, but for the telegraph shut out from all intercourse with mankind. The wire attached to the sounder on the little table across the room is the connecting link between the " outside barbarians " and ourselves. They are *doomed* to read (curiosity if not interest will lead them) the reports from Mount Washington. We have a saying that whatever is done is all for the " Benefit of Commerce."

December 25. There were no clouds above or around the summit. Below, and but a little lower than this peak, the clouds were dense and covered an extensive tract of country. Through the less dense portion of the lighter clouds, the sun's rays gave a peculiar rose-tint extremely beautiful in effect. This was my first cloud view, and it was a treat beyond expectation. About ten A. M., Mr. K. and myself went out for an observation. We had the pleasure of witnessing the formation of several coronæ, sometimes single but oftener three, even on one occasion *four* distinct circles, appearing and disappearing so rapidly that it was impossible to more than catch a glimpse of form and color. It was a phenomenon of rare beauty. Mr. K. devoted himself to the task of getting up a dinner worthy of the day. His efforts were entirely successful, and as the highest compliment we could pay him, we did full justice to the repast " our Blot " had prepared. The bill of fare embraced roast lamb, onions, canned peaches, corn-starch pudding, and sauces. It was not a bad dinner to sit down to on Mount Washington on Christmas day ! Mr. S. and I did the smoking for the whole party ; all for the " Benefit of Commerce."   S..

K., and N. made a *call* at the Tip-top House, but did not stay long, the wind was too severe. Mr. S. takes our four-footed friends, the sable and mice, under his especial care, and sees that they get all the waste food. They are our companions, though we see them but seldom.

January 10. After ten A. M. the summit was free from clouds, but below masses of clouds were driven along the valleys and over the lower summits, and above there was more or less of cirro-stratus. The clouds about and over gave grand effects of light and shade along the mountain ranges; they were particularly fine on Adams and Jefferson and near the Glen. The snow is nearly all off the houses and the rocks, — a great change in three days' time. I cannot let the day pass without a mention of the high temperature — at one P. M. it was 37°. Like April it seemed, but who knows what it will be to-morrow ?

January 14. Last night we saw a fine aurora, broken arches with streamers. Never before was one apparently so near; it certainly did look as though it was within reach. The driving masses of clouds passing between it and us made the view more interesting, as they filled the valley between us and the ridge north, nearly at our level. Some of the views to-day have been grand, although it has been more or less cloudy. The lichen-covered rocks look splendid this warm weather.

January 16.   Still raining. At eleven this fore-noon Mr. S. started out on a voyage of discovery, but it rained so hard and the walking was so diffi-cult that he soon came back. Didn't stop long however; he is too energetic a man to give up easily; so putting on an overcoat and otherwise pre-pared, he once more went out, determined to find the break in the wire, if he had to go to Littleton. Wished him good-luck, not expecting to see him for three or four days, and he was off. But we soon heard the click, click, click of the instrument, and then we knew that he had found the break. In half an hour he returned; the break was at the Gulf Tank.   Mr. Huntington went down to the spring to-day and brought up a pail of water. A week ago this was an arctic region, now it is more like April in the valleys of New Hampshire.

January 17.   The wind was high during the night, say eighty miles.   This A. M. at seven o'clock only seventy-five! — strong enough, however, to compel Mr. H. to sit while he measured the force of the wind, that he might not be carried over into Tucker-man's Ravine.   A trip to that famous locality is pleasant under some circumstances — on a fine summer day, for instance, — but not so agreeable on the wings of a winter gale. Has blown stiffly all day, yet we have taken the air several times — pleasant walks in the face of a fifty-mile breeze.

Perfectly clear at sunset. Had one of the best views of the shadow of Mount Washington yet obtained. The mountains far and near look dull and gray now, since the rains.

January 18. I have seen to-day a sea of clouds. It is a rare, a grand, a magnificent sight. At ten A. M. westward from a line due north and south, as far as the eye could see, the clouds presented the appearance of a frozen ocean. The surface level and motionless, apparently, but really moving eastward and only a little below the summit. In no direction west of a line north and south was there a glimpse of mountain or valley. Turning to the east the contrast was striking, for in this direction there was scarcely a single cloud, and the atmosphere was remarkably clear. Saco Valley was never more distinct, while the range comprising Clay, Jefferson, and Adams was completely hidden, but the Carter range loomed up as on a clear morning when not a single cloud can be seen, and far away the ocean was plainly visible. I went out south to a point of rocks and stood there almost over the clouds. Above were beautiful forms of cirrus clouds, very high.

January 19. Mr. H. called us out before sunrise to see the beauty of the morning; in truth it was wicked to miss such a glorious view as we had. Perfectly clear and nearly calm. Never before have I seen the shadow of the mountain so grand on the western sky, never so charming the purple tints at break of day. Never so impressive have been the shaded outlines, the lights and shadows on the mountains and in the valleys as on this memorable morning. Sunset was but the complement of the morning, and the evening is beautiful as ever night can be; the stars shine with a light as soft as June, — all, all, is beautiful. Who would not live on Mount Washington? Who would not brave danger, endure hardship, and the loss of social ties for the pleasure of these clear winter days upon the mountain summit? H. and S. took their constitutional in the shape of a sled-ride down toward the Glen, about a mile ride, making some of the way 2.40. It is slightly hazardous, but full of fun and very exciting.

January 21. Mr. S. started early for the camp at the base of the mountain, but met with a serious accident, badly spraining his ankle near Jacob's Ladder, so that he had to return. How fortunate that he did not break his leg, as we should have known nothing of it, and had he not been able to crawl to the camp he surely must have perished! We should not have been alarmed if he had not returned, for it is no unusual thing for the one going down to stay over night.

January 22. Having a gale to-day, and not

only a high wind, but a temperature below anything I have ever experienced before, now at nine P. M. —34° inside the door. The wind is eighty miles, blowing steadily. At two P. M. wind seventy-two, Professor H. measured the velocity. He had to sit with a line around him, myself at the other end indoors, as an anchor; even then it was almost impossible for him to keep his position. Temperature —31°. I put up a pendulum this morning in our room, it is four feet long, and the rod passes through a sheet of card board, on which are marked the points of compass. The oscillations when the wind blew in gusts were in every direction, changing suddenly, and sometimes had a rotary motion. When the wind was steady the oscillations were northwest and southeast. With two fires the room is cold to-night. Had a long talk with Littleton and Concord, all anxious to know how cold it is here.

January 23. The wind raged all night. The house rocked fearfully, but as we had no fear of a wreck, it did not disturb us much. Sometimes it would seem as if things were going by the board, but an inspection showed everything all right. It is a sublime affair, such a gale, — only we do not care to have it repeated too often. Nobody was hurt or scared, though there was not much sleep for our party, with such an uproar of the elements.

Evidently the spirits of the mountain are angry at this invasion of their domain. Toward morning the wind ceased, and all day it has been nearly calm. The temperature outside —43°. Professor H. and myself sat up all night to keep fires going. The pendulum gave oscillation of an inch and a half at times during the night. Temperature to-night ten P. M. —40°; a changeable climate this.

January 27. Stormy all day, wind from forty to sixty-eight miles per hour. H. measured the force of the wind at seven P. M. How he stood up against it is hard to tell, — came in covered with frost and snow. To-night we had some fearful gusts, the house creaked in every joint, and the ice was thrown against the side of the building in terrific showers.

Crash went a pane of glass, in a minute another, and then a third. Lively times for awhile, but fortunately the windows are double, and the inner ones escaped. We fitted some boards in case they should be needed, but soon after the wind moderated.

January 30. It is a quiet, mild, clear day. Clouds beautiful, bright, and fleecy, floating gracefully past the summit. At four P. M. one dense cloud stretched from Mount Washington to the Green Mountains.

January 31. The most glorious sunrise this winter. To the east was a sea of clouds, somewhat broken and much lower than usual. The protruding peaks resembled islands more than ever before. Over Northern New Hampshire and Maine, and along the coast, the clouds were very dense, but their upper surface as the sun shone across them was of dazzling brightness, while singular forms of cirrus clouds overcast the sky. Low in the west it was intensely black, and detached masses of clouds floated along the northern horizon. For an hour after sunrise all these cloud forms were constantly changing in color, — purple and crimson, leaden hues and rose-tints, almost black and dazzling white.

February 1. Clouds on the summit till noon, then it suddenly cleared up. Early in the forenoon the wind was fully fifty miles an hour ; at noon it was nearly calm and till nine P. M., not above 20. At nine P. M. the thermometer indicated —16°. Mr. Huntington went to the camp for mail, this morning, and returned at one P. M. bringing nothing. No one has been out to the White Mountain House this week. Mr. Smith has been making repairs on the line. It is his first day out since the 21st ult. S. has sent off all delayed messages this evening.

From 3.30 P. M. to sunset there were the finest cloud displays possible. Eastward heavy masses of cloud in color from gray to an intense black ; west, detached cirro-stratus presenting every shade and color. Along the northern horizon a clear, white light rested ; the west was burning bright in crimson, purple, and gold, while far south, fading out toward the east into gray, the color was a delicate rose-tint. Below to the west, far as we could see, the whole country was covered with cloud. The icy peaks glow and glisten in the bright sunlight. The transitions of shades and tints, the colors burning into the radiant sunset, surpassing anything we have seen yet for a sunset scene, mark this as a day never to be forgotten. As I write it seems like a dream-picture.

Thursday, February 2, 10 p. m. This has been one of the indifferent days, of which there are fortunately few. Just now it looks as though the night would prove the counterpart of the day, for it is " blowing great guns." All day the wind has been light, and it was nearly calm this evening till half an hour since, when, without any warning the gale began, not with a rising wind, but a single blast that shook the house to its foundations. I said that we had no warning of its approach, we had notice of it in the falling of the barometer.

A moment before the first blast, some one called attention to the quiet night, remarking that the storm would not probably reach us before morning, when conversation was suddenly interrupted by the uproar of the elements. We had a hearty laugh at the expense of the party who predicted a pleasant night. Now, eleven o'clock, the wind has risen to the dignity of a gale. As the temperature is —20° out-doors, and too low for comfort in this room, we are going to replenish the fires and retire to our more comfortable beds.

A wind blowing sixty miles an hour is quite as agreeable as these calm, cloudy days, when if one goes out there is nothing to see, or, if from choice remains in-doors, it is to sit in the twilight gloom of the little room. In cloudy weather we frequently light up at three o'clock. Think I had better toast my half-frozen feet and go to bed, as Professor and S. have already done.

Friday, February 3. Well, it did blow last night, making some of the time such a racket out-doors and in-doors too for that matter, that sleep was out of question. Must have been high as ninety during several of the heaviest gusts. For a change we get to-day the most severe snow-storm of the winter, so far. The wind is northwest, the point from which our storms and hurricanes come. At no time has the temperature been higher than 5°; it was —25° this morning at seven o'clock.

S. and myself are yet on the sick-list, so all the hard work falls to Professor H. To add to the discomfort of our situation the line failed last night, just after S. got off the Press despatch. Cold as it is, and has been all day, Professor H. made six trips down the railway repairing line.　His method was to find and repair a break, then run for the house, get thoroughly warmed and rested, and then out for another attempt.　The last time he went to the Gulf, below there he did not dare go.　So, as there is at least one more splice to make, far as any good for to-night telegraphing goes, his labors were of no avail.　S. and I have taken things quietly, spending the day in reading.

It is not a trifling duty for a day like this, to keep the fires going.　The wind has not been high through the day, but is now, nine o'clock, rising. The intense cold of to-day makes our little, dark, rough-finished room, seem a very cosy place.

Saturday, February 4, 9 P. M.　The wind rising toward morning has held its own all day, at no time being below seventy-five, and since 8.30 acts as though it was ambitious to attain the ninety mile standard.　This has been so cold a day that we found Dr. Kane's voyages most suitable reading.　At seven A. M. —33°.　From five P. M. to this last observation it has gradually worked down to —40°.　We have not suffered from the cold, simply because we have not exposed ourselves.　In the room at no time has the temperature been lower than 35°, and most of the time we have managed to keep it up to about 60°.　To do this we have the stoves at a red heat; the thermometer hangs pre-

cisely five feet from the stove; ten feet from the
stove at the floor to-day the temperature was only
12°, and at the same time was 65° in other parts
of the room. Of course the quantity of coal consumed is greatly in excess of the usual daily allow-
ance. Did we use wood for fuel in such weather
it would be an impossibility to keep ourselves comfortable.

Professor H. has taken the anemometer out for
a three minutes' airing at the several regular hours
of observation. I timed him the last hour. I
much prefer to be the timer in a wind like this,
than the one to hold the anemometer. Had hard
work to reach the house, — don't think he will care
to try it again to-night. Evidently we shall catch
it, as the wind is steadily rising and the barometer
falling rapidly.

The cloud was dense in the forenoon, light in
the evening to seven o'clock, and now there is no
upper current of cloud, but the valleys are full.
The moon never shone more brightly. But what a
wind, — will wait till morning and then I may have
something to say. S. is watching the barometer
and reading. Professor reads awhile, then takes a
look out. I am going to bed.

Midnight. Really, there is quite a breeze just
now. Some of the gusts, from what we know of
the measured force, must be fully up to one hun-

dred miles per hour. In fact it is a first-class hurricane. The wind is northwest, and as the house is broadside to it the full force is felt. At times it seems as though everything was going to wreck.

We go to the door and look out, — it is the most we can do; to step beyond, with nothing for a holdfast, one would take passage on the wings of the wind in the direction of Tuckerman's Ravine. However unwillingly one might go, such would be the result if he should venture outside, so irresistible is the fury of wind.

Find that I froze my fingers while *sawing* off a piece of pork for our "Sunday baked beans;" was out only five minutes. It was like cutting into a block of gypsum to saw off that piece of pork. Wish we had engaged a competent "cullared pusson" to take charge of the culinary department, for none of us are first-class cooks.

What varied sounds the wind has as it changes: now howling, screeching, roaring, as though the building was surrounded by demoniac spirits bent upon our destruction. We shout across the room to be heard. Now it suddenly lulls and moaning and sighing it dies away. Then quickly gathering strength it blows as if it would hurl the house from the summit. The timbers creak and groan and the windows rattle; tho walls bend inward; and as the wind lets go its hold rebound with a jerk that starts the joints again. The noise is like rifle-firing in fifty different directions, at the same moment; in the room, — a moment ago close by me as I sat here, leaning against the wall, now in the outer room or up aloft, and outside as well. Then there is the trembling and groaning of the whole building, which is constant. Everything movable is on the move. Books drop from the shelves, we pick them up, replace them only to do it again and again. Professor has just looked at the thermometer, finds the temperature lower than at last observation, is now —40°. Professor and S. are taking hourly observations. When we hear an unusually loud report in the outer room one goes to inspect, — nothing has given away yet. I am going to bed, to get warm if not to sleep.

Sunday, February 5. From one to two A. M. the wind was higher than during the early part of the night. Some of the gusts must have been above 100, possibly 110. The tempest roared and thundered. It had precisely the sound of the ocean waves breaking on a rocky shore. And the building too had the motion of a ship scudding before a gale. At three A. M., the temperature had fallen to —59° and the barometer stood at 22.810, attached thermometer 62°. Barometer was lowest yesterday at eight A. M., when it was 22.508, and attached thermometer 32°. Now, seven A. M., the thermometer indicates —25°. and the wind has fallen to 70. By accident the spirit thermometer has not yet been received. But this has been the only day when the mercurial instrument has not been perfectly reliable. The valleys are full of stratus clouds; charged with frost as they are, occasionally sweeping over the summit, they completely cover one in a moment, hair, beard, and clothing; when the face is exposed it feels like the touch of a hot iron. To breathe this frosty air is very unpleasant. A full inhalation induces a severe coughing fit. Our butter-tubs stand in the outer-room; this morning we cut a piece of butter for breakfast, using a chisel and hammer! — it was like cutting into a stone.

Nine A. M. Talked over the events of the past night at the breakfast table, recalling many laughable incidents, and agreeing that we rather enjoyed the night's experience than otherwise, that it was a sublime affair (having full confidence that the house would stand, the storm had no terrors for us); but all things considered, were unanimous in the opinion that once a fortnight was quite often enough for such grand displays of the storm-king's power. Of all the nights since this party came here the last exceeds every one.

Nine P. M. It has been a rough day; down in the world, people would say a severe one; so should we but for the recollection of last night.

MEASURING THE WIND.

Sergeant Smith measuring the wind when the velocity was 88 miles to the hour. The sun shone brightly. Mt. Adams is the prominent snowy peak in the distance.

Our coal-bin is under two feet of snow, and anywhere in that room the snow is six inches deep.

The wind is falling and temperature rising; it seems as though we should get a good night's rest, — no one will object in the least.

Monday, February 6. The highest temperature to-day, 12°, and the lowest now, nine P. M., 2°, is a very acceptable change. Wind 50 in forenoon, now 20, — is good as a calm. It is clear, and the moonlight is that of the mountain, seen only at this or higher elevations.

They have put the line in order to-day, and Professor sent an interesting Press despatch. Wonder if our situation excites any comment, especially as we have held no communication with the lower world for three days. S. has cleared off his Washington reports, — a dozen of them. I have improved the time in writing letters. Professor set some glass this afternoon, out doors; — the wind at 40 and thermometer 8°.

Tuesday, February 7. A glorious sunrise; a quiet, warm day, and at sunset almost equal to that of the 1st inst. Temperature at two P. M. 62° in the sun. Change of temperature since Sunday of 121°!

This afternoon I finished the work of setting glass begun by Professor yesterday; worked without gloves and was warm enough. Heard the whistle of an engine on the Grand Trunk road; seldom the sound of an engine whistle reaches us, or any sound from the busy world. For anything of sight or sound below, we might as well be living on the shore of Morton's Polar Sea.

Professor went to the station this forenoon, came back at two P. M., — no mail for us. The snow is deep, but the crust is hard, so he made an easy trip of it. S. made extensive repairs on the line this forenoon; now it is all right till the next heavy gale. It is working better than ever to-night.

I have given some time this afternoon to the study of cloud formations. Days like this are so rare that we improve every opportunity for investigation. Gales, storms, hurricanes, all clear off with a north wind, — a wind gentle and soft as the south wind of the lower regions. How can this be explained? It is S.S.W. to-night and two miles per hour, a marked contrast to Sunday morning! Mr. Holden, "Ranger" of the "Boston Journal," telegraphs from Littleton that we may look for him to-morrow. Great is the rejoicing here, for a visitor is a god-send, and none more welcome than Mr. H.

Wednesday, February 8. Ten P. M. There is evidently a snow-storm along the coast, the northern edge within fifty miles of us. This forenoon we could see the storm as it moved eastward. It was cloudy and clear by turns on the summits, that is, the lower current of cloud rested at times over us. The valleys east were full, and the upper stratum overcast the entire country far as could be seen. Wind S.S.W., from 20 to 50. Temperature from 14° at seven A. M., to 20° at two P. M. Interesting to watch the progress of the storm, and to see the lower current of cloud driven by an easterly wind running under the higher stratum which, of course, was moving *toward* the northeast. Lake Winnipiseogee showing dimly, all the country beyond hidden from sight.

Professor left immediately after breakfast for the station — Marshfield, — to escort our expected guests, Messrs. Holden, Cogswell, and our whilom companion, Clough. S. and I busy making things "ship-shape" around the house ; laid in a supply of ice, enough for three days' consumption. Are obliged to look sharp in fair weather and lay in an ample stock of ice, for it sometimes happens that we cannot replenish for several days.

At noon the party arrived; they received from us a right hearty welcome. They brought a large mail, and a contribution of magazines and papers. Some of the dailies are a fortnight old, yet we read them with as much eagerness as we do the evening paper at home.

Ours was as jolly a dinner-party as ever met at " Young's " or " Parker's." And the evening has

passed pleasantly; we had something to tell our
friends of mountain life, and they, in return, had
much to relate of events occurring since we left the
region below the clouds.

Arrangements are being made for the night;
our accommodations are limited: it is two in each
bed and two on the floor. S. and I sleep on the
floor; as we are used to roughing it, doubtless we
shall sleep soundly.

Thursday, February 9. Nine P. M. Cloudy
all day, wind moderate, temperature high as 26°.
The cloud on the mountain so dense that it was
impossible to see ten rods in any direction. The
frost-work is fine.

Had a roast-turkey dinner with all the side
dishes that our mountain larder could supply. I
must note — if I desire to be considered " truthful
James " — that our *roasted* bird was *baked*. The
united verdict was, that it was a capitally got up
meal. Fun and good humor made everything pass
agreeably, and we did not miss the many little ac-
cessories supposed to be necessary to a well-ordered
table.

It is a pleasure to have company in this out-of-
the-world-place. And I sincerely hope that we
may be able to treat our friends to some one or
more of the Mount Washington novelties, a gorgeous sunrise or brilliant sunset, a superior show of

frost-work, or failing in these, something in the line of hurricanes. It is a pity they should be at the trouble of making the ascent at this inclement season and not take back something of the experience which falls to our lot daily, something to endure or enjoy, as the case may be.

The line has been down to-day between Littleton and Concord, this time it is *not* the Mount Washington cable.

The papers say that fears were entertained for our safety during the time the line was down. Knowing better than the good people below all about the matter, we had not the least anxiety.

Friday, February 10. The wind high all day, 88 at two P. M.; Holden having the honor of measuring its velocity; Professor timing him. H. acknowledges perfect satisfaction as regards Mount Washington winter winds. Now, seven P. M., the wind is rapidly rising. Been cloudy all day; a dense cloud on the summit charged with frost.

Have done very little writing to-day, any of us, but we find the time passing quickly in the society of our visitors. In conversation, our party most resembles a Debating Club doing up six months' business in a three days' session.

12.30. It is past midnight and we are beginning to talk of retiring. About eight o'clock the wind had worked up to the ninety mile rate, and then commenced a furious bombardment of ice from the summit and frost-work from off the house. The house shook and trembled as the fiercer blasts beat against it. Pieces of ice were driven between the bars protecting the windows, and at last by one heavy discharge three panes were broken. As good luck would have it the broken lights were in the room above. The roar of the wind as it rushed through the opening was enough to wake a Rip Van Winkle.

Professor, Clough, Smith, and myself were out in a moment, and after having the " hurricane " lantern blown out — which is warranted to burn the brighter the higher the wind, — and twice extinguished, we succeeded in nailing boards over the aperture. Still the bombardment was going on for an hour, but no more glass was broken. The supply of ammunition was exhausted by ten o'clock, and then, though the wind was terrific, we did not mind the gale.

Professor, Cogswell, and Clough went to bed; Clough not to stay there long, for Holden, Smith, and myself were having too pleasant a time chatting and reading around the table. Only when a more than usually heavy gust struck, did we pay any attention to what was going on outside. Half an hour ago we made coffee and partook of a lunch; now we think of retiring. The line failed

just after H.'s " Journal " despatch went.   One
thing sure, — our friends have had the enjoyment of
a very respectable, if not a first-class gale.   It does
not seem now as if it would rise to the rank of that
of December, January, or the one of last week.
The temperature at nine P. M. was —20°.   Hourly
observations to-day.

And now we are going to bed to hear the wind
blow, if not to sleep.

February 11.   It has been a rough, disagreeable day; a dense cloud on the summit till late in
the evening.   But as if to compensate us for being
shut in and seeing nothing all day, there has been
during the entire evening a magnificent aurora.
Now — nine, P. M. — the temperature is —21°;
not above zero at any time during these last
twenty-four hours.

Clough and Smith made an attempt to repair the
line this morning, but were forced to give in before
they had gone far.

We had for pudding on our table this noon, the
Christmas gift of Mrs. ——— .   Our guests pro-
nounced it excellent.   Following a griddle-cake
breakfast, this is truly " high " living.   Subsisting in
the main, as we do, on canned beef, hard-tack, and
coffee, such trifles make " talk " in this household.

Monday, February 13.   Evening.   So busy in
the forenoon yesterday, writing letters, and lastly,

helping the party in their preparations for the descent, that I found no time for the Journal. In the afternoon, had the magazines to read.

The party left at 11.20. S. and I watched them going down as long as we could see them, and then returned to the house, perhaps a little envious; a little more thoughtful, more silent we certainly were than usual, though this is not the first time we have lived by ourselves. Really, these few days have passed most agreeably.

The dinner was eaten in silence, and then we read till ten o'clock, neither feeling in a mood for conversation.

Soon after the party had gone, a snow-storm set in. It had been cloudy all the morning, and snowing to six A. M. There is a foot of light snow, the largest quantity at any one time this month.

The day fine with little wind, and a temperature of 25° in the sun and 5° in shade at two P. M. A nearly clear sky above, the valleys clouded over at sunrise. The clouds in the morning did not present any remarkable features for this locality, but from three to half-past four P. M., there was an extensive " sea of clouds." It extended from a point sixty miles north, far as the ocean east, bounded only by the horizon. This summit was alone above the cloud. It was to the eye a frozen polar ocean, here and there a lofty mountain of ice rising from the apparent dead level surface. The setting sun, throwing a silvery light along the cloud, dispelled the illusion. Perfectly clear overhead all day, — our sunny day contrasts strongly with the cold, gloomy, cloudy one below. If we have much cloud here, it is not always sunshine there.

There is a cosy spot which I visited to-day, five minutes walk from the hotel in a southerly direction. It is a large boulder, six or eight feet high and as many wide, forming a perfect wind-break. Light as the wind was, we were chilled through while on the summit, but under the shelter of this rock it was warm enough, and then the outlook is one of the best.

The evening is calm, and it seems strange to have so quiet a night, yet the change is appreciated by us. A bright, starlight night. We have been out to enjoy its beauty. These days and nights like this are all too rare to lose one of them. The telegrams are sent. S. gets one from Littleton, who says, " cloudy here all day." Also one from the Professor, reporting the party at Littleton this morning. These, to us, important messages, we discuss as I write, and " guessing " as to the weather for to-morrow, we close the day's labors and think of retiring.

Tuesday, February 14. Relieving, in a large measure, the monotony of mountain life in winter,

are cloud views. To-day we had in early morning a " sea of clouds," and later, the pleasure of
watching and noting the progress of a storm.   The
under current below the level of the summit, as it
came in from the ocean, and its advance westerly ;
far south the storm-cloud moving toward the northeast, snowing over Lake Winnipiscogee two hours
before it did here, was a sight worth seeing.   Some
idea of the grandeur of an advancing storm may
be obtained from a description ; but a clear conception of it, only by seeing it.   Snowing at 5.30
P. M. Concord and Boston report " snow."   S. has
had a long talk with each of these operators.

Had Hanover to-night. Professor Hitchcock, for
the Scientific Association, has taken by telegraph,
the pulsations, heart, and wrist, of the " members
resident."   Wind southwest, not above fourteen ;
highest temperature 18° at two in the afternoon,
and 7° at seven in the evening.   Barometer nearly
stationary.

Wednesday, February 15.   The storm was but
for the night. Clear at seven in the morning ; temperature 5°, and wind N.N.W.   Fine ocean view
this morning.   Northwest wind all day, rough but
not cold.   Many and sudden changes of temperature, as for instance, at six in the evening 13°, and
nine o'clock, 20°. Littleton reports, " quite warm in
L. ; " we wish it might be here.   Interesting cloud

formations which I record elsewhere. A heavy cloud lying low in the south to-night.

By request of Professor Hitchcock, we sent a long despatch to the Dartmouth Scientific Association this evening. S. has had his hands full to-night, sending and receiving more messages than many regular offices do in two days.

Repairing the line to-day, he found a great depth of snow a mile down the road.

Thursday, February 16. A storm of snow and rain. It rains here with the thermometer at 22°, as it did to-day, and snows with it at 30°, as might be supposed. Why it should rain at 22° is hard to explain. Wind steady, southwest through the day, but at 8.20 evening, changed suddenly to northwest, in gusts, sixty to eighty miles per hour. At nine p. m., still snowing. Forgot to mention last night, that at 6.30 p. m., I read from the " Atlantic " in the open air. Our days are about forty-six minutes longer than they are at the sea-level. And this reminds me of the gentleman in B., who expressed much sympathy for us on account of the *short* days we should have, half an hour shorter, he said. I accepted his expressions of commiseration without trying to set him right as to the facts.

Neither S. or myself have written at all; read an hour or two, turned post-laundress for an hour, doing my own washing — it is every one for himself in this institution, — then I cut S.'s hair, which he could not well do for himself, and so went the day. But would not our friends make themselves merry, especially our lady friends, to see us get a dinner, or at the wash-tub, or playing the part of a tidy house-keeper as we dust the parlor furniture and mantel ornaments ! Ours is a queer style of living ; if we have many pleasures which others know nothing of, there are some deprivations and not a few hard-ships to offset the advantages. We shall never forget the grand, sublime, and beautiful scenes of this place, and shall remember what living on Mount Washington in winter means. It will have a significance for us, if not for others. Littleton sends us the news that four gentlemen are on their way to Mount Washington ; does not say who they are.

Friday, February 17. Blustering weather, that is, only rough for Mount Washington, but would pass for a gale down below.

About noon the expected visitors arrived. They were favored in having the wind to help them, as a southwest wind is the worse, one having to face it. Northwest to-day. These gentlemen are Messrs. Walter and Chas. L. Aiken, Geo. C. Procter, of Franklin, New Hampshire, and Michael Mularvey, of Marshfield, New Hampshire. They brought us a large mail. Stopped to dinner, but returned to M., instead of spending the night here, as we hoped they would do. It was a disappointment to us, for we had counted on keeping them over night.

Done nothing but write a few letters this evening. It is calm or nearly so; calm as it ever is here, — never is quite that. The line is down somewhere. A storm is brewing.

Tuesday, February 21. Have not written a line for three days; or since Saturday, when we had a tough snow-storm and a wind all day that held us imprisoned much against the will of either, S. because the line was down, and I, from a decided preference to out-door life. In the afternoon and to a late hour in the evening we were busy with household duties.

Sunday proved clear and calm, a bright sunny day, yet the temperature was at no time higher than 8°. We had breakfast, then S. went out to repair breaks in the cable and I sat down to my writing. The line must be repaired as soon as possible after a break, and if the first fair day is Sunday, as it happens to be this time, it becomes proper Sunday labor. Then, what could I do better than to answer some one or more of the dozen letters awaiting replies?

S. said when he left that he should not go far, and should be in by one P. M. Did not come, but two o'clock did. After taking the usual observations

I went down the railway.   Found him at the Gulf
Tank.   He had been hard at work since early morning ; the line was in an awful condition — broken in
nearly a hundred places.

Last Saturday night's gale must have been a
hurricane over that part of the mountain.   Perhaps
it was worse here than we imagined, but we sleep
so soundly even in the heaviest gales, that the night
might have been one of the most tempestuous and
we wholly unconscious of the raging storm.

It was my first long walk since Christmas-week,
after which date I was confined to the house till
within a few days.   Weary from the unwonted exercise, I sat awhile seeing him at work, then becoming chilled I slowly made my way home.   Found
the fires down and the house cold.   S. came in
soon after hungry and tired, his feet half frozen and
fingers quite so.   Tried to start a fire in the cook-
stove till our patience failed, and we voted ourselves
a cold dinner.   Nor was it until bed-time that we
had raised the temperature of the room to anything
like comfort.   Went to bed early — past ten o'clock,
for S. takes an observation at that hour, and we
always sit up as late as ten P. M., — and woke
Monday morning to find it cold and windy, with a
dense cloud on the mountain.

No work on the cable, though S. made one attempt, contrary to my advice, and was driven back

after going a short distance, — came in covered with snow and frost. Writing to-day and when tired of that smoked. The room has been warm, but it is stinging cold outside. A fierce snow-storm all day.

This Tuesday morning we were out at day-break. A cold morning, temperature at seven A. M.—8°; the fires troubled us; had a cold breakfast, a warm one is a matter of the highest importance to us.

Then S. went down to finish repairs, returning at noon. Got off all delayed telegrams at two P. M. He has labored under disadvantages, but persistently, for ten hours.

Littleton says that Hanover has inquired for us every day.

When S. left this morning the thermometer read —4° and wind 20 ; at the Gulf Tank it was so warm he had to lay aside overcoat and gloves, —no wind there, — the snow was melting and the water running down the centre rail ; quite a contrast to the summit, yet only one mile distant, —meteorologically speaking, he was 300 miles south of his mountain home, though in sight of it.

After dinner laid in a large lot of ice, and then we had some cooking to do. " Housework " done, we took a walk. Fine weather, for a change. Beautiful cloud-views this afternoon. Light, fleecy clouds floating over Mount Monroe, dissolved before reaching Tuckerman's Ravine. They passed between us and the sun, showing the prismatic colors, then as they rolled eastward gradually faded out and changed to a cold gray. The transitions of light and shade were inexpressibly beautiful, enough to give sensations of pleasure to the dullest observer and drive an artist crazy with delight.

The buildings are cased in ice and frost-work of most elegant forms, resembling rocks, flowers, leaves, shells, and the wings of birds. Some are in Italian marble, others in alabaster. In another place I have written out a description in full.

Wednesday, February 22. The only perfectly clear day this month; cool, the mean temperature being but 1.7°. These clear days, and if nearly calm, so much the better, are the chief attractions, or rather among them, for cloud-views count in the list. On such days even the most distant mountain peaks are clearly outlined. Katahdin is to-day plainly seen, as are some mountains in Canada as distant. The view is not often good in a southerly direction, — it is not to-day. The mountains belonging to this group show grandly in the bright sunlight.

S. has been working on the line and I have spent the day in writing. In such weather this is a pleasant winter residence.

Anniversary of Washington's birth-day, and we

had not thought of it until now! We might have raised our little flag in honor of the day ; it would have been " quite the thing."

Thursday, February 23. A nearly clear day here, but people below over a wide extent of country had a cloudy one. So much we had the advantage over them. Highest temperature at nine P. M. 23°, wind westerly, at no time higher that 45, barometer 23.90, higher than for many days.

Writing for *Work and Play*, the most difficult writing I ever tried my hand at, — prefer to write for adult readers. As this is a very excellent location for observation, one may fill pages daily with notes, but it is the worst possible place to work up anything fit for publication. There is so much to see : now it is a wonderful cloud-view; then the summit is covered for a half hour, perhaps ; next the sun shines, and we know that if we go out some new revelation awaits us, a new surprise to distract the attention from the work in hand.

This evening, the bright starlight tempted me out. I did not propose to go far away from the buildings, but the night was so clear, so calm, and the stars shone with such brilliancy, I was induced to extend my walk down the mountain in a southerly direction, till out of sight of home.

If any person is curious to know what solitude means, to have a full realization of the term let that one come here, and spend a half hour away from sight or sound of the busy world, — make himself believe for the nonce that he is the only one human being on the mountain, and if he does not confess that the word has a deeper meaning than ever he had thought, he is either more or less than human.

Friday, February 24. A dense cloud on the mountain, so that indoors we had a twilight gloom disappearing only for an hour in the afternoon. The day was so spring-like that we did not stay in the house. This morning I went down the railway to look after the line, there is trouble with it again. S. came down soon after, overtaking me at Lizzie Bourne's monument.

As we could not leave the house unguarded, he went further and I returned. Where he left me the cloud was so dense that it was difficult to distinguish any object a short distance below. Yet he passed out of the cloud into fair weather only a little way lower down; at the Gulf he entered the cloud again and encountered a heavy rain. Snow is melting and a thousand tiny rills are making music on the mountain.

The wind southwest, and a soft April wind too. This afternoon we had to go no farther than the Glen stables to enjoy the warm sunshine, while here it was chilly, cloudy, and damp.

From nine A. M. to three P. M. the temperature varied but a degree or two from 37°; the barometer steady.

Saturday, February 25. Dull and gloomy, for a dense cloud rested on the mountain all day. Wind 74 at two P. M. It was fair at Littleton. In a day like this one can read if he does nothing more. Two or three days like this tend to make us think of our daily life as being in the least possible degree monotonous. One will do, but more become unendurable.

Sunday, February 26. A morning perfect as a morning of winter can well be. Clouds in the valleys, the ocean visible for a long distance up and down the coast and far out to sea. About nine A. M. a heavy cloud commenced to move inland, one portion of it moving up the Saco valley; its progress was so slow that it did not shut the Glen House in till seven P. M. Heavy upper current southwest and thick in the south. Wind west to two P. M., then southwest and rising. The thermometer indicated 25° at two P. M.

The frost-work made last night has more the form of feathers this time. If the snow and frost of the summit was as uninteresting as that of the lowlands, Mount Washington would lose one of its greatest charms. What studies for an artist in the various forms the frost-work presents! I made a very beautiful model for a vase of frost leaves, a day or two ago, simply taking four leaves of equal size, which were a little wider at the extremity than the base, and slightly concave. A more exquisite design it would be hard to find in Nature's Book.

Monday, February 27. This time we are favored with a rain-storm, pouring when it was calm, and in driving sheets after the wind rose to the agreeable rate of eighty-four miles per hour. At nine A. M. it changed to snow, and then it was by turns, rain for a moment, quickly changing to snow and suddenly rain again; but the snow obtained the mastery. The barometer fluctuated as it often does, falling in the afternoon.

We brought water from the spring this morning, the first since some time in January, I think. The wind was not so high as later in the day; it was getting water under difficulties, however. Shut in all day, but we had enough to do to keep us busy; so although a disagreeable day the time did not hang heavy on our hands.

Hanover telegraphs the welcome news of " Peace in Europe," and also the pleasing intelligence that Mr. Huntington is on his way to Mount Washington. We shall ply him with questions, S. says, for we are wholly ignorant of what is transpiring outside our little world. Our labors are limited to a few things done over and over day after day; observations on clouds, winds, and storms in addition, which last vary from time to time; our pleasures and recreations consist almost solely in walks around the narrow bounds of the summit, and in reading. We find a pleasure in correspondence, but our letters are one, two, three, sometimes four weeks old when we get them. I lately received a letter from England of the same date with one written less than two hundred miles distant. Professor H. has seen the world since we have and most assuredly will bring a full budget of news.

Tuesday, February 28. This is one of those days which make us contented with our home. It cleared off early in the morning. Wind from fifty to seventy miles per hour. The mean temperature for this day is 0; this cold weather combined with the high wind compelled us to remain in the house. I took the time for writing and did not go out at all until four P. M., when I got in a very small quantity of ice — the wind so strong that I lost the pail once, and my foothold a dozen times. Not troubled by " callers " to-day.

The frost-work is again fine and the house, if not a marble palace, looks like a building fashioned from purest marble, no part of the chains, wooden braces, nor finish to be seen.

CHAPTER XIV.

March 1st.

IT is spring at last, and how quickly the winter has passed, though no more pleasantly to me than to the others. I had thought, as is often the case under like circumstances, that time would rather drag. Welcome to the spring! — not that I am at all anxious to see May 1, for this is altogether too pleasant living here to wish to have time pass rapidly, but spring-time is ever welcome. Even Mount Washington, in spring, has its own peculiar pleasure, it is presumable, as has the "lower world." Snowing all day, quite a furious storm even for this "home of storms." So we write to-day. From early morning to three in the afternoon, we had been at our work, when just as the subject of dinner was up, we heard voices in the outer room. It proved to be a party of whom we had heard by telegraph — Mr. K. and Mr. Wilson, editor of the "Philadelphia Photographer," and our friend "Mike." They had a hard time coming up. They brought a mail.

March 2. All were out early to witness a sunrise of rare grandeur. The valleys were full of clouds, and occasionally there would a cloud pass over us driving rapidly over into the ravine. Snowing all the afternoon. Our visitors left.

March 3. A storm seemed to be brewing last night at a late hour, and early it came, — a heavy rain-storm. Toward noon the wind rose, and at one P. M. it blew ninety-six miles per hour. How the wind roared in the flue! How the house shook! Had to shout across the room to be heard. It was grand, however. From four o'clock the wind abated. At six P. M. S. and I went for water and got wet through, — night calm.

March 4. A fine morning and warm. Had a fine view of the ocean by aid of a telescope. This glass was kindly loaned to us by a gentleman in Boston, made by R. B. Tolles, and is a splendid one for its size. Mr. S. went out to make some repairs on the cable. Our fires work badly to-day; no draft, had a cold dinner. O, the trials of house-keeping! Think I shall board in future. After all, house-work is not such an art as the ladies would have us masculines believe. Made bread to-night, and now — eleven P. M. — am waiting for the beans to boil.

March 5. Dense clouds on the mountain in the morning but clear in the afternoon. Looked for our

mail, thinking that some of our friends from Marshfield would be up, and when we heard voices outside
felt sure of it.   Went to wait on them, found they
were from the Glen House, and had come up on the
carriage-road.   Had two dogs with them, one an old
but fine specimen of the Newfoundland race, who
in his younger days had performed the responsible
duties of a mail-carrier between the Glen House
and Gorham, a distance of eight miles; he was
completely used up.   Treated both men and dogs to
a good dinner, and they started back at four P. M.

March 7th.   A fair, blustering day.   As we expected Professor H. we waited with our dinner
till three P. M.; he arrived at four P. M., and
brought Dr. Rogers and Mr. Nutter of Lancaster,
N. H., with him.   Spent the evening very pleasantly
reading our letters and papers.

March 9.   Another day peculiar to Mount
Washington.   All day the clouds have been driving over the summit.   There would be times
when it was perfectly clear.   Wind from forty to
fifty miles, and temperature as high as 43° in the
shade.

March 11.   The morning was so fine that we
felt invited out.   The rocks look charming in their
alpine-dress of beautiful, pale green, moss lichen.
The snow is nearly all gone.   We were so fortunate as to discover a fine bunch of Greenland

sandwort, one in bloom. I took up some of each for house-plants, that our parlor may boast its winter-garden.

March 15. Many have been the magnificent sunrises this winter, none more so than that of this morning. The day has been calm and nearly clear, and along the north mountains are in view that are not often seen, and some never before this winter. Heard this morning the astonishing news that New Hampshire has gone democratic.

March 16. Rainy much of the day and this evening. Mr. H. and Mr. S. out repairing the cable.

March 23. This morning there was a thick stratum of clouds eastward, at a moderate elevation above the summit. By eight A. M. it was quite dense. At nine A. M. snow-squalls to the northeast, and the clouds gradually settling in the valleys; eleven o'clock thick on the Carter Range; by twelve, clouds all about, except on the summit. By two P. M. the mountain was in the clouds. The formation — for I can call it nothing else — and progress of the storm was very interesting. The clouds were at a higher elevation than has generally been the case; cirro-stratus; color gray; uniform in density nearly over the entire field of view. Thick along the southeast, east, and northeast long before it shut down elsewhere. Evidently the

lower current of wind was from the east, while the
wind on the summit was west-northwest. It was
two hours from the time the Carter Range shut in
before the summit was enveloped. The clouds
poured over Mount Adams, and later over the
dividing ridge between Mounts Washington and
Clay. They seemed to curve, as they passed over
these mountain tops, as though the upper currents
of air conformed to the irregularities of surface.
When there are two strata of clouds, they unite
before the snow or rain falls, as a rule, though to-
day snow fell an hour previous to the clouds settling on the mountain.

March 31. A glorious sunrise. The Glen valley was full of clouds, and further east heavy masses
of clouds covered the entire country as far as we
could see. In other directions the clouds were few.
As the sun shone over the clouds eastward, the dark
heavy masses were tipped with light of silver brightness, while the borders were almost black, and the
sun shone brightly on the protruding mountain tops,
throwing deep purple shadows westward.

Saturday, April 1. What a change from last
night to this morning; then, at nine P. M. wind
fifty, temperature 3° ; with every prospect for a cold
day to follow. The wind is westerly. Although
it is not above forty-nine, the cracking reports of
the joints of the frame are loud enough to shake

weak nerves. Really they are startling, more so in a comparative calm than when the wind is blowing a gale.

These reports are never frequent in steady cold nor settled warm weather. They occur oftener as a cold term is changing to warm, and *vice versa*, due in the one case to the expansion and in the other to the contraction of the wood. Last evening one was so heavy as to shake the house like a sudden gust in a storm.

To-day 64° in the sun at eleven A. M., afterwards cooler, 15° at nine P. M. Thawing all day in the sun, snow going rapidly. Thick along the south and east all day. A northeast wind to-night, seldom from that quarter. Light wind all day. These are the days calculated, if any are, to make us discontented, they so remind us of spring-time —and here?

Clough has had the good fortune to get several fine negatives. S. and I *stood* for figures in two, S. pointing to the icicles on the roof.

Monday, April 3. Another charming day. Clough has gone to Littleton to return in a few days. S. and I baked a chicken for our principal dish on this day's dinner bill of fare. Too fine this morning to write, such a day is too rich in beautiful scenery to waste time in-doors. Our luxuries are few : in our larder, none; neither are there any in parlor, library, or bed-chamber — yes, one in the parlor, — a cane-seat *rocking-chair*. No true-born Yankee would think of housekeeping without one.

But beyond the confines of these four walls we have choice things, in the grand scenery, cloud painting, sunrises and sunsets, moonlight such as is never seen but on mountain peaks.

After dinner we went to the Tip-top House ; the view was magnificent. A soft haze over the whole expanse of country far as we could see north and south, east and west. Such is the atmosphere here, that although the thermometer in the shade marked 27°, I wore neither hat or coat, yet was warm enough. So fine a day suppose I pull on my boots and run down to Tuckerman's Ravine? But then the steeps are glare ice, and it would be a rather hazardous undertaking; it might involve a broken leg or neck, and then *possibly* in either case, my companions would deem me an incumbrance, which is a consideration of account. How cozy ; what a home-like air our dark, narrow, meanly furnished quarters have in a storm or when the wind blows ninety miles an hour ; but in such a day as this how like a prison-cell the place looks !

Tuesday, April 4. All the forenoon till one P. M. the summit was in a dense cloud. Suddenly it lifted or passed off, and then we had the most gorgeous display of cloud-scenes we have yet witnessed. Eastward masses of cumuli rested over the valleys and the mountains. Why not call them *mountains of cloud?* Certainly. They rose far above our level, six thousand or perhaps eight thousand feet higher than this peak! They conformed to the heights over which they lay and seemed to envelop other mountains nearly as lofty as their upper limits. The illusion was perfect, and Mount Washington, in comparison, was a diminutive spur or outlying peak of this great mountain range. Without ever having seen the Alps I understood them better for having seen these cloud mountains. In other directions there were masses.

The sun runs high, but we know nothing of spring. Truly it is more like winter than some of the time in March. Then there was no snow, now everywhere there is snow and ice.

Professor raised our little flag the other day on the summit for the benefit of some friends in Lancaster. He has no design of establishing an independent government, but S. and I have quietly done so, and this banner floating from the top of the mountain is that of the new Republic of Washington. We are getting along finely. We only lack three things to make our new government a success: a national debt, internal revenue, and two custom-houses, one on the carriage road and the other on the railway.

Wednesday, April 5. The wind blew a gale last night, — had just gone to bed when it commenced. The building had a heavy coating of ice on the east side and tons on the roof. Soon as the wind rose the ice began to fall. We were awake when the grand crash came, at first a few pieces, then with a roar like the stormy wind half of the great body on the roof started, and falling made everything tremble. The beds shook as in the hurricane of February. If we had not known the strength of the building — and severely it has been tested, — we might have thought that the roof had fallen in. It was startling to hear the roar and crash, and there was not for a while much disposition to sleep.

All day there has been a furious storm of snow — at one time wind 86 and temperature low as 2°. Nine P. M. wind 60, and clear.

This afternoon we were surprised by the arrival of Messrs. Clough and Cheney. They were somewhat frost-bitten, ears, fingers, and feet, and it was doubtful, for a half hour, how badly. But now they are all right, though their hands and ears are considerably swollen. It is the toughest storm in which any party has made the ascent this winter.

Professor H. pays no attention to the state of the weather in making his many journeys up and down, but he has never had a day quite so bad as this ; a day like this, or worse, would not stop him if he had arranged to make the trip.

Thursday, April 6. A clear sunrise — cold; only 3°, the wind 20, and the morning view that of December. Though clear, the sun gave little heat, — a pale, white, rayless light; the sky a light blue, and so clear that it seemed almost as though we could see beyond its bounds, or *through it* into the regions of space.

Sunday, April 9. After a bean breakfast, a party of four, Messrs. H., Andrews, Cheney, and myself, went to Tuckerman's Ravine. Professor led the way and took us to the head of the ravine, where we saw the snow arch that is to be in July, but now quite a stream poured over the cliff. All but Professor took part in rolling stones down the side of the ravine. We followed down the ravine on the north side to a bold point of rocks, some two hundred feet in height. Standing on this, we had a fine view. The ravine looks much more grand than it does from the side opposite; and one should see it from several points of view before describing its claims to admiration. Hermit Lake is breaking up, and we could see through the trees the tiny stream which winds through the ravine and loses itself in the forests below. Down the mountain side, a thousand little rills, feeders of mighty rivers, make sweet music, sweeter to my

ear from my long stay where there is only ice and
snow. Going down we had the pleasure of a little
slide on the snow, a quarter of a mile or less, long
enough, however. Coming up we had to climb, of
course. At noon, Messrs. Andrews, Clough, and
Cheney left for home.

Wednesday, April 12. A stormy day, snowing
much of the time, and the wind as high as 60.
Frost work forming again, and it really seems much
like winter. None of us cared to go far to-day, so
I got a pail of water from the spring near the house
and took a look at the frost-work; that is all the
out-door exercise I have taken. Now we shall
have a plenty as long as we stay ; we get it from a
hole among the rocks and it is of excellent quality.
We have not really suffered from the want of water
at any time, but it has been rather rough sometimes
getting ice.

Saturday, April 15. The rule holds good, no two
days alike on Mount Washington. Professor called
us out to see the sunrise. Over Berlin and all the
country in that direction lay the most beautiful
cumuli clouds. The shadow of Mount Washington
was clearly outlined on the sky far above the horizon, and we might imagine for the last three days —
while a dense cloud has covered the mountains and
hills — that an array of giants had been at work cutting every mountain ridge into sharper outline,

for they never before seemed to stand up chiseled so sharply. Chocorua seemed miles nearer than usual, resplendent in the bright sunlight. Through every rift in the clouds the sides of the chain north showed finely, while the summits were a blaze of light.

The Glen and shaded sides of Carter Range were as dark as night, while just above the clouds were gorgeous with the play of colors. Let a painter throw as much light into a mountain view, or give such tints to the clouds, and shade as deeply as nature did in the picture she gave us this morning, and everybody would say " exaggerated."

Ten hours we had splendid cloud effects in every direction. Cumuli north, in every form beautiful and fantastic, and colors as though some radiant angel had thrown aside his robe of light.

But so much glory could not last, a cloud shut down, and we were snow-bound and cloud enveloped the remainder of the day.

Wednesday, April 19. A splendid day ; have been to the station ; a rough road to travel, but took the day for the trip. Dined at the lumber camp, and got back at six o'clock. Took down mail and brought some back, though little for myself. Not in luck for once, — can stand it if my correspondents can.

Wednesday, April 26. Professor Hitchcock, E. C. Burbeck, and Alonzo Hall climbed the summit

to-day, bringing with them a bouquet of scarlet
geraniums and trailing arbutus, sent by a friend of
the Expedition.

Thursday, April 27.   Went down the Crawford
bridle-path to Mount Monroe ; then crossed Bigelow's lawn, and walked to Boott's Spur — not quite
to the extreme point.   Saw a few birds ; couldn't
make *them* out — don't know if they cared whether
I did or not ; don't know as they had any curiosity to ascertain who or what I was.   Too much
snow to find how the plants are coming on this
spring-like weather.   Found willows at the head
of Tuckerman's ravine, showing their catkins half
opened.   Reached the summit at two P. M., —
found S. down sick ; he has been ill since Sunday.   Professor Hitchcock and Mr. Burbeck came
in at five o'clock, quite tired ; had been to Mount
Adams.   Tough snow-storm to-night.   Fine cloud
effects this afternoon, as there was in the morning.
Take morning views on hearsay, as I did not rise
till breakfast-time.   The others rose at 5.30.   I had
a fearful headache last night.   Enjoyed my lonely
walk to-day,— monarch of all I surveyed.   It seems
odd to see birds, while the adjacent peaks and
others beyond are covered with snow, and to feel
that it is really spring down in the world.   Wind
at Boott's Spur, southeast, thirty miles per hour
when I left ; here same direction, eighteen miles per

hour, while at the same moment on their way from Mount Adams Messrs. Hitchcock and Burbeck encountered the wind moving at the rate of forty or fifty miles per hour.

Friday, April 28. Cloudy all day on the summit and at times rainy. At four P. M. started down the railroad expecting to meet Mr. Huntington and Mr. Holden. Went as far as Gulf Tank; encountered wind, rain, and sleet; had to keep in motion or freeze. Came back at 6.15, wet and covered with ice. Went down again at seven, sliding most of the way. When I reached the Tank, the clouds passed off, but the storm was still raging below; had a magnificent view. To show the changes in temperature here, in a few feet of altitude, I note my trips down to-day and up as well. Left the house at 4.30 P. M., wind thirty miles, at the Lizzie Bourne monument forty, at the Gulf House ruins and below, fully sixty, thus reversing the order of things in regard to wind. Thermometer on the summit 28°; frost-work forming some distance below the Monument. At the Gulf Tank, when the sun came out, as it did several times, the ice on my cap would thaw completely; then while the cloud was passing, icicles two inches in length would form on the visor. It was difficult to walk or even stand against the wind below the Gulf House ruins. Returning, the wind was not so violent; rain as far as the plateau, where they collect water for the engine in summer; mist on the summit, with thermometer 28° at 6.50. Went down again at seven P. M., cloud to the head of the Gulf and thawing as far as the tank, and water dropping from the trestle. A dead calm all the way. Every appearance of a rain-storm in the valley, probably as high as Waumbek, for at times the storm-cloud came up to the very spot where I stood. The two H.'s did not arrive, but night did, and I came back to the summit, quite well satisfied with my last trip.

Saturday, April 29. One of the finest mornings of the winter. At first a sea of clouds east and northeast, later also on the west; at seven A. M. in every direction.

Professor Hitchcock and myself sat on the roof of the Tip-top House. A luminous corona, showing from one to three distinct circles with the prismatic colors, was thrown upon the clouds around our shadows. It was in some respects like the spectre of the Bröchen. In the afternoon the clouds cast their shadows on the mountains and over the valleys; of late this has been quite common, as the cumuli assume summer forms.

Mr. Burbeck left this morning. Mr. Huntington, L. L. Holden, and E. Thompson came up. Mr. H. brought us all the late magazines, but no letters. Had rain at depot last night and high wind.

CORONA, SEEN APRIL 28.

The dark cone is shadow of observer with glory about the head. Above the foreground is the shadow of the mountain, while the large circle is the colored prism or Corona resting on clouds, and partially obscuring the two shadows.

The sable was out this morning, but did not stop long to show himself. It is the first time I have seen him. S. has seen two; they look plump and hearty, as though Mount Washington was a healthy climate for them.

Sunday, April 30. Snowing most of the time — not a gleam of sunshine; four inches of snow has fallen. Sunday passed much as Sundays do down in the world when people don't go to church. We have had the past month more clouds than sunshine, more snow than rain; light winds and few gales, the clouds often dense on the summit when clear below. Now only on the higher peaks, in the deep ravines, and a few places on wooded slopes is there snow.

Monday, May 1. A fine sunrise for " May morning." Clouds all about, and the summit was enveloped, but here it was thin so that the sunlight streaming through gave the morning something the aspect of the sunrise scene of March 1st, only that was far more grand. This morning a sea of cloud covered the whole extent of country, north and south, east and west, Mount Washington alone rising above the aerial ocean. Over Mount Adams the cloud was higher than the summit of Washington; on the other side Tuckerman's Ravine looked twice as prominent as usual, and like the deep, black gulf it is, when clouds overshadow it. The lighter clouds passing between us and the sun threw a twilight gloom over all, then as they sailed away down the valley a golden flood of light diffused itself over the mountain and cloudy sea below. The misty clouds above were constantly changing from gray to purple, and occasionally crimson tinged their edges.

Mr. H. and Mr. Holden saw from the summit, westward, a corona, similar to that observed by Professor Hitchcock and myself a few mornings since. This morning there was the shadow of Mount Washington on the clouds. It is a pleasing spectacle, but by no means so interesting as when the mountain is shadowed on the eastern sky. Beautiful frost-work formed last night; even the surface of the snow as well as rocks and buildings is covered with it. May-day, and still it is winter; every aspect is that of midwinter. The spring near the Observatory remains frozen solid, and so we daily melt ice for use, and yet down the mountain a half mile there is seldom a day when the streams are not running.

About one P. M. the clear sky disappeared and clouds prevailed over sunshine the rest of the day, — snowing at intervals through the afternoon, and quite severely in the evening.

Prof. Hitchcock left for Hanover, at noon, before the storm set in. Soon after he went a man from the depot came up with a message to transmit to Franklin, N. H. Good for the Mount Washington office, that people should come to this far-away place to communicate with the world! Our visitor reports a heavy rain at Marshfield yesterday.

Tuesday, May 2. A wintry sunrise scene, then clouds on the mountains, passing off at noon. Taking advantage of the day, Mr. Holden and myself set out for Tuckerman's. Found more snow than on the 9th ult. Sunlight, bright and warm there, but over Washington a dense cloud most of the afternoon. The air spring-like, as were the surroundings; little snow except at the head of the Ravine, where the arch will be looked for in vain next summer, unless May makes up for the short-comings of winter. Hermit Lake really breaking up, and the stream open above. We could see the pretty cascade some distance above the lake and hear the rushing waters, now loudly, as the wind arose, now softly murmuring as it fell. Half way down the northern side, under a sheltering rock, we lunched on hard-tack and sugar, drinking the pure water of a little rill which ran down among the rocks. Then for an hour we climbed the crags, getting views from many different points. Found fine specimens of mosses and secured a few specimens of insects, two of which were the more interesting, as they were new to me. Came away at three P. M., too early

15

to go home, so decided on a trip to the northeastern spur of Washington. Passed a deep spring of excellent water which in my jaunts I had never seen, then visited the ravine beyond, — our first visit. In some respects this is even more interesting than Tuckerman's, for what is lacking in extent is made up in the boldness of outline, its steep, sloping northern side and sheer precipice of two hundred feet or more on the south. Seven seconds was the time taken, by repeated trials, for a stone to reach the bottom. Professor says that it bears no name. We propose that *Huntington's Ravine* shall be its future designation. A " thousand rills " run down its western side — the head, — joining in forming a stream below. Away, among the wood, half a mile perhaps, the rushing sound of a cascade was distinctly heard. Professor says that it is a very beautiful fall, and scarcely ever visited. This ravine is worth exploring.

Went to the extreme point of the spur, — Mount Washington summit. The Glen and Great Gulf are all well seen from this point. Home at five P. M., much of the way through a cloud, satisfied with our rambles on the mountain.

Prof. Hitchcock telegraphs his arrival at Littleton.

Temperature at seven P. M. 26°. A dense, black cloud lying along the south indicates a storm not far distant.

Wednesday, May 3. Snowing all night and cloudy all day, — a dull, quiet day, more disagreeable than the fiercest storm. We have all spoiled much good paper to-day, — Professor, Holden, Thompson, and myself. Mr. Smith sick, seems no better; a rough place to be sick, in — safe from the doctors, he has that comfort!

At 5.30 p. m. we — Professor and I — got in a supply of ice. At the time, the cloud was so dense that from the Tip-top House the Observatory could not be seen; fifteen minutes later the cloud passed off and there was a most magnificent outlook. Below, an ocean of cloud, calm and unruffled as an inland lake; above, but quite low, the upper current of storm-cloud; far away north, a line of clear sky; south, heavy masses of cloud shutting out the distance. We could mark the line of a storm bearing down upon this section, a grand sight. At nine p. m. snowing.

Thursday, May 4. Another tough snow-storm; we enjoy it; might as well find pleasure in it, for endure these frequent changes we must if not enjoy them. One fine day is full compensation for a week of stormy wintry weather, and then, what did we come here for but to study storms? Wind got up to 48 and temperature down to 21°.

One pair of birds have made the house their home of late. To-day especially they have hardly been out. This afternoon they have sung several songs for our benefit. They are quite tame. To-night they sit on the beam over this room close by the flue, and we can occasionally hear them twitter, softly calling to each other.

Prof. Hitchcock reports by telegraph, rain at Hanover all day. Now, ten P. M., the storm is increasing in fury and really might almost rank with those of last December.

Professor and Mr. H. were out this morning at 4.30; had a rare sunrise to repay them for rising at so unseasonable an hour; the rest of us preferred our morning nap, so we only had the storm, for the cloud shut down at six o'clock.

Friday, May 5. The storm — snowing in such a wintry way last night — turned to rain toward morning and has been rainy all day. About seven P. M. the cloud lifted, settled, or dissipated, — cannot say which as I was not out at the time. Then we had a grand sea of cloud — a display we never tire of, — north and west far as the horizon, south for nearly an hundred miles, and east quite to central Maine. Excepting Lafayette and Adams, and a bit of the Saco valley, the whole country was befogged. The upper strata of clouds were mixed in the most confused manner; it would have puzzled Espy to have given them names, and for that matter names were of little consequence, for the coloring was that which gave them the greatest interest in our eyes. I did, however, write out in its proper place a dry description ; the colors and shades ran through the list ; such changes, such inter-mingling of colors, the brilliancy, the delicacy, was beyond belief. The time 7.30. Then there was repeated, on the dull, cold, gray clouds below, the changing hues of the higher clouds, from a pearly whiteness to rose, fading out to gray, not once. but several times, the last lingering beams slowly dying away into the blackness of night. As late as eight o'clock, after the stars could be seen in the east, the lower clouds retained some color.

The wind was west here, not higher than five, yet in the valleys it must have been much stronger, judging by the velocity of the clouds ; besides we could hear distinctly its almost roar. While west the clouds had a rapid movement, over Ellis River they were stationary.

S. has been ill to-day. T.'s lame foot is better, and everything in our little world has moved in the usual regular course. To-morrow, if fair, some of us go to Mount Adams. The mountains are covered with snow. Surely, it cannot yet be spring !

Saturday, May 6. Mr. Holden and myself have made that long contemplated trip to Mount

Adams. Just what object we had in going I cannot say, neither can he tell, for when I put the
question to him as we were toiling up one of the
ugly steeps of Mount Jefferson on our homeward
way, he said — *nothing.* So I am confident that
he had nothing to say.

This is the only explanation I can give, as I sit
here to-night, foot-sore, wet, and weary, with the
day's tramp fresh in mind : Mount Adams, in the
majestic style he has been wearing for the past
week, while we have made our minor tours around
the ravines of this mountain, seemed to defy us ;
and so without unnecessary delay we were determined to dine or lunch the first fair day on Mount
Adams. Then, Prof. Hitchcock and Mr. Burbeck
had paid the old fellow a visit, — the first persons,
probably, who ever made the trip in April, and if
they were the first visitors of this season, there
was no reason why we should not be the second
party.

This morning was one of the best for the intended journey, — clear, calm, and warm. The
thermometer at eight o'clock indicated 85° in the
sun, — warmest morning this spring. Though clear
above, the valleys were full of cloud; we did not
fear to be clouded in, as we had a compass. Filling
our pockets with hard-tack and taking a canteen
for water, at about nine o'clock we started. The

wind was northwest here ; at the foot of Mount Clay it was east and chilling. So far the walking was excellent, the snow hard as ice. There we stood, on the level of the clouds to the west and above those east. Skirting along the east side of the first peak of Clay we made slow progress. While resting, the clouds settled in the Gulf, and we had a good point from which to get a clear idea of the immensity of the mountain — Washington, — and of the depth and breadth of the Gulf. As the distance is short, visitors ascending the mountain might find themselves well repaid if they would not only view the Gulf from the head, which is a very advantageous position, but also from Mount Adams, — so we agreed as we sat there. Going to the highest point of the dividing ridge of Clay and Jefferson, we could hear on the one side the rushing, roaring sound of the falls in the Gulf and the smoother flow of Jefferson brook on the other. We could see nothing, as all below was covered by clouds.

In places the mountain side was free from snow, in others the snow was many feet deep. On the more level places it was thawing, and before we reached the base of Jefferson our boots were thoroughly soaked. Climbing Jefferson we rested, and while so doing amused ourselves in building *our* monument in case we should perish on the way. At the summit we found the wind to be northwest, as we afterwards found it on Mount Adams, while both going over and returning it was easterly at lower levels.

There we saw that Lafayette was under a cloud, and that on the west the great body of cloud had risen nearly to the summit of Washington. I have been here long enough to learn that when Washington is enveloped, it means a cloudy day for Mount Adams. While debating whether to go on or give up the trip, a dense and extended body of cloud passed between us and Adams, and this decided us to push on. Down the steep eastern side of Jefferson in sunshine is bad enough, in the twilight gloom of a dense, damp cloud, that wets one as though he had been immersed in an ice chilled bath, it is anything but agreeable. But the cloud passing, we were so fortunate as to reach the head of the ravine between Jefferson and Adams just in time to get a good view of its huge dimensions. There we could almost see, under the cloud, the forest at the foot of the mountains. Again the cloud shut in and we went on.

And now our tramp was over the dwarf trees — we took the south side of the ridge — and through the snow, sometimes waist-deep, always over our boot-tops. Coming out of the cloud once more, and for the last time, we saw the lofty summit of Mount Washington, then far above the clouds, and we heard the cheers of our comrades at the Observatory. We could hardly credit our ears, for it is nearly or quite three and a half miles in an air line from point to point. But the successive cheers came to us so clearly that we could doubt no longer, and then we sent back an answering shout. How hot it was under the shelter of the mountain-side! not a puff of wind, but plenty of ice-cold water, and of that we drank freely. Adams seemed miles away, and the harder we toiled the less near seemed the goal. Half a mile of this weary work over the snowy plateau, and we began to climb the rocks again, — this was easy compared with plunging through the snow, — and resting often, we, at one P. M., gained the summit. To repay for our long walk, we saw a sea of cloud that we might have seen without going a rod from the door, if we had been content to stay at home.

But we had something which we cannot have on Mount Washington, — *an idea of the immensity of the monarch himself* — the grandeur, the overshadowing majesty of this king among kingly mountains. This view alone was worth all the day's toil. I have seen Washington from several points; this I deem the best.

A gentle summer breeze played about the peak and the sun shone bright above, but beyond the narrow limits of the mountains, the cloud rested everywhere.

About two o'clock we saw by the increasing volume of cloud that we were likely to be forced to find our road back by the aid of the compass, and unwillingly we turned our faces homeward. Going down we remembered the advice of Professor Hitchcock, to keep the height of land, and doing so made an easy descent.

At the base of Jefferson again encountered a dense cloud, which came along just in time to catch us. Didn't Jefferson loom twice as high for our weariness — twice as high as the measurements make it? It did ; but an hour's toil, and we stood on the summit, then far above the cloud. Adams showed only the highest point, and elsewhere all was in cloud ; even for a time Washington was hidden. And then the downward way to the peaks of Clay — three in the morning — thirty we thought before we crossed the last and stood facing our summit home ; and how lost in the cloud as the last height of Clay deceiving us, we supposed it to be our own Mount Washington ; shall we ever forget these and the incidents of the day? Think not — not soon. That glorious lighting up of the western sky as the sun went down — the moment when sky and cloud became so intermingled and the whole was like a sea of molten gold reflected on a sky of crimson, blue, and gold ; and the closing scene the Battle of the Clouds, when east and west met over the ridge of Clay, and darting sharp flashes of electric fire from one to the other, then closing, the west drove back the east — a grand *finale* to so gorgeous a sunset.

We found on reaching home that the members of the party here had seen us through the Tolles and Army telescopes much of the day; saw us raise our flag on Adams; saw us as we lunched; and in fact knew our every movement, whenever the clouds permitted them to see us. They did not claim to have overheard our conversation — it is a wonder they did not, possessing such excellent telescopes !

They were out watching for us, and, as we came up the track, greeted us with congratulations. We have narrated to them our adventures, trifling as they are, and they have related the doings on the summit the livelong day; the sudden changes of relative humidity; that the temperature was 56° at one time; and how they all have spent the day : these little things make the excitements of life on Mount Washington, insignificant as they may appear to the world outside our circle. Found many insects, even on the summit of Adams.

I am going to bed to dream of falling down the snow-slide at the head of the Gulf, which little feat I might have performed but for the greater caution of my friend Holden.

I must add one item.   H. and myself have passed judgment on the mountains we visited to-day. Briefly it is, that Clay is a blunder — a failure as a mountain — the whole family of Clay being represented in its many yet useless peaks — useless for any purpose but to worry the toiling traveler ; that Jefferson is well worth a visit, and Adams, above all, grand.   The whole route is interesting for its wild scenery, often rising to the sublime.   Bold cliffs, deep ravines, high rocks and beetling crags, cozy nooks and places where the sun never sends a beam.   Now, 10.30 P. M., it is *raining* ; what a country !

Sunday, May 7.   The barometer fell 50-100ths from last night at nine o'clock to this morning at seven o'clock.   Wind rising at three A. M., reaching the highest velocity at two P. M., which was 67 ; highest recorded for some time, quite strongly reminding us of the winter months. Snowing all day ; the whirling, driving clouds of snow made it far from pleasant to stay out for three minutes, the time occupied in taking the force of the wind. Mr. Holden had that honor conferred more than once upon him.

At five P. M. the cloud passed off and we could see that not the mountains alone, but the lower country as well, was " snow-bound."   At 9.40

P. M., snowing again. Temperature, two P. M., 21°
highest for the day; and 19°, at nine P. M.

No church-bells rang out for us the call to morning service. Really, now I write of church-bells
ringing for Sunday service, it strikes my fancy that
I should enjoy hearing them; since the 19th December I have not heard them — may not for a
month to come.

As there was no church-going for us, H. and I
slept late, and rose tired and lame from the ten-
mile tramp of yesterday. Ten miles! if properly
distributed, they would make fifty on a decent road!

Littleton reported, at 4.30 P. M., that it had
been rainy, but was clearing away.

Nine P. M. We have had a quiet Sunday in-
doors; anything but that outside now; none of
the family have attended church, nor have we had
callers. We have passed the day in reading. The
wind is higher than an hour ago and we may get a
rough night.

Monday, May 8. We did have a rough night,
called the wind 80 at midnight. Of course there
was considerable pressure on the house, and the re-
sultant creaking and cracking of the building, the
jarring and rocking, were all very creditable for a
May storm.

Temperature, seven A. M., 15°. Professor found
the wind-vane, it was carried away last night by

the spindle breaking — a quarter-inch rod. The wind last night was at no time below 60, and as high much of the time to-day; since three **P. M.** rising, and the barometer rapidly falling; at two **P. M.** it was 23.035, the lowest for some weeks. At two **P. M.** temperature 18° and wind 62. Ten **P. M.**, snowing, and wind more moderate. The frost-work is heavy and fine; on the house it points in every conceivable direction, showing that it was formed in the eddies, and of course against the wind.

None on the sick-list to-day. Holden is embargoed but manages to make himself comfortable. The Handel and Haydn Society will have to excuse him to-morrow night. He could not desert if he would, and I do not think he will try it, to-night at least.

A wild-cat was here last night; did not come in, but contented himself with caterwauling outside the premises. It might, possibly, have thought it was paying us a high compliment in so vigorous an exhibition of its musical powers; if so, never a more mistaken puss. More likely there was a dispute between Master Sable, whom we consider one of our party, and said feline as to the right of way, or for the ownership of a poor little mouse. H. and I saw their tracks Saturday, just below the summit; we have seen them before, but more generally since May came in.

Tuesday, May 9. Clouds off and on till five P. M., when they disappeared entirely. The wind fell away towards midnight, and has been steady to-day at about 35, though now, nine P. M., nearly calm. Wind northwest all day; it may storm by to-morrow.

Mountain peaks white as winter, but the valleys are bare — even at the Glen House there is no snow. A fine aurora to-night — arch, without dark underlying cloud or streamers.

And the frost-work has seldom been more beautiful. Thompson and I measured some feathers to-day. On a tall pole at the Tip-top House, found them thirty-six inches in length, and on a rock south of the house, forty-nine in length and fifteen broad. This last formation is very beautiful, but does not present such varied shapes as during the winter and last month. Yet there has never been the time when the trestle of the railway just below the observatory, or the Bourne monument, gave a better idea of the exceeding beauty of the finer specimens of this most charming feature of the winter scenery of the mountains. They might be pure, solid frost-work, for all one can see of either wood or stone.

Messrs. Holden and Thompson left this afternoon at one o'clock. Both S. and myself have been on the sick-list to-day.

Our birds have been merry to-day; they sing sweetly and appear to enjoy these comfortable quarters like sensible birds as they are. They do not think of venturing out during storms or when the weather is at all inclement. Monday night one of these birds roomed with us, making the anemometer its perch; seemed perfectly at home after it had concluded to stay.

This morning was fine, pleasant, nothing remarkable about it, unless to see the sun once more was an event worth recording, and most assuredly, we shall soon begin to think even a clear sunrise to be quite an event; for " cloud on the mountain," is the almost daily entry in the Register. And so after all the fine morning it commenced to snow at 9 o'clock, and continued to all day at intervals, and · we had the usual amount of cloud.

Professor found to-day some beautiful frost-wings; just as perfect in form and feathering as a real wing; they were very beautiful indeed.

Thursday, May 11. A wintry sky and winter scenery this morning; the sky a pale blue and the sunshine that of December. The clouds presented an infinite variety of shades — gray, brown, and dingy black; distant mountains showed clear-cut outlines ; snowy peaks of the higher mountains glisten in the morning light. Looking beyond them we see a change; the Androscoggin is broader and its waters sparkle in the play of sunlight; the valleys are bare and brown. Last winter the river was a silver thread, the lowlands white as are these summits now. Only these differences between a pleasant morning last December and this. 20° at seven A. M.

Soon the clouds settled down and we were shut in the remainder of the day till near sunset. Then the sun tried to throw a little glow over the scene, but miserably failed and angrily went to bed — the clouds, though broken, were too dense.

Later in the evening it was clear, and the stars shone brilliantly; starlight on the mountain is not the passionless thing it is below the clouds. A rare, rare evening.

Mr. Huntington expects to leave us soon. How quickly the winter has passed spite of storms, hurricanes, and clouds — of discomfort, and rather hard fare and the many deprivations. S. is still far from well. To endure, without suffering in some respect, the sudden changes of weather, one needs an iron constitution; and any one that stays here should have a will equally as strong. It is hard on an invalid — I can bear testimony to that.

Temperature 27° at two P. M. and the same at nine P. M.

Friday, May 12. A sunrise bright and fair as ever poet raved about or painter dreamed. And

the day was lovely simply because it was spring-like ;
the sunset charming. Half an hour before sunset
a crimson glow came creeping out of the west and
diffused itself over the broad expanse of country
north. Mount Washington was under the shadow
of the heavy upper stratum of cloud, but the crimson light resting on mountains and valleys, lakes
and rivers, below and far across the Canada border,
so nearly touched Mount Washington that its
southern bounds were within twenty miles. Later,
the crimson was followed by broad bands of varying
brown and purple, the shades constantly changing,
and finally, as the sun went down, all color faded
into gray. The south lay under a dense, black
cloud; in the east was the darkness of night, intensely deep, the gloom the more from contrast
with the radiant west. In the evening an interesting auroral display — streamers with a dark underlying cloud broken on its upper edge.

The last Press telegram goes to-night. Nor
shall we any longer have pleasant evening chats
with Professor Hitchcock at Hanover. S. is at the
depot to-night, and the telegraph has no word for
us.

Professor and I writing all day ; wished much
to take a walk, but were unable.

Saturday, May 13. A really fine sunrise — but
here it does not follow by any means that the day

will prove the same, and so about nine A. M. there were " clouds on the mountain " and snow-squalls much of the time afterwards. The wind worked up to 50 at 10.30 P. M., when we concluded to let it blow, as we could not prevent it so doing, and now we are going to bed.

Well, if the half-dozen almanacs on the shelf did not say that it was May we might think we had missed one of the winter months. How the wind howls — charming for " merrie month of May ! "

If Thomson — the poet I mean — not my friend T., who is *not* a poet — were here to-night he would sing another strain than —

> " Forth fly the tepid airs ; and unconfined,
> Unbinding earth, the moving softness strays."

Not a bit of it. But this is the climate of Labrador, and there is no reason to find fault with it — a most excellent climate too — of its kind.

Sunday, May 14. The wind was high as 80, if not higher, during the night. All day, as usual, it has been cloudy, and frost-work forming. Temperature at seven A. M. was 11°, and highest for the day at nine P. M., 21°. At no time the wind lower than 46. Mr. Huntington left at nine A. M. in the face of a forty-eight mile gale and the temperature only 14°. I am anxious for his safety and shall be till S. returns.

To-night, for the first time, I am keeping " watch and ward " on the mountain top alone. Am rather pleased with the novelty of the situation ; and quite enjoy the gale. I have been listening to winds and studying the many different sounds. There is the uninterrupted rumble of the wind and click and creak of the frame of the building more particularly noticeable in the outer room. As heard here it is like the sound of factory machinery as one may hear it on a summer's day, at a distance. The windows and boarding as they give and rebound creak intermittently. Without are the chains clanking, thumping, and rattling, sometimes sounding like a ship's cable running out in casting anchor. When the wind blows steadily it gives the building a rocking motion ; eddying, it converts the vibratory to a jarring action. Now scarcely audible, its sound is that of summer breeze, a gentle murmur; now husky and muffled as the wind which precedes the storm, now high-sounding and clamorous, it rises and gives the house a violent shaking, bringing out clearly its every creak and groan from the straining frame ; the walls give back a dull booming, like distant artillery practice, as they rebound when the wind lets go its hold. Now it dies away into a soft whisper and for a few minutes there is a lull — a dead calm more disagreeable in its death-like stillness than the roar and howl of the hurricane in its fiercest anger.

And this night's gale is similar to the heavy ones, the hurricanes, differing only in the greater force of those.

As I sit here to-night I do not feel as though I was alone ; admit to a slight degree of sadness as I saw Mr. Huntington go out into the storm. I had so much anxiety on his account — that perhaps prevented my thinking much about this parting being final so far as Mount Washington is concerned.

I have wished that my bird-companions would sing a little song, but it is too cold. They appear to be very comfortable and contented. When I go into their room, they seem glad to see me and give an answering chirp to my greetings.

The wind now is about 50 or 55. I have made the last observation, and am going to bed to sleep just as soundly as though there were a half-dozen good fellows to keep me company.

CONCLUSION.

The winter's work is done. We trust that has not been time and labor lost. Storms of unparalleled severity, when for days in succession the summit was enveloped in clouds and the hurricanes lasted longer and were more violent than any yet recorded in the United States, together with very low temperatures, have been a part of our experience.

Just such an experience has seldom before been
the lot of human beings. Though interesting, these
grand atmospheric disturbances are not the most
enjoyable features of mountain life.

And ours has been the good fortune to witness
some of the most magnificent winter scenery upon
which mortal eyes ever rested; scenery of tran-
scendent grandeur, and views surpassingly beautiful.

There were mornings when the atmosphere was
so transparent and the sky so pure a blue, with not
a fleck of cloud, the snowy mountain-peaks so daz-
zlingly white, their forms so clearly outlined and
standing up in such bold relief, that they seemed
the creation of yesterday; and mornings when
earth and sky, forests, lakes, and rivers, and the
clouds above wore a radiance and richness of color
never seen in other than mountain regions and
from the loftiest elevations.

There were days when the shifting views of each
hour furnished new wonders and new beauties, in
the play of sunlight and changing cloud-forms, every
hour a picture in itself and perfect in details. Sunsets, too, when an ocean of cloud surrounded this
island-like summit, the only one of all the many
high peaks visible above the cloud billows, all else
of earth hidden from sight; there were times when
this aerial sea was burnished silver, smooth and

calm, and times when its tossing waves were tipped with crimson and golden fire.

There were mornings and evenings and whole days when the winds were hushed and a soft haze rested over everything, making the distant out-look much like that of summer.

Although our situation has been very much an isolated one, and the area of our little world limited, our daily life has not been without incident or void of interest, to us at least. But now, our work being done, we go down to the busy world once more. And though we look forward to the change with anticipations of pleasure, we shall half-regretfully turn our backs upon this majestic old mountain whose cloud-enveloped summit has so long been our home.

The days of canned-beef, " hard-tack," and coffee will soon be counted among the things of the past. Gone are the long days and longer nights when the stoves failed to comfortably warm the little room, though we kept them at a red heat, and when the thermometer indicated 65° near the stove, and 4° at the floor ten feet distant. So are the long periods when we received no news from below the clouds, and the longer weeks when no visitor could think of making our quarters his temporary home.

Days of storm and gloom and piercing cold ; times when the line is down and we are then as

effectually cut off from communication with mankind as if we were dwellers on another planet, —
these are days never to be forgotten. And there
have been those days which we shall ever remember for their splendors, and beautiful ones that
seemed more of heaven than earth, and nights
which made the complement of such days.

A party of three brought into so close relations
as we were, incur the risk of finding each other disagreeable companions, especially where, as in this
case, they happened to be entire strangers. Our
intercourse has ever been pleasant. It is doubtful
if three coming together by chance, often find their
tastes and sympathies so generally in harmony.

Having an equal interest in the work, and feeling
our situation to be one where we were mutually
dependent for help in sickness, for our pleasures,
for companionship, for everything that made our
isolated life endurable, we have passed the winter
pleasantly.

Though less intimately connected with us, we
consider the other members of the party as belonging to the Observatory, and we shall ever remember
with pleasure the happy days spent in their society.

The larger part of the time there was telegraphic
communication with Littleton, and this had a tendency to make us more contented than we should
otherwise have been. Triweekly the line was con-

nected with the private office of Professor Hitchcock at Hanover, and daily with L. Through the kind offices of the operator at L., Mr. Currier, who has been very obliging, and the thoughtfulness of Professor Hitchcock, we received both foreign and home news. Reading telegraphic news from Paris, as soon as people in the seaboard cities, was not an uncommon occurrence. News thus received has a flavor to it that people who have the daily papers cannot appreciate.

In closing, I would remark that this Journal was never intended for publication, being merely daily notes for future reference; hence its imperfections. I have culled from each day's record such portions as seemed most suitable for this work. Meteorological notes are generally omitted for the reason that the subject is fully treated in other chapters.

Long descriptions of scenery for like cause are not given. To me, my journal is a portfolio of sketches, and these pen jottings faithfully picture the scenes I have witnessed, however much they may lack expression to those who have not seen these or similar scenes.

The record of our daily life has rarely been transferred to these pages, in fact but little of it recorded. Its trials and vexations and petty cares are so very like those of any family living under civilized rules and governed by the customs bred of habit, which even living on a mountain in winter one does not willingly give up, — they are so like these, that the mistress of any household in the land may with safety exercise the Yankee privilege of " guessing," with the assurance that she cannot guess far from the truth.

In making the selections I have aimed to give the reader some idea of what mountain scenery in winter is, and also what life on the mountain is, from our daily experience.

My wish is that every one so desiring might see something of the winter scenery of the mountains. May the day be not far distant when a hotel shall be maintained here in winter as well as in summer !

CHAPTER XV.

HAVING made a visit to the scientific party on Mount Washington early in February, I was desirous of looking in upon them again sometime about the incoming of the " merrie month of May," when the rigors of winter were supposed, in the lower world, at least, to have melted before the blandness of spring. With this end in view, I set out from Boston, Thursday, April 27. It was a bright, sunny, genial morning, filled with the joyful promises of the summer soon to come. The workers in the fields had thrown off their coats while following the plough, and the passengers were content to admit the pure, bracing air through the open car windows. It seemed impossible that a single day's journey could bring forth the slightest reminder of winter, now long past and gone. Any one who has taken the railroad ride from Boston mountainward, through Lowell and up the Merrimac valley to Concord, and thence over the Boston, Concord, and Montreal Railroad, need not be told of the delights of the journey. For miles one is borne along the banks of the broad, swelling Merrimac, amid scenes of peaceful beauty, with brief halts at the busy marts which have sprung up here and there by its side. By noon the shores of the broad and beautiful Lake Winnipiscogee are reached, and across its fair expanse we catch some glorious glimpses of the lower ranges of mountains. Farther northward we join the Pemigewasset and Baker's Rivers and are soon ushered into the presence of some of the noble hills which form the western outposts of the Franconia range. Emerging from among these, we strike across to the banks of the Connecticut, in the seemingly boundless town of Haverhill, and after gaining the enchanting view which opens for a long distance southward, once more seek the companionship of the hills by winding along the course of the swift gliding Ammonoosuc, almost to the heart of the great mountains themselves. The journey is at all times enjoyable, and especially so was it at this time, when the clear spring atmosphere gave even to far distant objects great distinctness. At Manchester I was joined by Professor Huntington, who had come down from the mountain a day or two before to fulfill a lecture engagement, and at Wells River, Mr. Eben Thompson, a member of the Scientific Class of Dartmouth College, was added to our little party.

WINTER LINGERS IN THE LAP OF SPRING.

Leaving the cars at Whitefield, the nearest rail-road point on the western approach to Mount Washington, we carried out our prearranged programme of driving over to the White Mountain House the same evening, despite gathering clouds which threatened a severe storm. We had not proceeded far on our twelve miles' ride before the storm burst upon us in great fury, and for the greater part of the way we were compelled to face the fierce assaults of rain, hail, and sleet. The ferocity of the storm was greater on the summits of the Carroll hills than anywhere else, except, perhaps, on the entrance to the plateau below the White Mountain House, where the wind swept up from the direction of the Notch with really tremendous force. In both places the hail beat against our faces like showers of needle points. By the time we had reached the White Mountain House we were chilled to the extent that we could hardly move, and drenched to the very skin. The ground was whitened by snow and the wintry landscape was in very strange contrast with the vernal and sunny scenes of the morning. We awoke Friday morning to find the storm somewhat abated, and the snow already melted, and in order that we might lose no time in gaining the top of the mountain, we drove over to the depot of the Mount Washington Railway, seven miles distant from the White Mountain House, immediately after breakfast. It was decidedly cold when we arrived at that point, and there were occasional showers, but we cared less for a low temperature, even though it had approached the winter standard, than for a high wind which prevailed, and which would have blown directly in our faces, half way up the mountain. Dark, angry looking clouds were flitting down the valley at no very great altitude, and the tree tops bent and writhed under the fitful blasts. Altogether, it seemed an unfavorable time to attempt the ascent, and we settled down quite comfortably at the log-hut with the railway workmen, determined to await more propitious weather. We were not a little vexed to learn upon reaching the summit the day after, that while the elements had been so turbulent in the valley, it had been calm and pleasant above the clouds.

THE ASCENT.

Saturday dawned more auspiciously, and refreshed by a good night's rest, we were in good condition for our upward journey. Dense clouds still rested upon the mountain, but there were no indications that either wind or storm would impede us, and the temperature was more springlike — too warm, in fact, for violent exercise, as we soon discovered. The morning mists had transformed the valley below us into a lake of silver, which remained calm and motionless through the early morning and until the sun's heat caused the vapors to rise and dissipate. Breakfast over, our preparations for departure were quickly made, for they consisted of little else than the buckling on of knapsacks and the grasping of spiked staffs. Crossing the little stream above the station, and following up the logging road a few rods, we gained the railway track at a point above the high trestle-work. Thenceforward we kept upon the track, a course we could easily take, since the snow had melted from the ties and stringers. Walking up the mountain over the railway — stepping from tie to tie — is fatiguing work, and in places where the trestle-work is very high, quite dangerous under certain circumstances, but it is the most expeditious way of getting over the ground, and on the whole the easiest, provided frequent halts are made to rest. As we crept slowly upward, we paused many times to gaze upon the glorious panorama which was gradually unfolding itself to our view. The lower banks of mist were rising from the valleys and were being wafted about in little clouds, or vanished altogether. Above us were leaden clouds shutting out the sun, and other great masses of cloud appeared in the west. The Franconia range stood out in noble outline against the western horizon, and farther distant in the north-west were some of the Green Mountain peaks, though there was less distinctness than usual in the remote view on account of the general cloudiness. At one time Lafayette seemed transformed into a volcano by a little fleecy cloud which ascended from its peak like a puff of smoke. No snow was encountered until we had nearly reached the Waumbek station, and then it appeared in little patches, in one or two places some distance above that point, completely covering the track.

Not far above the Waumbek station we reached the lower surface of the cloud which hung about the mountain, and everything remained in obscuration until we emerged into the sunlight a short distance below the head of the Great Gulf. As we approached the upper surface of the vapory mass, a fine solar bow, showing all the prismatic colors, with a supernumerary bow, was thrown on the dense mists below. The cloudy mass was twelve or fifteen hundred feet thick, and while we had been enveloped in its misty folds, it had extended farther westward, forming a continuous, boundless sea, relieved only here and there by the tallest peaks, which rose like islands from the surface. Washington, Jefferson, Adams, and Madison lifted their proud heads far above the cloud ocean, like bold promontories on a rugged, rock-bound coast. When we reached a sufficiently high point to look eastward, we found that nearly the whole expanse in that direction was also overspread by the billowy masses, though at a lower level, as usual.

In the rarefied air about the summit of the mountain any exertion is fatiguing, and pedestrianizing up a steep grade becomes all the more difficult, but happily, for a considerable distance above the Great Gulf and until the Lizzie Bourne monument is passed, the ascent is much more gradual than below, and the weary traveller becomes better prepared for the final pull to the summit. We reached our destination in excellent time considering our leisurely way of travelling, for we had stopped many times for the double purpose of resting and enjoying the strange and beautiful scenes spread out before us. Professor Hitchcock and Mr. Nelson met us a little distance below the Lizzie Bourne monument, and, after extending a very cordial greeting, relieved us of our knapsacks, encumbrances we were by this time very ready to part with, for they were heavily laden with clothing, mail matter, provisions, etc. At the summit we received another warm welcome from Sergeant Smith.

We could not have had a more favorable time for our ascent. There was scarcely a perceptible breeze at the summit, and at no time during the

morning had the velocity of the wind exceeded
more than a mile an hour. The temperature was
unusually high, having been recorded at 39° at
seven o'clock A. M. — three degrees warmer than
at the foot of the mountain, — with a slight downward tendency in subsequent observations.

MORE BEAUTIFUL CLOUD SCENES.

For hours after our arrival there was a succession of the most glorious cloud pictures, and it was
a rich and rare pastime to watch their ever-varying
effects.   Westward dense masses of cloud still
stretched out as far as the eye could discern, while
the vapory formations eastward of the mountain
range, upon the topmost pinnacle of which we were
standing, beside being at a lower level, were less
dense and in a more disturbed state. Masses of
cloud breaking away from the vast sea in the west,
were driven around Mount Washington and the
other high peaks, before the slight breeze, and
poured into Oakes' Gulf, Tuckerman's Ravine,
and the Great Gulf, like huge, noiseless cataracts.
There was a greater movement of air in the
Pinkham Notch than anywhere else, and the two
currents meeting at that point, fleecy mists were
thrown hundreds — perhaps thousands — of feet in
the air like spray.   Now and then huge rifts would
appear in the southeast, opening most glorious vistas

down the valley of the Saco. Once the misty curtain was rent asunder from Mount Carrigain on the west, to beyond Pequawket on the east, and the atmosphere being exceedingly clear, the view encompassed by those points was very extensive, reaching even to Wachusett Mountain in Massachusetts, while with a powerful glass we could see all that was going on in Jackson and in the village of North Conway. Later in the afternoon, the clouds cleared away along the valleys of the Androscoggin and the Connecticut, opening new scenes of loveliness.

A RAMBLE ABOUT THE SUMMIT.

I took an early stroll about the plateau forming the summit, visiting the Tip-top and Summit houses, and other points. While on the mountain in February, I found it a very easy matter to wander about in any direction, the ice and frost covering all inequalities, and making comparatively an even surface. When we arrived on this visit, all the large rocks were bare, snow filling only the interstices, although a furious snow-storm had occurred only a week before. The mountain-top presented a mottled appearance. In places along the railway and among the rocks, the old snow remained to the depth of two or three feet, and in occasional drifts still deeper. There was a huge drift in front

of the Tip-top House, obscuring nearly the whole
of the door, and another on the easterly side of the
Summit House, but aside from these, the buildings
were almost bare. There were a few lingering
beauties of frost-work, but this as well as the snow
had for the most part disappeared. It was a much
more difficult task to go about over the rocks now
than in February, but the exertion, however great,
well repaid one, for there were many strange sights
to see.

A CHANGE OF SCENE.

The succeeding day brought a very great change
in the weather, and a corresponding change in the
aspect of familiar objects about the summit. A
snow-storm set in sometime in the course of the
night, and by morning, every rock and building
was once more adorned with a white mantle. The
delicate frost-work had also begun to form again,
but the falling snow soon obscured its beauties.
This storm was succeeded by others of still greater
severity in the course of my ten days' sojourn at
the summit, and in a short time, the landscape was
rendered exceedingly wintry, in fact surpassing
everything of the kind I saw in February. The
huge rocks were almost entirely hidden by the
snow, which in some places was piled up in tremendous drifts. The drift against the easterly end of
the Tip-top House extended to the upper windows,

and it was no very difficult matter to clamber up the side of the building, over the snow and ice, to the very ridgepole.   A few rods down the carriage road, between the two stables, a drift formed at least twenty feet in depth, making an even surface over the steep incline at that place.   The buildings became entirely coated over with snow, ice, and frost-work.   The latter began to form in great abundance a few days after our arrival, and the delicate, feathery formations attached themselves to every object — buildings, rocks, telegraph posts and wires, the railway trestle-work, and even to the surface of the snow itself.   On the ninth of May we measured masses of the frost-work which were between four and five feet in length.   The telegraph posts just below the summit presented a singular appearance, fringed with the beautiful white masses, and in many places the formations on the trestle-work extended out to a considerable distance.   The little post which marks the highest point of the mountain, a rod or so northward of the Tip-top House, assumed the form of a harp with the strings running the wrong way.   The pile of stones at the southerly verge of the plateau, which Mr. Clough has christened the " Arctic Sentinel," sustained its new found title very appropriately, for scarcely a vestige of the stones could be seen through the thick masses of frost.   The rude pile of stones which marks the spot where poor Lizzie Bourne perished, September 14, 1855, was also transformed into an object of great beauty,— a more fitting monument to the sad and mournful event. The frost-king had adorned every stone with strange and beautiful forms of spotless purity and whiteness, and surmounted the whole with a crystal cross. Every chain and support about the houses became objects of the rarest beauty, and a barrel left standing beside the Tip-top House assumed a fantastic shape with the delicate, white, feathery masses growing out upon it. An old telegraph pole standing in the rear of the house, which, by splicing, had been made to serve the purpose of a flag-staff, likewise became a thing of picturesque beauty, a fantastic fringe extending from it to the length of from a foot to three or four feet, while the width of the mass scarcely exceeded the thickness of the pole itself. The staff was broken and the flag itself tattered and torn, but to all adhered the same strange forms. As the " frost feathers " form directly toward the wind, even the tip of the wind-vane became encrusted with them and the instrument was rendered useless until they were removed.

HOW WE PASSED MAY-DAY.

The residents of the mountain-top were stirring on the morning of May-day, quite as early as the people of the country below, who were supposed to be in quest of the traditional May-flower, but with a somewhat different object in view, for outward appearances suggested any possible pastime except going "Maying." Early rising was one of the virtues rigidly practiced at the summit, and any visitor who failed to conform readily to the custom was quite sure to comply when the "Nevada militia" mounted guard, a military performance superintended by Sergeant Smith, and consisting in a very great part of a drum solo executed on a large tin can. Encased in overcoats, mufflers, and mittens, some of us spent the early morning hours out of doors, in the crisp, pure air, admiring the ever varying cloud scenes and the gorgeous sunrise, and studying the beautiful forms of frost-work created during the previous night. Before the middle of the forenoon clouds again enveloped the mountain, shutting out everything below, above, and around us, and snow again began to fall. After dinner some of the younger members of the party tried coasting down the carriage-road. A sled was brought out from the depot, and the sport was entered into with considerable zest. Sliding down over the road fifteen or twenty rods, or across lots over the huge drifts formed just below the summit on the east side, was easy enough, but at such an altitude, dragging a sled up-hill through the snow

is a trifle too much like work to be called a pastime,
and it was soon abandoned. The greater part of
the day was passed within doors, where the members of the scientific party were kept quite constantly employed, for the preparation of this volume
had already been entered upon. In-door confine-
ment at the summit during the winter, was made
far more tolerable than it might have become in
other localities, on account of the excellent library
made up for use by the different members of the
expedition. About noon Professor Hitchcock took
his departure on his return to Hanover, and in the
afternoon a fresh visitor arrived, an employee of
the railway company, who had come up from the
station at the base of the mountain, into the clouds,
to communicate by telegraph with another resident
of the lower world. It seemed a strange errand,
but by climbing the mountain side, a long journey
to Whitefield or Bethlehem had been saved, and
much time also gained, since the telegraph station
at the summit was the only one open short of
those points.

SUNRISE AND SUNSET GLORIES.

Notwithstanding the quick succession of storms
which accompanied my visit, I was permitted to
enjoy several days of delightfully clear weather,
although at such times even, the country below us

was for the most part obscured by clouds. We also had several fine sunrises and sunsets, — such as no mortal ever gazed upon below. The morning of May-day was delightful. It was clear overhead, the storm having ceased during the night, but the surrounding country was still obscured. A perfect ocean of clouds covered all save the very highest peaks. Of the Franconia range, Lafayette and Moosilauke only were visible. The nearer mountains were clearly to be defined on the cloud surface, which everywhere seemed to follow the contour of the hills and valleys. A cloud cap upon Mount Adams extended higher than the top of Mount Washington. Tuckerman's Ravine and the Pinkham Notch became deep, black gulfs, being filled with clouds at a lower level. The sun had already risen and had begun to flash its bright rays over the vast cloud sea. Occasionally little masses of cloud would drift over our heads before the light westerly breeze, obscuring the sun for a moment, and as the mists disappeared eastward, they became a golden flood of light. The topmost points of cloud were tinged with a delicate purple, and little, fleecy masses of vapor breaking away from the great body below, would rise here and there into the blue ether, like mysterious spectres. Walking out to the western verge of the little plateau, we discovered the shadow of the mountain upon the clouds resting northward of Mount Monroe. Our own shadows were surrounded — or rather the heads were encircled — by a corona displaying the prismatic hues, and occasionally a bow was shown on the drifting mists above. The lower half of our shadows, of a more intense blackness than the rest, was cast upon the shadowy form of the mountain. A similar phenomenon had been observed only a few mornings previous by Professor Hitchcock. Such exhibitions are, however, exceedingly rare.

A few nights after, we enjoyed another glorious spectacle. The summit was enshrouded in clouds when the sun went down, but they floated away soon after, disclosing a scene of indescribable beauty and grandeur. A vast sea of leaden clouds lay at our feet, covering every valley and every mountain peak except our own. Above us was another cloud stratum, and we looked out from between the two upon a fairy picture. Over Mount Monroe and the chain of mountains running down to the Notch, poured with the stillness of death a vast Niagara. The whole western horizon was aglow with light. The sun had left a sea of gold, while upon either side were delicate tints of purple, crimson, blue, and green, the whole forming a picture such as no painter ever produced. It seemed like a foretaste of the bright, beautiful land of the future, — an opening of the pearly gates leading to the haven of eternal rest and peace. Like everything else in winter scenery about the mountains, every feature of loveliness was intensified many fold. Turning from the glorious scene to the eastern horizon was like being transported from the regions of light to the very depths of darkness. Night had long since settled there, and the dark, shadowy forms of cloud appeared like spirits of evil banished from the heavenly paradise we had just gazed upon. The broad band of light in the west began to contract, and the bright colors faded little by little. The clouds around us were at times flushed with a roseate hue, while those above us, in the west, were tinged with a brighter, though yet a pale light. After an ashy pallor had settled upon the clouds below, there was a reviving light — a faint flush which lighted up the misty surface in a strange, supernatural way, — and at length the gloom of night stole across the whole scene.

AN EXCURSION TO TUCKERMAN'S RAVINE.

Taking advantage of a warm and pleasant afternoon, I made an excursion to the head and the north side of Tuckerman's Ravine, accompanied by Mr. Nelson. The temperature was comparatively mild at the summit, ranging from 26° at seven A. M., up to 34° at two P. M., and down to 25° at seven P. M. We proceeded down the carriage road a little distance, and then struck off directly down the mountain side over a course that would be impassable in summer. In places, the snow was five or six feet deep, and the sun had made it so soft that we occasionally sank to a considerable depth. At times we had to proceed with much care and caution for fear of starting the whole mass in a slide. We soon reached the plateau below, which was covered with snow only in places, and turning our steps southward, quickly made our way over the intervening mile to the Ravine. It was warm and spring-like behind the cone of Mount Washington, and the snows of the summit were melting into countless little streams which murmured among the rocks beneath our feet, or saturated the lichens and sedges to the condition of a well filled sponge. One needs to be well clad about the feet to travel among the mountains in either winter or spring. Skirting the head of the tremendous abyss, we reached the north brink, and making our way as best we could through the deep snow and over the stunted trees, descended a considerable distance. The snow covering the jagged, little trees was so soft that we frequently broke through to the depth of several feet, and perchance became entangled in the branches. We found a more practicable way back, and managed to avoid both trees and snow by keeping to the rocks.

It is not my purpose to attempt any description of the vast, rocky amphitheatre, for few White Mountain visitors have neglected to view it with their own eyes, and furthermore, language is weak in describing such stupendous features in mountain scenery. A great number of little rills trickled down the walls of the Ravine, forming into a stream of considerable size, which made merry music as it danced along its rocky, precipitous bed, on its way to the bright and inviting valley below, and the deeper bass of the larger cascades came up to our ears softened by the distance. The Titanic barriers of the Ravine formed the frame of a most beautiful picture which included some of the most lovely portions of the Saco valley and the Conway meadows, with a background of mountains. Glancing upward to the lofty brow of Mount Washington, we seemed transported from the region of spring to the home of hoary winter — from the verdant tree-tops and pleasant meadows adown the Saco, to the seemingly exhaustless stores of snow garnered from the cold and cheerless clouds, which even now enshrouded the summit like an impenetrable gray mantle. The winter snows had poured over the head of the Ravine and remained in a huge bank reaching from the bottom to the very top, but the quantity was probably less than is usual at the same time of the year, and subsequent warm weather diminished it greatly.

From Tuckerman's Ravine we retraced our steps for a mile or so, and visited another enormous chasm, of which visitors to Mount Washington ordinarily hear little and see less. In fact, it is not discernible from any of the travelled roads or paths. It is much narrower than Tuckerman's, but to appearances, nearly if not fully as deep, and the walls are equally as precipitous — in one place actually overhanging. The head of the ravine, unlike Tuckerman's, forms an angle, and affords but little lodgment for the snow. Before returning to the summit, we also paid a visit to the northernmost spur of the mountain, opposite Mount Adams, making our way back across lots, reaching the protecting roof of the Observatory soon after sunset.

A DAY'S TRAMP AMID THE CLOUDS.

Saturday, May 6th, was an unusually warm day at the summit, the thermometer once standing at 56° in the shade. There were clouds below as usual, and the sun's heat refracted therefrom with increased power. Prof. Hitchcock and a companion had made an excursion to Mount Adams a week previous, and Mr. Nelson and myself determined to perform the same journey. We indulged in the vain hope that the clouds would dissipate or pass away before we reached our destination, although the entire country, except a little patch down the

Saco valley, in the direction of Jackson and North Conway, was obscured when we set out from the Observatory, about nine o'clock. Proceeding down the railway as far as the Gulf Tank, we struck off northward, by the head of the Great Gulf, and thence onward to Mount Clay. There is no beaten track between Mount Washington and Mount Adams, but the way cannot easily be missed under ordinary circumstances, for the traveller has only to keep along the ridges of Mount Clay, Mount Jefferson, and Mount Adams successively, until the high peak of the latter is reached. The whole distance lies far above the line of trees, and for the greater part above an elevation of five thousand feet from the sea-level. Mount Adams is the next highest peak of the White Mountain range to Mount Washington, its elevation being 5,794 feet. To reach it by the route above mentioned, we were compelled to walk fully five miles, and to overcome the following inequalities, according to Mr. Vose's measurements of the elevation of the several peaks and gaps: First, we had to descend about 874 feet from the summit of Mount Washington to the gap between Washington and Clay, elevation 5,417 feet; then ascend 136 feet to the summit of Clay, elevation 5,553 feet; descend 574 feet to the gap between Clay and Jefferson, elevation 4,979 feet; ascend 735 feet to the highest point of Jefferson, elevation 5,714 feet; descend 775 feet to the gap between Jefferson and Adams, elevation 4,939 feet; and finally ascend 855 feet to the top of Mount Adams. These figures, however, fail to represent the actual amount of up-hill and down-hill work to be accomplished, for there is a succession of lesser peaks, each of which must in turn be scaled. Most persons who visit the mountains are inclined to look contemptuously upon Mount Clay, regarding it as an insignificant pile of stones compared with its proud neighbors, Washington and Jefferson. Let them but undertake a journey over it, as we did, and they will certainly change their opinions. There is seemingly enough of it to represent every member of the Clay family, dead or living. It is a long ridge of little peaks made up of rough, jagged rocks, which are most uncomfortable to clamber over. The snow was in some places several feet in depth, and long before we reached the sides of Mount Adams, where it appeared to be the deepest, it had grown very soft and yielding. In crossing the plateau on the south side of Mount Adams, instead of keeping upon the ridge at a greater elevation, as we should have done, we frequently found ourselves entangled in the branches of the stunted trees.

Arriving at the top of the little heap of stones forming the summit, about noon, we were not a little disappointed to discover that the whole of the surrounding country was still covered by clouds. A broad furrow, stretching miles away both northward and eastward, indicated where the Androscoggin valley was situated, but nought could be seen of the river itself. The cloud line generally rested about four thousand feet high, or about on a level with the limit of trees on the mountain sides, so that the sections seen were only the rocky, snow-clad peaks. Mount Washington stood forth in grand majesty, although we could see only its upper half. The long ridge of Mount Carter lifted itself above the surface of the shadowy sea, looking " very like a whale ! " Some of the snow capped peaks of Maine were also to be seen, but all else, save the nearer White Mountain range, was sunk beneath the vast ocean which stretched far away on every side.

We devoured our dinner of " hard-tack," washing it down with pure snow-water, and then inscribing our names upon an old sardine box which had evidently served as a sort of visitors' register for nearly a dozen years, started to return. Tumultuous clouds rose angrily in the southwest, as if to drive us back from their domain. The prospect of having to grope our way back over an uncertain path, in the clouds, was not particularly pleasant, but it was one we were compelled to accept, for we

were soon engulfed by the huge, fleecy masses
which rose in the west and drifted over the mountains. While upon Mount Adams, and at other
points in our journey, we heard the shouts of our
friends on Mount Washington very distinctly, notwithstanding the distance from peak to peak, in a
direct line, is at least three miles, and we were told
on our return that our progress had been watched
very minutely with the aid of the telescopes, our
staffs and footprints in the snow, even, being discernible. Up and down the sides of Lafayette, and
across the greater part of Clay, we were compelled
to grope our way through the clouds. Where the
snow remained we could retrace our footsteps, but
these frequently led over trackless rocks or bare
patches of sedge. The ridge in places is narrow,
and a deviation from the proper course might lead
us into the deep ravines on either side. The clouds
gathered thicker and thicker, at times clearing away
sufficiently, however, to show us our course ahead,
and by fixing our pathway at such times with a compass, following our foot-prints where they could be
traced in the snow, or guiding ourselves on the
ridge between the falling waters which could be
heard on either side, we finally reached the railway,
which is a sure and safe pilot to the summit of
Mount Washington. It was a long, weary journey,
however, and we did not reach the depot until after
seven o'clock.

In ascending the cone of Mount Washington, we again got above the cloud level, and enjoyed a rare sunset scene. We also witnessed a veritable battle of the clouds. The wind, which had been very light throughout the day, had appeared to come from different directions at different points — now from the east, in another place from the north or northwest, and again from the west or southwest. We had ascended a little distance above the Gulf Tank, when we turned and observed two ghostly armies approaching each other — one from the direction of Mount Monroe, and the other from out the depths of the Great Gulf. Noiselessly they marched onward, and the conflict came near the gap between Mounts Washington and Clay. The battle was short and decisive. Little fragments of cloud, like wreaths of smoke, were flung high in air, and there seemed a momentary indecision, but the fleecy forms from the southwest were soon fleeing before the fast gathering hosts of the east, until all were commingled in one shadowy mass.

MORE WINTRY WEATHER.

In the course of the twenty-four hours succeeding our visit to Mount Adams, we had an opportunity to reflect upon the changeableness and uncertainty of mountain weather. After a genial and delightful day on the 6th, the summit became envel-

oped in clouds in the early evening, and rain began
to fall by nine o'clock. Before morning the rain
turned to snow, and a furious gale set in. The
thermometer which had indicated 56° Saturday
morning had descended to 25° at the same hour
Sunday morning, and Monday morning it marked
15°. For nearly forty-eight hours the snow fell,
or rather drifted over the summit in clouds, and the
tempest raged with great fury. Huge banks of
snow formed against the sides of the buildings and
along the line of the railway, more than replacing
those which had almost disappeared under the warm
influence of Saturday's sun. After nightfall on
Sunday the storm seemed to increase in force, and
it was thought that the wind at times reached a
velocity of nearly if not quite ninety miles an hour.
Beneath the force of the terrific blasts, the building
which sheltered us trembled and writhed like a ship
in an ocean tempest. No one ventured out of doors
except to make the required observations with the
anemometer, and there were times when it would
have been impossible to withstand the fury of the
storm. Warmth and comfort reigned within, but
the creaking of the timbers and chains and the
surging, seething roar of the storm were frightful to
hear. Each plank and timber in the whole structure
seemed to have a particular creak and groan of its
own, and a thousand demons appeared to rage with-

out. Yet the storm was much less severe than
many which had been encountered at the summit
during the winter. I had chanced to be present
during a much more furious assault of the elements, in February, but nevertheless, the storm of
May 7th and 8th was something long to be remem
bered.

THE DESCENT.

Having already been detained at the mountain-
top longer than I desired, in consequence of the
storm, I availed myself of the earliest abatement of
the tempest to descend. To have attempted the
journey on Monday would have been both difficult
and dangerous, and it is doubtful if it could have
been performed in such a storm. On Tuesday, the
9th, it continued cloudy at the summit, but the
storm had passed. Immense quantities of snow had
fallen and the average depth for a mile and a half
down the mountain side was at least three feet. It
was unsafe walking upon the railway, for the snow
made the ties and stringers slippery and treacher-
ous, and it became necessary to take to the rocks.
From the summit to Jacob's Ladder, the best course
was to keep beside the railway. At that point the
old Fabyan bridle-path is crossed, and this formed
an easier route until the railway was again reached,
a short distance above the Waumbek station. The

snow was very deep far down into the forests, and it made a pitfall of every hole and crevice, but there was an advantage in having soft places to fall upon. As I had neglected to provide myself with snow-shoes, I could make but slow progress through the deep snows, but upon the lower slopes there was a much less quantity of snow, and the little there was made a better surface to walk upon than the bare rocks and earth alone would have furnished.

Emerging from the cloud which enwrapped the summit in its icy folds, I beheld a most glorious scene. At first the misty curtain was withdrawn just far enough to bring the valley of the Ammonoosuc and the more distant green hills of Vermont into view — a landscape of incomparable beauty, framed and tinged by the neutral gray of the drifting mists. Soon the surrounding peaks were added to the picture. A snowy mantle was spread over them all, and little patches of sunlight played about their summits or shot down their slopes like shafts of burnished silver. The frost formations near the summit of Mount Washington were very extensive and very beautiful. In the forests below they were more delicate, and seemingly more beautiful still. They covered every bush, twig, and bit of hanging moss, while the snow which had fallen upon the branches formed a canopy of the same spotless purity. One looked through long vistas of exquisitely carved columns and arches, here and there bedecked with a sprig of living emerald, and intertwined with curtains and festoonings of ermine. It was surely a glimpse into fairy-land.

There were some two inches of snow about the depot at the foot of the mountain, but in the seven miles' walk from thence to the White Mountain House — from which point further locomotion was had by horse power to a railroad connection at Whitefield — all trace of winter, save in the view backward toward the mountains, was lost. It was a sudden transition from midwinter back to spring. In the clear atmosphere the mountain chain we were fast leaving behind us stood out in bold relief, and we lingered long upon the brow of the hill, half a mile up the turnpike from the Notch road, to enjoy the beautiful prospect that spot above all others affords.

PART THIRD.

METEOROLOGY OF MOUNT WASHINGTON.

INTRODUCTION.

THAT a knowledge of the climatology of a country is intimately connected with the welfare of its people, is not to-day a mooted question. From being a matter of mere conjecture it has come to be a subject of inquiry and investigation. Many things have a bearing upon the question: electric phenomena; the formation, course, and progress of storms; the average temperature and rainfall, and the fluctuations to which the elements are subject. Indirectly, the knowledge derived from the investigation of these phenomena, is a benefit to all, but especially is it of direct advantage to the two most important vocations, — commerce and agriculture. Although the different phenomena of meteorology have occupied the attention of mankind from time immemorial, it is most frequently only the application of the laws of physics to a particular class of phenomena, " therefore it

could make no real progress until other sciences,
and especially physics, were sufficiently advanced
to constitute a satisfactory body of doctrines."

The discoveries in electricity, the most important
branch of physics for meteorology, date back scarcely
a century, and hardly twenty years have elapsed
since scientific societies and governments commenced systematic operations. The knowledge of
storms furnished by Redfield, Reid, etc., "suggested
the possibility of inaugurating a system of weather
observations, and of using the results for the benefit
of commerce and navigation both on the sea and
land. The giving effect to this idea, as Buchan
remarks, constitutes the splendid contribution to
practical meteorology made by Admiral Fitzroy in
February, 1861, by the system of storm-warnings
or forecasts, which has since been adopted by almost
every country in Europe." The Congress of the
United States, in April 1870, passed a law establishing a "Bureau of Telegrams and Reports for the
benefit of Commerce." "With quiet activity," it
was speedily organized and equipped.

The last of October it had its corps of observers
in the field, and on the first of November the first
official storm-warnings were made. Scarcely half
a dozen forecasts were published, when it was evident that this was the most important service ever
organized by the government.

The observations taken by individuals, each working after a method of his own, are interesting in themselves, but lacking uniformity they are of little value as compared with those taken under one organization, each observer being furnished with standard instruments, and all taking observations simultaneously. The observations taken under the direction of the British Board of Admiralty, the Smithsonian Institution, and the United States Storm Signal Service, with their trained, educated observers, everything reduced to a perfect system, and giving daily reports and forecasts of storms, will reduce meteorology to such an exact science that the probabilities, which are drawn from observations taken, will amount to almost an absolute certainty. My object in occupying Mount Washington, was if possible, by studying the upper currents of the air, to add something to our knowledge of meteorology. Is there any one that doubts, but that our atmospheric disturbances are governed by fixed laws? If they are, then, if we are able to understand these laws we ought just as surely to be able to give forecasts of the weather, as to foretell the changes of the planets. That we were not mistaken in supposing Mount Washington to be a desirable point for meteorological observations, the following extract from a letter from Professor Cleveland Abbe, Director of the Cincinnati Observatory and Assistant in the Signal Service will show : —

" Thus far, as regards the cold period, I am able to verify your statement, and also to add that the cloudy, drizzly and cold raw weather continues here below a few hours after it begins to moderate overhead. The cold upper winds, as reported from Cheyenne and Mount Washington, are sure to be followed by cold, cloudy weather for a long distance south. The hygrometric observations from the mountain stations are however of still more importance. Although these require very large correction, which are not given in Guyot's tables, yet I manage daily to derive information which foretells the coming storm, and would do so far more accurately had we two other stations distant one to three hundred miles. Especially do I value the Mount Washington record in the study of the rapidity of the motion of small areas of high and low pressure. This has been to me the most important part of my work since I entered upon my duties in January, and I feel the great advantage that we possess over the English meteorological observers, in that we, at once, have been able to enter upon the study of that which they after many years experience are only now able to begin to study. I think, my dear sir, that meteorology and our Signal Service are under great obligations to you for your successful efforts to carry on your meteorological observations during the winter on Mount Washington."

CHAPTER XVI.

THE FROST-WORK AND CLOUDS.

THE frost-work is one of the most remark-able phenomena of this high altitude. It is difficult to convey in words any idea of its wonderful form and beauty. It was not easy at first to understand how it could be formed, but from the study given to it last winter, and the op-portunities we have had of observing its formation this, we are able to give a plausible, if not a cor-rect theory to account for this, the most plastic of all the handiwork of nature.

HOW FORMED.

At our first observation, we see that it forms only when the wind is northward, *i. e.* at some point be-tween north and west or north and east, and never when the wind is southward. It begins with mere points, on everything the wind reaches: on the rocks, on the snow, on the railway, and on every part of the buildings, even on the glass. On the south side of the buildings and the high rocks it is very slight,

as the wind reaches there only in eddying gusts.
When the surface is rough, the points, as they begin are an inch or more apart; when smooth it
almost entirely covers the surface at the very beginning, but soon only a few points elongate, so that
on whatever surface it begins to form, it has very
soon the same general appearance, presenting
everywhere the same beautiful, feathery-like forms.

> " Thus Nature works, as if defying art ;
>   And in defiance of her rival powers,
>   Performing such inimitable feats,
>   As she with all her rules can never reach."

When the ice which has formed on the rocks is
transparent and the frost-work forms on this, we can
often see in the interstices of the frost-work, which
is purely white, the gray rocks and the many
colored lichens, the whole making a picture of rare
beauty. In going up the mountain we do not see the
frost-work until we get some distance above the limit
of the trees; it is nearly a mile before it is seen in
its characteristic forms, and it is only immediately
about the summit that it presents its most attractive
features. We notice also, that it always forms
toward the wind, never from it, and the rapidity
with which it forms, and the great length of the
horizontal masses, is truly wonderful. We placed a
round stick, an inch in diameter, in a vertical position, where it was exposed to the full force of the

FROST FEATHERS

Formed against the northwest wind.

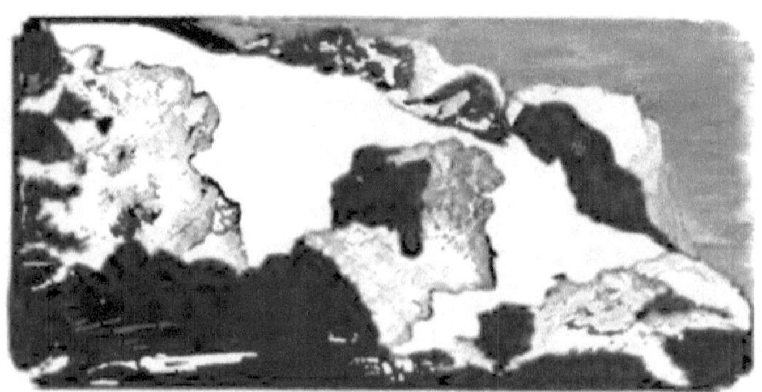

SOLID ICE

Formed upon the rocks when the wind came from the South.

wind, and in less than two days some of the horizontal icicles — we call them icicles for the want of a more appropriate name — were two feet in length and scarcely any thicker than the stick itself. They formed on every part of the stick that was exposed, but of course some points were much longer than others. They remained several days, but with a change of wind they were blown off. On the piles of stones south of the house, these horizontal masses are sometimes five or six feet in length. Although these masses are often as hard as the hardest ice, yet throughout they are as white as the purest snow.

On the southern exposures, instead of the frost-work — especially on the telegraph poles along the railway, — there are only masses of pure ice, which have always a peculiar hue of greenish blue, which is in striking contrast with the pure white of the frost-work on the side opposite.

In the early part of December, when the thermometer ranged from 25° to 29°, and the wind was southward, the ice formed to the thickness of a foot or more on the telegraph poles near the house. These icy masses are formed evidently by the condensation of the vapor of the atmosphere, as it is not uncommon for the air to be above the point of saturation. The frost-work is also formed by the condensation of vapor, but besides the vapor, the air must be filled with minute spiculæ of ice. As the vapor condenses these are caught, and thus the horizontal, feathery masses are formed. This accounts for the facts that we have observed, namely, that it forms when the wind is northward and always toward the wind.

THE CLOUDS.

Mountains without clouds are spiritless and tame. It is true, that on high summits even under a noonday sun, when there is some haze in the atmosphere, we get an idea of immensity that we could not before comprehend, but on the same heights with clouds floating gracefully around the distant peaks or their shadows flitting across illimitable forests, we have besides, a beauty and a grandeur, of which one who has never looked upon a cloud-scene from a mountain-summit " has as little imagination or understanding as he has of the scenery of another planet than his own." I suppose we might stay here a lifetime and not see a single cloud effect repeated ; we might see something similar, but in its details each would be unlike that which preceded it. Hence the attraction is ever new, and each succeeding day reveals new glories not seen before. In summer, often in the morning, the fogs lie along the valleys, over the lakes and streams. When the sun warms the air, these fogs rise and form clouds that pass over the summits and float away to be redissolved as they meet the warmer currents of the air, or to be augmented, when they meet the cooler currents. In winter the cloud effects are quite different from those of summer. Often we stand on the summit and look forth upon an illimitable sea of mist glittering in the bright sunlight, while every peak, except that on which we stand, is concealed by clouds. So it is not uncommon for it to be a dark day in the valleys while on the summit we are in the bright sunlight. Sometimes the clouds are two thousand feet below the summit of Mount Washington; in that case innumerable mountain peaks protrude and seem like islands in an ocean bounded only by the sky. In winter these cloud-effects continue often a whole day almost unchanged.

These scenes naturally suggest Bayard Taylor's " Hymn to the Air, — "

" What is the scenery of earth to thine ?
    Here all is fixed in everlasting shapes ;
But where the realms of gorgeous cloudland shine,
    There stretch afar thy sun-illumined capes,
Embaying reaches of the amber seas
    Of sunset, on whose tranquil bosom lie
    The happy islands of the upper sky,
The halcyon shores of thine Atlantides.
Anon the airy headlands change, and drift
    Into sublimer forms, that slowly heave
    Their toppling masses up the front of eve,
Crag heaped on crag, with many a fiery rift,
    And hoary summits, throned beyond the reach

> Of Alps or Caucasus; again they change,
> And down the vast, interminable range
> Of towers and palaces, transcending each,
> The workmanship of Fable-land we see
> The "crystal hyaline" of Heaven's own floor, —
> The radiance of far Eternity
> Reflected on thy shore!"

At times the whole country westward is covered with clouds which are moving eastward, but when they pass the ridge that runs south to the Notch they are redissolved as they meet the warmer currents, and the air is then as transparent as if there was but a single cloud westward. It has not, to my knowledge, ever rained or snowed in the valleys when there was only a single stratum of cloud spread over the country at this low elevation. It has been noticed by aeronauts, "that when there is rain from a sky completely covered with clouds, there is always a similar range of clouds situated above at a certain height; and that on the contrary, when it does not rain, although the sky presents below the same appearance, the space situated imdiately above, as a dominant character, has a great extent of clear sky, with a sun unobstructed by a single cloud. This explains why a similar state of things frequently exists, — a very cloudy, overcast sky without a drop of rain."

CLOUDS FROM THE OCEAN.

It is one of the sublime scenes on Mount Washington, to watch the clouds as they come moving in solid phalanx from the ocean. The upper surface is generally higher than Mount Pleasant in Maine, hardly as high as the summit of Pequawket, or the Carter Range. When lower than the Carter Range it is frequently the case that the clouds come into the deep ravines between Mount Washington and the Carter Range, both from the north and the south. In every instance when the clouds have come in thus from the sea, there has been a storm the same day or the day following, not only on the mountain but throughout New England. When the clouds have come thus from the eastward, the wind on Mount Washington has been west or southwest. The clouds, when a storm has approached from the south, have always been at a high elevation, and they seem to be continually augmented as they come northward, extending over the high mountain summits; although far above them, a column would be formed from each summit to the mass above. The gradual formation of the cloud is easily explained. The moisture-laden atmosphere from the south, coming in contact with the colder currents north, the vapor is condensed. In the vicinity of the snow-clad mountain summits, it

is quite probable that there is a colder stratum of
air, hence the column extending to the clouds above.
Instead of a great sea of mist, or a storm gradually
approaching, the clouds may be driven by fierce
winds into " boiling heaps of illuminated mist,
furrowed by a thousand colossal ravines," or dashed
against the jutting cliffs and crags, being thrown
like spray hundreds of feet into the air to be caught
again by the wind and hurled down into the seething depths. No pen, no pencil, can portray the
grandeur of the scene, when these clouds are
touched with rose-tinted amber light, while into the
depths of the chasms formed by the whirling mist,
shadows fall dark as night, or when the sea of clouds
with " mighty icebergs floating in it," extends as
far as the eye can reach, or the forest-clad peaks
protruding above its surface, the bosom of the
sea apparently as smooth as polished marble, then
perchance agitated by slightly undulating swells, or
rolling in waves burnished with silver and tipped
with gold.

The coronæ encircling the sun, the luminous
glow surrounding our shadows as they are thrown
far out upon the clouds, the supernumerary bows
continuing for hours, and many cloud scenes, are
described by Mr. Nelson in his journal.

CHAPTER XVII.

THE WIND.

ERY few persons have any idea of the velocity of the wind or its pressure. The greatest velocity that has been measured at the Observatory at Central Park, New York City, is forty-five miles per hour. As the Observatory is in an exposed situation and near the sea-board it is reasonable to conclude that this is the greatest velocity, except in very rare instances, anywhere on the Atlantic slope, where the elevation is not much above the sea level. The pressure for this velocity at the level of the sea when the barometer is at its mean height, is six pounds per square foot.

THE VELOCITY AND PRESSURE AT LOW ELEVATIONS.

As the pressure varies as the square of the velocity, when the velocity of the wind is twenty miles per hour, its force is four times as great as that of a wind blowing ten miles per hour. When the wind is blowing from sixty to seventy miles per hour, it requires a man of considerable physical strength to be able to stand against it, for the pressure then near the level of the sea, is from eighteen to twenty-four pounds per square foot. If a person presents a surface of six square feet and knows his physical strength, he can easily tell how great a velocity he can withstand.

It is a very different thing, however, being merely able to stand bracing one's self, and going against the wind, for in this case, we have as it were, to push the weight of the pressure of the wind before us.

THE VELOCITY AND PRESSURE AT HIGH ELEVATIONS.

The summit of the mountain is rarely free from winds, and they have a greater velocity than at any point where they have ever been measured, except those measured by Mr. Clough and myself on Moosilauke, last winter. One reason why it is so much greater here than elsewhere, is from the fact, that in the valleys the wind is generally unsteady, blowing in gusts, while here, during the most violent winds, there is not the slightest lull, until the storm has reached its culmination, then there are lulls which continually lengthen until the storm ceases.

" During the most violent storms the wind has exceeded a hundred miles per hour, and the average height of the barometer may be stated at twenty-three inches.

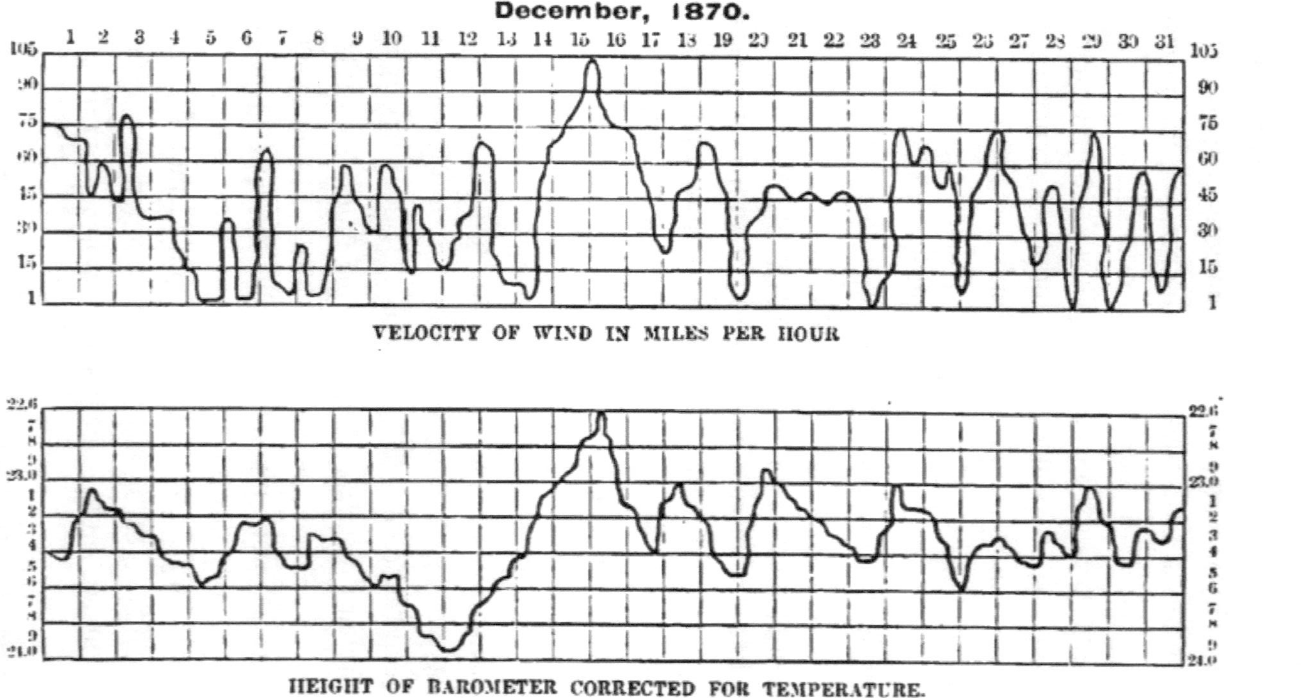

December, 1870.
VELOCITY OF WIND IN MILES PER HOUR
HEIGHT OF BAROMETER CORRECTED FOR TEMPERATURE.

" With a velocity of one hundred miles per hour at the level of the sea, the pressure on a square foot is fifty pounds. But in estimating the pressure at the summit we must make a reduction in accordance with the principle that the power of a moving fluid to remove an obstacle is in proportion to the square of its density. Taking the average pressure at the level of the sea during these storms at twenty-nine inches, we must reduce the tabular pressure of fifty pounds as follows : $50 \times (\frac{29}{30})^2 = 31.45$. That is, a velocity of one hundred miles per hour at the summit, would gave a pressure of 31.45 pounds to the square foot; and this pressure corresponds by the same table to a velocity at the level of the sea of 79.3 miles an hour. Hence we see that a velocity of 79.3 miles an hour at the level of the sea would do the same damage as a velocity of one hundred miles on the summit." Calms are very rare and generally of short duration. They occur when the wind is on the point of changing. At times the changes are very sudden ; the wind may be southeast and in an hour there will be a stiff breeze from the northwest, which soon increases to a gale. This change of the wind from a point, to that directly opposite, is not uncommon. The prevailing winds have been northwest, and the most violent, with one exception, have come from that direction or a few points farther north.

As the side of the house presents a surface of more than six hundred square feet, the pressure of the wind, when it reaches its greatest velocity, is tremendous, and it puts the house to the severest test, especially when it comes in heavy gusts.

After a time of light wind, when the building is full of frost and the joints are frozen, a heavy wind loosens the joints with a report that is startling, so sharp that, until we become accustomed to it, we can hardly believe but that the house is coming down over our heads. These reports, with the almost constant roar of the wind, are trying to weak nerves, and even if a person has considerable courage it is sometimes difficult to be perfectly cool, particularly when the thermometer gets below —40, as the chances of escape are very small should the house be crushed. But in general it only furnishes excitement enough to keep off the *ennui* incident to an isolated life.

REMARKABLE WINDS WHEN CLEAR.

Nothing has surprised me more than the fierce winds we have when it is perfectly clear. We expect them when there are clouds on the mountain, but we have had the wind more than eighty miles per hour when there was not a single cloud above the summit. The wind at such times is rarely a steady pressure, as it is during a period of storm.

No war of the elements is so remarkable as when these invisible elements rage with such fury around this high summit on a clear, cold, moonlight night in midwinter. At such times the sky is intensely blue, the moon looks coldly down, and the stars shine as nowhere else, except at high altitudes and in northern latitudes. Besides the roar of the wind and the creaking of the house, the wind seems to be trying its utmost to draw the coals upward through the stove-pipe, for it tugs and pulls and jerks, and now, as if gathering all its force, it gives one long, steady pull, but the coals are too heavy for it. With light wood it would certainly succeed, if not in taking the wood away, at least in taking every spark of fire, — for this was done several times during my stay on Moosilauke. Now the sound is a hoarse deafening roar, that dies away into a plaintive moan ; now it screeches and howls as though all the witches of Macbeth were therein confined, but in an instant the sound ceases, only however to be renewed by others so weird and strange that one almost believes that the ghosts of the aborigines, who were guilty of having ascended where only the lichens grow, still hover about the summit ; for they had a tradition that such would never reach the hunting ground beyond the sunset, but must wander forever around the mountain they had dared profane. Now it seizes the damper in the pipe, which rattles and vibrates, and seems to offer no resistance to the passing currents of the air.

Thus the wind through the pipe roars and shrieks, growls and howls, pipes and hums, grating and jarring, creeking and twanging, then gently breathing with a plaintive moan, while outside it comes in waves as the ocean beats in heavy surges on the shore. Almost every one who has been here in summer has noticed, when at intervals there are clouds passing over the mountain, that the wind blows with greater velocity while the clouds are on the mountain. This is probably due to the greater humidity, as it is well known that an excess of aqueous vapor gives rise to currents in the atmosphere. As the motion of the atmosphere is from the place where it contains least vapor to that where there is the most vapor, this may be the cause of the prevailing northwest winds. On account of the proximity of the ocean there must be an excess of vapor there as compared with the currents on the summit of Mount Washington.

THE WIND AND THE BAROMETER.

From my observations here and on Moosilauke, it is quite certain that during periods of storm there is a close connection between the velocity of the wind and the rise and fall of the barometer. By a period of storm we mean the time embraced in any severe and extensive commotion of the atmosphere. These commotions here usually last from twelve to thirty-six hours, and may extend to forty-eight hours before the barometer rises to its mean height. For each period of storm during our observations, I have constructed two curves on the same time scale, one representing the velocity of the wind, the other the rise and fall of the barometer, and find that the ordinates of these curves almost exactly correspond. In one instance the barometer went up when there was a lull in the midst of the storm, but went down as the velocity of the wind again increased, which it continued to do for half an hour, when there were frequent lulls, accompanied by a gradual rise in the barometer until the storm ceased. Why is it that the barograms correspond so exactly with the velocity of the wind?

An explanation of this curious phenomena is given by Mr. F. Gaston, F. R. S., in the Proceedings of the British Association : —

" The answer to this question will best be conveyed by a consideration of what we should expect the movements of the mercurial column to be if a suitably made barometer were plunged into troubled water. Its movements would not correspond to each ripple that passed vertically above its cistern, because it would be affected by all the disturbance in an area of surface water whose radius is a function of the depth of immersion. If it were plunged to the depth of many fathoms the mercury would wholly cease to oscillate, because the average level of the area with which it sympathizes would be constant however much its surface might be broken up into undulations. If it were immersed to a suitable depth, the mercury would foretell the advent of each wave of exceptional size, before an exceptional height of water had arrived vertically above the barometer. It is easy and interesting to make an experiment to the same effect, by dipping a glass tube, open at both ends, straight into a pan of water and disturbing the water with the hand. When the tube is dipped but a short way in, the water it encloses harmonizes in its oscillations with the water that surrounds it, but this harmony is diminished and the oscillations in the tube become more sluggish, as the tube is immersed more deeply, and at length they disappear altogether. In precisely the same way I believe the mercury in the barometer sympathizes with atmospheric disturbance throughout a wide circle."

CHAPTER XVIII.

STORMS.

T is difficult to convey in words any vivid idea of the terrific grandeur of the storms in winter upon the summit of Mount Washington. They have probably been more severe than any ever before experienced, especially when the cold is taken as one of the elements. The storm of the 18th of October is noticed on page 167. There was a storm of some severity the 24th of November, when I was alone on the mountain. But the most severe storm, of all that we had, occurred on the 15th of December, and as it was the first terrific storm since the house had been built which we occupied, we did not feel that security, that we should in one that had stood the force of the storms in winters past.. The other houses are of stone, ours of wood, and besides presented a much greater surface to the wind than any building ever before erected on the summit. Two of the party had never been on a mountain summit during a winter storm, so they would be likely to describe it more vividly than a person who had witnessed many : —

"We have had probably as severe a tornado as will visit us during the winter. The velocity of the wind was recorded at seven o'clock in the evening, and it was ninety-two miles per hour. After that time it was not safe to venture out with the anemometer, unless we wanted to take an air-line passage to Tuckerman's Ravine ; for the wind kept increasing until toward morning, when it blew a terrific hurricane. Mr. Huntington and Mr. Clough, both having had considerable of this kind of experience, say it must have blown, at the highest point, one hundred and ten to one-hundred and twenty miles per hour. We expected at any moment to have the building come down about our heads, and were prepared to make an effort for our lives, having put hard-tack in our pockets, and armed with axe and saw, ready, in case we found it necessary, to cut our way out, getting also some of our thickest blankets ready for use, and preparing with considerable excitement for any emergency. The wind roared terribly, as if inspired with the power and spite of all the furies, and the wild rage was so deafening that we were obliged to shout to our utmost in order to be heard.

"Messrs. Huntington and Clough were both very cool, although I believe they thought the chances were more than even that we would have quarters elsewhere before morning; and Mr. Smith, the gentlemanly meteorological observer sent by the government to this station, was quite jolly, offering such consolation as this: 'If we were blown down into Tuckerman's Ravine, it would be for the "benefit of commerce," and so, of course, all right.' It seemed too much like cracking jokes while sitting up with a corpse, however, to be much relished. We watched all night, waiting anxiously the effect or result of the hurricane, and after a long night of such fearful tumult, morning brought us a little relief, by reducing the velocity of the wind to eighty-four miles per hour. We were duly thankful for this slight change, and at breakfast we congratulated each other on our narrow escape; for, if the building had been crushed, our chance for wishing any one a 'Merry Christmas' and 'Happy New Year' would have been very small; for the mercury was 15° below zero, and the barometer, the lowest recorded so far, 22.796. This remarkable fall will not happen often, but when it does, we shall keep housed.

"The immediate danger is passed, however, and our good cover has been severely tested, and has not been found wanting in point of strength. We have more confidence in it than we had before the storm."

During the storm so great was the force of the wind, that the three-inch planks which had been securely bolted across the opening where the train enters the building in summer, were pressed in four or more inches, while the end of the building and the side towards the wind, and finally the whole structure, had a vibratory motion not altogether pleasant.

THE STORM OF TWENTY-SECOND AND TWENTY-THIRD OF JANUARY.

We had another storm the twenty-second and twenty-third of January. Though the wind was not so fearful as the storm of December, yet the cold was more intense. The building had been tried by previous storms and we felt more secure. But the roar of the storm and the ice thrown against the building, like showers of grape, kept us wide awake. In the journal of this date will be found additional notes of this storm, and in the meteorological record it will be seen how uniform was the fall of the barometer, until the storm reached its culmination.

During the storm of the fourth and fifth of February the cold exceeded in intensity anything we had the whole winter. The gale began on Thursday, the second, quite suddenly, and reached its height on the fourth, about midnight, when the velocity of the wind was estimated at one hundred miles per hour, and the barometer was 22.464, the lowest recorded. To it was added the most intense cold ever experienced short of arctic regions, the thermometer indicating 59 below zero at three o'clock Sunday morning, the fifth.

THE COLD IN ARCTIC REGIONS.

In arctic regions, the intense cold " is breathless, still, and bright ; " and Dr. Carpenter in his " Human Physiology, says " " that in the experience of Arctic voyagers the temperature of —50° may be sustained when the air is perfectly still, with less inconvenience than is caused by air in motion at a temperature of 50° higher." The immunity from chilling influences is " chiefly attributable to the dryness and stillness of the atmosphere." But here we had neither dryness nor stillness, for the wind was at least eighty miles per hour, while the cold was most intense. Above it was perfectly clear, but below there was a dense haze which had more the appearance of smoke than clouds. During this period of cold, when the temperature was —21°, and the wind a little more than sixty miles per hour, my nose was frozen in less than three minutes, while standing with my back to the wind. Mr. Nelson, when the cold was most intense, had his fingers frost-bitten while cutting a piece of meat, directly over our room. When it is so intensely cold a person freezes without feeling the least sensation

of cold. During my stay on Moosilauke I made
the ascent of the mountain when the thermometer
was at zero, and the wind was seventy miles per
hour, though I was not exposed to the full force of
the wind until within a short distance of the house.
Here I went about forty rods from the house when
the thermometer was —16° and the wind above
sixty miles per hour. In the most intense cold we
had and when the velocity of the wind was so great,
it is probable that a person would become instantly
insensible.

During a gale on the 10th of February we
were not the only witnesses. " It was not accompanied by such intense cold, although the temperature was quite low, reaching 21° below zero at
seven o'clock the next morning. There was a
downward tendency in the barometer in the morning, and it was quite low throughout the afternoon
and until late in the evening, when the tempest began to abate. Its lowest point was 23.033, and its
variations followed the rise and fall of the wind
quite closely. The wind, which was blowing at the
rate of fifty-two miles an hour at seven A. M., increased to eighty-seven miles by the middle of the
forenoon. At noon it had decreased to forty-eight
miles, but at two P. M., it had begun business with
renewed vigor, eighty-eight miles being indicated.
At three o'clock, the anemometer marked seventy-
six miles, and at seven P. M., when the last obser-

vation with that instrument was taken, it had again reached eighty-eight miles. For the next hour or so the gale increased in fury, until it reached at least one hundred miles per hour. The wind howled and thundered without like an army of angry demons, while an incessant pelting of the building was kept up with pieces of ice and dislodged frost-work. At times it seemed as if the whole side of the depot was about to be crushed in. Added to the roaring of the storm there was seemingly an individual creak and groan for every plank in the whole structure, and a universal rattling of everything that could emit a sound. In the midst of the storm there came a sudden crash, followed by a rushing, seething noise, and it was discovered that a window had been broken. The aperture was closed by nailing boards across the inside, and further damage was prevented. With each occasional lull, the framework and supports of the structure, which had been strained to their utmost, sprang back to their places with another startling report."

The wind during the storms already mentioned, was northwest, or a little more towards the north. On the 3d of March the storm was from the S.S.E. and the wind reached a velocity of ninety-eight miles per hour, and the rain swept along in torrents, completely deluging the mountain. In March the mountain was more free from storms and clouds than any month during our stay. In April there

was only one very severe rain-storm, and that was
from the southwest on the 5th. A thunder-storm
on the 11th, which was quite severe in the valleys
adjacent did not reach the summit; the flashes of
lightning, however, could be seen, but the thunder
was heard only as a distant roar. As it was snowing on the mountain the storm must have been far
below us. It snowed nearly half the month, and
the storms were quite like those in the valleys in
winter, while here in the winter months it snowed
very little, and the snow-flakes seemed to be mere
spiculæ, fragments that below may have formed
regular flakes. So it seems altogether probable
that the snow clouds of winter are at quite a low
elevation. The first half of May was very much
like April, though the snow-storms were more frequent, and in places the drifts were of greater depth
than at any time previous. During the winter it
sometimes rained when the thermometer was 23°,
and snowed when it was 38°. In case of rain, the
clouds must have been driven up from a much
lower elevation. When the wind is seventy and
eighty miles per hour it does not take a cloud long
to come half a mile up the mountain.

Whether we watch the storm as it approaches,
or feel its force as it breaks in all its fury on the
summit, there is a grandeur and sublimity in these
manifestations that fills the mind with awe and
wonder.

CHAPTER XIX.

METEOROLOGICAL RECORD.

HESE tables comprise the observations taken on the summit of Mount Washington, lat. 44° 16′ 34″ north, long. 71° 20′. west, 6,291.7 feet above the level of the sea, during a period of six months, from November 12, 1870, to May 13, 1871. On account of our high elevation the record in regard to clouds necessarily differs from ordinary observations, in that the clouds were frequently below our level. Those we looked down upon, sometimes, undoubtedly seemed to us to be of a different kind from what they would to an observer looking at them from below. At no time during the winter months were we able to see that the clouds above the summit moved in a different direction from those immediately around us. In April and May, however, the clouds both above and below frequently moved in a different direction from those at the elevation of the summit. The other observations are the same as those taken at low elevations. In the last table are the thermograms [1] of the three winter months at Mount Washington; Montreal, Q. P., from observations by Chas. Smallwood, LL. D., D. C. L., etc.; Lunenburg, Vt., from observations by H. A. Cutting, M. D.; and Providence, R. I. from observations by Alexis Caswell, LL.D., etc. The observations were taken syncronously, except that the last column of the Providence observations, were taken at ten P. M. instead of nine P. M.   In this table the fractions have been omitted, though they have been used in calculating the mean.

THE INSTRUMENTS WE USED.

The anemometer, the instrument we used for measuring the velocity of the wind, which is here represented, consists essentially of four hemispherical cups, having their diametrical planes exposed to a passing current of air. They are carried by four horizontal arms attached to a vertical shaft, which is caused to rotate by the velocity of the wind.

---

[1] We have used the word thermograms for the record of the height of the mercury in the thermometer. We usually say the height of the thermometer, or simply the thermometer, as a name for this record. But thermometer is the name of the instrument, and is inappropriate as expressing a record of the height of the mercury in the tube. The word thermogram is derived from θέρμη, heat, and γραμμή, that which is written; so literally it means that which is written of the heat, hence the appropriateness of the word. We might follow the word barograms in the same way, but this is unnecessary.

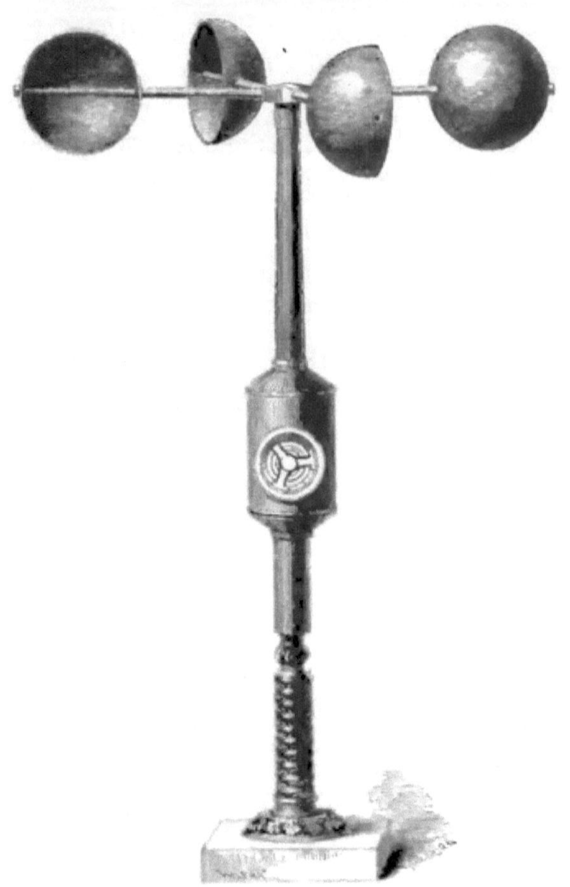

ANEMOMETER.

Dr. Robinson found that the cups, and, consequently, the axis to which they are attached, revolve with one third of the wind's velocity, which is here measured by a simple arrangement of two wheels, working in endless screws, and by means of two indices, shows on inspection of the dial, the velocity of the wind. The outer or front wheel, which revolves once for every five miles, is furnished with two graduated circles, the interior circle being subdivided to miles and tenths of miles, whilst the outer circle is divided into one hundred and one parts, each part being equivalent to five miles, so that it measures 505 miles of wind.

The stationary index, at the top of the dial, marks on the inner circle the number of miles — under five — and tenths, that the wind may have traversed, in addition to the miles shown by the traversing index, which revolves with the dial and indicates on the *outer* circle the transit of every five miles.

Thermometers are so well known that a description here is unnecessary. How low a temperature a mercurial thermometer will register correctly is a question. That the mercury here fell gradually to —59, and then rose again with the same regularity as in other extreme changes, is certain.

The Anemoscope or Wind-vane. We made many attempts to keep a vane on the building, but it was blown down every time it was put up. When the rod did not break the tail of the vane would become so loaded with ice that it would not turn to the wind. As a consequence a light vane had to be used which could be taken in to free it from ice.

The barometers we used here were manufactured by James Green of New York. The principle of these is also well known.

The Hygrometer. Though this instrument is common enough, very few persons perhaps, even among scientific men, fully appreciate its importance. Nearly every person has noticed that at certain times various substances attract the moisture of the atmosphere, or rather the particles of moisture enter the loose and open texture of substances exposed to the air and cause them to expand: wood swells, tobacco is sensibly affected, salt becomes moist, a rope contracts; these are for some persons a hygrometer, or "measure of moisture." The most simple mechanical device for measuring the moisture is a well-twisted elastic cord suspended with a small weight at the end. The rise and fall of the weight will show the variation of moisture in the air. In the weather-house, the man coming out in wet weather and the lady in dry; the contracting substance used in these is catgut or hair. A similar toy is the capuchin, in which the monk puts on his hood when the air is damp. But all animal substances deteriorate from time and exposure, and soon lose their hygrometric properties.

The instrument in most common use is the dry and wet bulb hygrometer. This, although perhaps suggested by others, was brought into general notice in England by Dr. John A. Mason. As modified by Glaisher it consists of two thermometers exactly similar and having a fine thread of mercury. One bulb is covered with a fine piece of muslin. From this a lamp-wick extends into a cup of water. When the mercury is below the freezing point the bulb is covered with a film of ice.

Dr. Schaeffer of Washington, D. C., has invented a revolving hygrometer which, especially in extremely warm or cold weather, seems preferable to any other. It differs from the last in that the bulbs are straight or oblong, instead of hemispherical. Water, at the temperature of the air or as near it as possible, is put upon one of the bulbs, with a camel's hair brush, then the instrument is revolved rapidly until the water evaporates, when the reading of the instrument is taken. The evaporation of water or ice takes from the bulb that amount of heat required for its conversion into vapor, and the consequent cold is shown by the fall of the mercury. This depression of the mercury measures strictly only the evaporating power of the air, as the latter depends on the amount of moisture in the atmosphere, and the depression of the wet bulb of the thermometer indirectly measures the humidity of the air.

The sanitary and the horticultural uses of the hygrometer deserve more attention than they have heretofore received. A hygrometer in our dwellings and public halls would tell us at once whether the requisite amount of moisture is present, for our sensations cannot guide us in regard to humidity.

The fact that the quantity of vapor is least during the winter months, and that at the same time the relative humidity is at its maximum, would to most persons probably seem paradoxical. But the relative humidity of the air depends not only on the amount of vapor it contains, but also on its degree of temperature.

The figures given in our tables for humidity is the ratio which the vapor actually present in the atmosphere bears to the amount which it would contain if it was saturated, that is, when there is present the utmost quantity of water it can contain in suspension.

Complete saturation is taken at 100, and it decreases from this to perfect dryness.

The difficulty we have experienced is from the want of tables calculated for low temperatures and fractions of a degree.

The accompanying cut represents " Edson's

HYGRODEIK.

Hygrodeik," an instrument adapted to general use. It differs from all other hygrometers in having a dial and pointer, showing at a glance the temperature, the relative humidity, the dew point, the absolute weight of vapor in cubic foot of air, and the elastic force of aqueous vapor. Thus simplified, it is adapted to meet every-day wants, and yet is susceptible of delicate adjustment for scientific purposes. Its principal uses are as a guide, — out-doors to aid in foretelling the weather, — in-doors to preserve health ; and in manufactories and store-houses, to prevent injury to goods or materials of any kind, by shrinking, swelling, rust, mildew, or any chemical change due to excess or deficiency of moisture.

METEOROLOGICAL TABLES.

NOVEMBER.

Date	Thermograms				Rain and Snow.	Clouds, 7 a. m.		Clouds, 2 p. m.		Clouds, 9 p. m.	
	7 a.m.	2 p.m.	9 p.m.	Mean.		Amount.	Kind.	Amount.	Kind.	Amount.	Kind.
13	19	18	21	19	–	9 below.	–	Clouds	on Mt.	Clouds	on Mt.
14	15	17	20	17	–	8 below.	–	8 below.	St.	Clouds	on Mt.
15	18	20	15	17	–	Light clouds	on Mt.	8 below.	–	4 below.	St.
16	15	14	14	14	–	1 below.	St.	2 below.	St.	3 below.	St.
17	15	19	14	16	–	2 below.	St.	6 below.	St.	4 below.	Clr.
18	19	18	19	18	Snowing at 1 p. m. and during night.	5 below.	St.	Clouds	on Mt.	Clouds	on Mt.
19	16	17	8	13	Snowing at 12½ p. m. and during night.	2 above. 3 below.	St.	Clouds	on Mt.	Clouds	on Mt.
20	9	14	14	12	–	Light clouds	on Mt.	7 above. St.& 1 below.	Cir.-st St.	10 above.	–
21	13	17	10	13	Snowing at 11 a. m.	Light clouds	on Mt.	Clouds	on Mt.	Clouds	on Mt.
22	11	10	9	10	Snow and sleet during night.	Light clouds	on Mt.	9 cir. above.	St.	Clouds	on Mt.
23	24	22	19	21	Frozen mist.	5 cir.	St.	Clouds	on Mt.	Clouds	on Mt.
24	9	7	6	7	Frozen mist.	Clouds	on Mt.	Clouds	on Mt.	Clouds	on Mt.
25	20	27	27	24	–	Clouds	on Mt.	8 above.	St.	10 above.	St.
26	23	24	22	24	–	1 above.	St.	Clouds	on Mt.	Clouds	on Mt.
27	24	24	19	22	Frozen mist.	10 above.	St.	Clouds	on Mt.	Clouds	on Mt.
28	15	17	21	17	–	Clouds	on Mt.	4 above.	St.	9 above.	St.
29	23	23	15	21	Snowing from 6 a. m to 8 p. m.	Clouds	on Mt.	Clouds	on Mt.	Clouds	on Mt.
30	–	5	9	4	–	Clouds	on Mt.	Light clouds	on Mt.	Clouds	on Mt.
Mean	–	–	–	16							

NOVEMBER.

Date.	WINDS.						BAROGRAMS AT 32°.			
	Direction. 7 A. M.	Miles per hour.	Direction. 2 P. M.	Miles per hour.	Direction. 9 P. M.	Miles per hour.	7 A. M.	2 P. M.	9 P. M.	Mean.
13	N.W.	24	N.W.	26	N.W.	22	23.264	23.424	23.180	23.289
14	W.	13	S.W.	42	S.W.	41	.298	.338	.324	.320
15	W.	5	W.	2	W.	1	.296	.364	.435	.365
16	W.	14	W.	15	W.	28	.468	.471	.588	.509
17	W.	16	W.	14	W.	2	.595	.702	.698	.663
18	W.	4	S.W.	6	S.W.	5	.664	.552	.486	.567
19	W.	7	N.W.	11	N.W.	14	.314	.180	.158	.217
20	W.	16	W.	18	N.W.	2	.427	.483	.546	.485
21	W.	12	W.	15	S.W.	46	.561	.500	.511	.524
22	S.	1	S.	3	S.	35	.863	.865	.775	.834
23	S.	27	S.W.	26	S.W.	36	.406	.204	.124	.244
24	W.	78	N.W.	76	N.W.	68	.022	.096	.295	.137
25	N.W.	25	N.W.	14	N.W.	12	.581	.598	.568	.582
26	W.	4	N.W.	16	N.W.	26	.483	.189	.301	.324
27	N.W.	47	N.W.	46	N.W.	14	.265	.273	.438	.325
28	N.W.	15	N.W.	17	N.W.	14	.586	.708	.794	.696
29	W.	5	W.	4	W.	17	.701	.655	.616	.657
30	N.W.	17	N.W.	24	N.W.	47	.609	.628	.663	.633
Mean	–	–	–	–	–	–	–	–	–	23.465

DECEMBER.

Date.	Thermograms.				Rain and Snow.	Clouds, 7 A. M.		Clouds, 2 P. M.		Clouds, 9 P. M.	
	7 A. M.	2 P. M.	9 A. M.	Mean.		Amount.	Kind.	Amount.	Kind.	Amount.	Kind.
1	14	16	13.5	14.5	—	0 above. 2 below.	 St.	0 above. 3 below.	– St.	0 above. 6 below.	– St.
2	15	16	15	15	—	Clouds	on Mt.	Clouds	on Mt.	Clouds	on Mt.
3	5	14	17	12	—	Clouds	on Mt.	Clouds	on Mt.	Clouds	on Mt.
4	17	18	16	17	—	Clouds	on Mt.	Clouds	on Mt.	Clouds	on Mt.
5	15	20	18	17.6	—	1 above. 7 below.	St.	Clouds	on Mt.	Clouds	on Mt.
6	22	22	15	19.6	—	Clouds	on Mt.	Clouds	on Mt.	Clouds	on Mt.
7	15	22	20	19	—	Light clouds	on Mt.	1 above. 8 below.	St.	0 above. 8 below.	–
8	16	18	15	16	—	Light clouds	on Mt.	Clouds	on Mt.	Clouds	on Mt.
9	12	13	11	12	—	Clouds	on Mt.	Clouds	on Mt.	Clouds	on Mt.
10	14	15	20	16	—	Light clouds	on Mt.	Light clouds	on Mt.	Light clouds	on Mt.
11	25	28.5	27	26.6	—	Light clouds	on Mt.	Light clouds	on Mt.	1 above. 8 below.	St. Cl.
12	17	20	20	19	—	Light clouds	on Mt.	Light clouds	on Mt.	Dense clouds	on Mt.
13	23	29	27	26.5	—	Dense clouds	on Mt.	0 above. 9 below.	–	Light clouds	on Mt.
14	22	22	14	18	Snow from 8 A. M. to 6 P. M.	Dense clouds	on Mt.	Dense clouds	on Mt.	Clouds	on Mt.
15	12	.5	— 7	1.8	—	Dense clouds	on Mt.	Dense clouds	on Mt.	Dense clouds	on Mt.
16	—10	— 6	—13	—10.5	—	Dense clouds	on Mt.	Dense clouds	on Mt.	Light clouds	on Mt.
17	1	5	4	3.5	—	0 above. 8 below.	–	Light clouds	on Mt.	Light clouds	on Mt.
18	4	— 1	— 4	— 1	—	Dense clouds	on Mt.	Light clouds	on Mt.	Dense clouds	on Mt.

19	0	9.5	11	7.1	–	–	0 above. 6 below.	–	1 above. 0 below.	– St.	5 above. 0 below.	–
20	15.5	20	14	15.5	Snow from 9 A. M. to 7 P. M.		Dense clouds	on Mt.	Dense clouds.		Dense clouds.	–
21	10	10	6	8	–	–	Dense clouds	on Mt.	Dense clouds	on Mt.	Dense clouds	on Mt.
22	0	—1	—5	—2.7	–	–	Dense clouds	on Mt.	Dense clouds	on Mt.	Dense clouds	on Mt.
23	—4	—2	—2	—2.5	–	–	0 above. 8 below.	–	5 above. 5 below.	Clr. St.	5 above. 2 below.	–
24	—10	—11	—15	—12.7	–	–	Light clouds	on Mt.	Light clouds	on Mt.	5 above. 0 below.	–
25	—14	—9	—7	—9	–	–	10 below. 1 above.	– St.	3 above. 0 below.	St.	0 below. 8 above.	–
26	—2	—1	–	—1	–	–	Light clouds	ou Mt	Light clouds	on Mt.	Dense clouds.	–
27	0	5	7	4	–	–	Dense clouds	on Mt.	8 above. 0 below.	St.	10 above. 2 below.	St.
28	6	9	11	9	–	–	Dense clouds	on Mt.	Light clouds	on Mt.	10 above. 3 below.	Cum. St.
29	6	3	1	3.7	–	–	Light clouds	on Mt.	5 above. 0 below.	Clr.	3 above. 3 below.	–
30	1	8	5	4.7	–	–	1 above. 0 below.	St.	8 above. 0 below.	St.	Light clouds	on Mt.
31	15	14	14	14	–	–	Light clouds	on Mt.	Dense clouds	on Mt.	Dense clouds	on Mt.
Sums				9.4								

DECEMBER.

Date.	WINDS.						BAROGRAMS AT 32°.				Relative Humidity.		
	Direction, 7 A. M.	Miles per hour, 7 A. M.	Direction, 2 P. M.	Miles per hour, 2 P. M.	Direction, 9 P. M.	Miles per hour, 9 P. M.	7 A. M.	2 P. M.	9 P. M.	Mean.			
1	W.	78	W.	70	W.	65	23.453	23.386	23.269	23.369	–	–	–
2	N.W.	46	W.	67	W.	48	.169	.144	.136	.149	–	–	–
3	N.W.	76	N.W.	47	N.W.	35	.258	.274	.384	.305	–	–	–
4	N.W.	37	N.W.	34	N.W.	31	.412	.468	.442	.440	–	–	–
5	W.	4	S.W.	4	S.	38	.611	.565	.391	.522	–	–	–
6	S.	4	N.W.	7	N.W.	80	.274	.274	.201	.249	–	–	–
7	N.N.W.	75	N.W.	12	S.	16	.413	.510	.508	.477	–	–	–
8	S.	24	S.E.	5	N.N.W.	45	.370	.340	.374	.362	–	–	–
9	N.	67	N.W.	49	N.W.	33	.421	.503	.583	.502	–	–	–
10	N.W.	64	N.W.	51	N.W.	15	.505	.484	.670	.553	–	–	–
11	E.	35	S.E.	27	S.S.E.	21	.904	.989	.007	.633	–	–	–
12	N.N.W.	24	E.	36	S.S.E.	67	.890	.772	.692	.785	–	100	85
13	S.	23	W.	14	N.W.	14	.612	.513	.465	.530	100	100	100
14	N.W.	6	N.W.	52	N.W.	63	.326	.115	.006	.169	100	73	91
15	W.	60	W.	65	W.	90	.058	22.897	22.734	22.896	22	55	19
16	N.W.	84	N.W.	65	N.W.	74	22.646	.938	.120	22.568	57	22	27
17	N.W.	48	N.W.	34	N.W.	26	23.226	23.378	23.173	23.259	100	50	74
18	S.W.	50	N.W.	47	N.W.	65	.008	.103	.180	23 097	74	43	64
19	N.	62	N.W.	36	S.	4	.347	.482	.497	23.442	69	46	79

20	S.	25	S W.	54	W.	42	.168	.973	.013	.385	64	41	73
21	S.W.	45	N.W.	63	N.W.	66	.048	.133	.200	.127	68	79	76
22	W.	63	S.W.	45	N.W.	44	.279	.344	.340	.321	39	22	31
23	N.	2	N.	3	N.	6	.370	.279	.220	.289	64	67	34
24	N.	78	N.	60	N.	63	.024	.064	.138	.075	53	51	52
25	N.	46	N.	61	W.	13	.348	.486	.616	.483	44	55	19
26	S.	47	S.W.	10	S W.	78	.439	.296	.331	.355	33	68	39
27	S.W.	45	S.W.	43	S.W.	25	.424	.412	.333	.390	39	50	76
28	W.	40	N.W.	39	Calm.	–	.306	.391	.398	.365	63	78	79
29	N.	45	N.	74	N.	44	.142	.008	.225	.125	100	19	41
30	Calm.	–	N.W.	12	S.S.W.	66	.355	.370	.278	.334	70	77	23
31	S.	25	S.	15	W.	60	.243	.239	.181	.221	82	82	63
Mean	–	–	–	–	–	–	–	–	–	23.315			

JANUARY.

Date.	Thermograms.				Rain and Snow.	Clouds, 7 A. M.		Clouds, 2 P. M.		Clouds, 9 P. M.	
	7 A. M.	2 P. M.	9 P. M.	Mean.		Amount.	Kind.	Amount.	Kind.	Amount.	Kind.
1	0	— 7	— 2	— 3	—	Light clouds	on Mt.	Clouds	on Mt.	Perfectly	clear.
2	10	9	— 7	8.2	—	Frozen	mist.	Clouds	on Mt.	Clouds	on Mt.
3	— 7	2	0	— 1.6	—	Light clouds.	—	8 above. 5 below.	St.	Clouds	on Mt.
4	—18	—13	—14	—14.8	—	0 above. 4 below.	—	Light clouds	on Mt.	Light clouds.	—
5	— 2	10	18	8 7	—	Light clouds	on Mt.	Clouds	on Mt.	8 above. 0 below.	St.
6	18	16	8	12.5	Frozen mist.	Clouds	on Mt.	Clouds	on Mt.	Clouds	on Mt.
7	— 6	— 7	— 8	— 7.2	—	Clouds	on Mt.	0 below. 1 above.	St.	0 above. 0 below.	—
8	— 6	— 4	— 5	— 5	—	1 above. 0 below.	St.	7 above. 0 below.	Cir.	1 above. 0 below.	Cir.
9	— 6	— 3	—11	— 7.7	—	0 above. 1 below.	St.	0 above. 1 below.	St.	0 above. 0 below.	—
10	— 2	0	4	.7	—	0 above. 0 below.	—	5 above. 0 below.	Cir.	5 above. 0 below.	—
11	13	23	25	21.5	—	3 above. 0 below.	St.	Clouds	on Mt.	Clouds	on Mt.
12	31	33	33	32.5	Frozen mist.	Clouds	on Mt.	Clouds	on Mt.	Clouds	on Mt.
13	34	36	38	36	—	—	—	10 above. 5 below.	St.	—	—
14	62	34	34	33.5	—	3 above. 2 below.	—	Clouds	on Mt.	10	St.
15	29	28	32	30.2	Light rain.	Dense cloud.	—	Clouds	on Mt.	Light rain.	—
16	82	33	31	31.7	—	Clouds	on Mt.	Clouds	on Mt	Clouds	on Mt.

17	1	8	— 1	2.7	—		Light clouds on Mt.	0 above. 4 below. St.	Clear. —
18	— 4	— .5	0.	1.5	—	—	Light clouds on Mt.	3 2 below. Clr.	Clear. —
19	8	9	10	8	—	—	Clear. —	4 above. 1 below. Clr. St.	8 above. 0 below. —
20	15	17	15	15.5	—	—	1 above. 30 below. Clr. St.	8 above. 1 below. —	Hazy. —
21	13	15	7	10.5	—	—	Clouds on Mt.	Clouds on Mt.	Clouds on Mt.
22	— 5	—27	—41.5	—28.5	—	—	Clouds on Mt.	Clouds on Mt.	2 below. —
23	—85	— 4	1	— 2.6		—	0 above. 2 below. —	9 above 0 below —	2 above. 0 below. —
24	.5	0	— 8	— 2.5	Snow all day.		Clouds on Mt.	Clouds on Mt.	Clouds on Mt.
25	—18	—28	—15	—15.9	—	—	Clear. —	Clear. —	Clear. —
26	0	+ 5	6.5	3.8	Snowing 2 P. M.		9 above. —	10 above. 0 below. —	Clouds on Mt.
27	5	— 4.5	—13	— 4.5	—	—	Clouds on Mt.	Clouds on Mt.	Clouds on Mt.
28	—14	— 5	3.5	— 5.6	—	—	0 above 3 below. —	1 above. Clr.	Hazy. —
29	8	7	8	6.5	—	—	Light clouds on Mt.	Light clouds on Mt.	Clouds on Mt.
30	7	13	11	10.5	—	—	Light clouds on Mt.	10 above. 8 below. St. Clr.	Very light clouds on Mt.
31	23	20	34	27.7	—	—	4 above. 10 below. Clr. Cum.	8 above. 8 below —	Light clouds on Mt.
Means	—	—	—	6.1					

JANUARY.

Date.	WINDS.						BAROGRAMS, at 32°.				RELATIVE HUMIDITY.		
	Direction, 7 A.M.	Miles per hour, 7 A.M.	Direction, 2 P.M.	Miles per hour, 2 P.M.	Direction, 9 P.M.	Miles per hour, 9 P.M.	7 A.M.	2 P.M.	9 P.M.	Mean.	7 A.M.	2 P.M.	9 P.M.
1	N.	67	N.	60	N.	56	23.165	23.173	23.373	23.237	46	2	36.9
2	S.	34	S.W.	60	S.W.	78	.370	.107	.078	.185	100	56	77
3	N.	79	S.W.	35	S.W.	4	.087	.291	.313	.231	28	43	39
4	N.W.	24	W.	63	W.	46	.318	.349	.409	.359	33	60	44
5	S.S.W.	46	S.	37	S.	62	.459	.359	.258	359	84	79	84
6	W.	25	W.	37	W.S.W.	64	.359	.320	.294	.324	100	82	77
7	N.W.	69	W.	48	W.N.W.	32	.264	.347	.467	.359	61	61	15
8	Calm.	0	S.W.	4	N.W.	2	.464	.410	.456	.443	22	28	62
9	N.	27	N.	36	N.	35	.477	.462	.501	.480	22	31	53
10	W.	38	W.	39	N.W.	11	.502	.487	.556	.515	34	39	48
11	W.	22	S W.	48	S.W.	45	.616	.613	.490	.573	81	100	87
12	S.W.	34	S.W.	50	S.W.	35	.914	.991	24.133	24.012	89	89	94
13	W.	12	S.W.	25	W.N.W.	26	24.168	24.165	.123	.152	89	90	94
14	N.W.	40	W.N.W.	12	W.N.W.	12	.089	.083	.107	.098	94	89	89
15	S.S.E.	38	E.S.E.	53	S.S.W.	58	23.995	23.800	23.707	23.834	100	100	100
16	S.S.W.	42	S.W.	25	S.W.	5	23.617	.514	.433	.521	100	100	100
17	N.N.W.	75	N.W.	68	N.N.W.	65	.208	.383	.473	.358	41	55	61
18	N.W.	33	N.W.	32	N.W.	19	.434	.698	.862	.665	36	70	39
19	W.	8	W.	17	S.S.W.	20	.965	.577	.990	.844	46	59	67
20	W.	34	W.	29	W.	36	.873	.745	.684	.767	46	74	46
21	W.	14	N.W.	22	W.N.W.	27	.510	.353	.185	.242	81	82	76

22	N.W.	64	N.	72	N.W.	88	22.860	22.649	22.755	22.755	25	100	–
23	N.W.	65	N.W.	86	N.N.E.	1	23.043	23.397	23.575	23.338	–	28	55
24	S.W.	17	S.W	36	W.	29	.514	.451	.437	.467	84	39	15
25	S.S.W.	55	N.W.	69	N.N.W.	52	.294	.395	.522	.404	–	–	–
26	N.	16	S.W.	12	S.	28	.756	.688	.532	.659	89	50	64
27	W.N.W.	29	W.	46	W.N.W.	40	.358	.042	.153	.184	50	65	23
28	N.W.	60	N.W.	36	S.W.	14.5	.291	.563	.588	.481	–	53	43
29	S.	25	S.S.W.	34	W.S.W.	44	.470	.422	.428	.440	46	64	66
30	N.W.	54	N.W.	14	S.S.W.	25	.514	.675	.685	.625	76	62	79
31	W.S.W.	25	S.W.	70	W.S.W.	54	.622	.464	.331	.472	86	93	89
Mean	–	–	–	–	–	–	–	–	–	23.499	–	–	–

FEBRUARY.

Date.	Thermograms.				Rain and snow.	Clouds, 7 A. M.		Clouds, 2 P. M.		Clouds, 9 P. M.	
	7 A. M.	2 P. M.	9 P. M.	Mean.		Amount.	Kind.	Amount.	Kind.	Amount.	Kind.
1	19	20	14	17	— —	Light clouds	on Mt.	2 above. 5 below.	Cir. St.	0 above. 1 below.	— St.
2	16	15	14	15	— —	1 above. 10 below.	Cir.	8 above. 3 below.	—	Light clouds	on Mt.
3	—19	— 3	5	— 6	Snow at 9 P. M.	—	—	Clouds	on Mt.	all day.	—
4	—31	—34	—40	—35	— —	—	—	Clouds	on Mt.	all day.	—
5	—25	—11	— 1	—12	— —	0 above. 6 below.	—	Light clouds	on Mt.	0 above. 4 below.	— Cum.
6	10	13	15	13	— —	0 above. 4 below.	— St.	0 above. 4 below.	—	0	—
7	14	16	11	13	— —	3 above. 1 below.	Cir. St.	0	—	0	—
8	15	14	18	16	Snow at 2 P. M.	8 above. 0 below.	—	Clouds	on Mt.	Clouds	on Mt.
9	18	20	18	18	Frozen mist.	—	—	Clouds	on Mt.	all day.	—
10	0	— 3	— 9	— 4	Frozen mist.	—	—	Clouds	on Mt.	all day.	—
11	—21	—13	— 8	—14	— —	Clouds	on Mt.	Clouds	on Mt.	0 above. 5 below.	— St.
12	— 2	14	9	7	Snow from 2 P. M. to 12 M.	0	—	Light clouds	on Mt.	Clouds	on Mt.
13	0	5	4	3	— —	Light clouds	on Mt.	0 above. 8 below.	—	0 above. 1 below.	— St.
14	7	14	8	9	Snow from 2 P. M. to 9 P. M.	10 above. 5 below.	St. Cum.	2 above. 8 below.	Cir. Cum.	Dense clouds	on Mt.
15	0	13	20	11	— —	0 above. 10 below.	Cum.	1 above. 0 below.	Cir.	9 above. 0 below.	St.
16	14	17	9	13.5	— —			Clouds	on Mt.	all day	

					Remarks						
17	4	12	14	10	–	4 above. 0 below.	Cum. & St.	0 above. 1 below.	St.	8 above. 0 below.	St.
18	13	27	17	19	Snow all night.	–	–	Clouds	on Mt.	all day.	
19	− 5	5	3	1	–	3 above. 0 below.	Cir.	5 above. 0 below.	Cir. St.	Clouds	on Mt.
20	8	4	2	3	Frozen mist.	–	–	Dense clouds	on Mt.	all day.	–
21	2	− 3	− 8	− 3	–	3 above. 0 below.	Cir.	0	–	0	–
22	4	− 2	3	1.7	–	0	–	0	–	0	–
23	9	19	25	19.5	–	1 above. 0 below.	Cir. St.	3 above. 0 below.	Cir.	4 above. 0 below.	Cir.
24	35	35	33	34	Rain in the A. M.	–	–	Clouds	on Mt.	all day.	–
25	22	19	13	16.9	–	–	–	Clouds	on Mt.	all day.	–
26	7	21	25	19.5	–	7 above. 8 below.	St. Cum.	7 above. 0 below.	St.	Light clouds	on Mt.
27	26	15	6	13	Heavy rain from 7 A. M. to 9 A. M.	–	–	Clouds	on Mt.	all day.	–
28	8	0	− 8	0	–	Light clouds	on Mt.	0 above. 4 below.	St.	0	–
Mean	–	–	–	7.1							

FEBRUARY.

Date.	Winds.						Barograms, at 32°.				Relative Humidity.		
	Direction, 7 A. M.	Miles per hour, 7 A. M.	Direction, 2 P. M.	Miles per hour, 2 P. M.	Direction, 9 P. M.	Miles per hour, 9 P. M.	7 A. M.	2 P. M.	9 P. M.	Means.	7 A. M.	2 P. M.	9 P. M.
1	W.	55	W.	10	W.S.W.	9	23.325	23.507	23.614	23.482	84.5	70.2	82.9
2	W.	16	W.	27	N.W.	60	.562	.328	22.968	.286	82.9	82.3	81.0
3	N.W.	70	N.W.	62	W.S.W.	48	22.749	22.722	.776	22.749		65.8	75.0
4	N.W.	69	N.W.	64	N.W.	65	.457	.601	.644	.567	–	–	–
5	N.W.	84	N.W.	88	W.N.W.	40	.877	23.000	23.225	23.034	54.4	29.5	68.3
6	W.N.W.	50	N.W.	36	N.	28	23.361	.424	.626	.470	89.4	81.0	66.8
7	W.N.W.	12	W.N.W.	8	W.S.W.	1	.746	.757	.786	.763	81.6	65.9	78.7
8	S.W.	19	S.S.W.	44	S.S.W.	28	.515	.620	.645	.595	64.8	81.6	84.0
9	S.S.E.	15	S.W.	18	W.	36	.356	.356	.258	.323	100	70.2	84.0
10	N.W.	52	N.W.	88	N.W.	88	.159	.033	.039	.077	69.5	47.6	55.7
11	N.W.	64	N.W.	58	N.W.	51	.187	.397	.513	.366	–	19.4	15.6
12	W.	24	W.	6	Calm.	0	.589	.431	.312	.444	67.1	81.6	89.0
13	W.	21	N.	14	Calm.	0	.350	.463	.599	.472	69.5	87.2	60.2
14	S.W.	5	S.S.W.	4	N.W.	17	.571	.483	.448	.499	76.9	81.6	77.7
15	W.	33	S.W.	24	S.W.	14	.495	.615	.624	.578	39.3	62.3	70.2
16	W.	34	S.W.	46	N.N.W.	53	.371	.230	.209	.270	100	78.7	78.4
17	N.W.	51	N.W.	24	S.S.W.	19	.448	.640	.645	.578	48.0	80.4	63.5
18	S.S.W.	62	S.S.W.	66	W.	62	.111	22.810	22.813	22.911	72.1	94.0	83.4
19	N.W.	43	W.	28	W.	37	.184	23.274	23.283	23.247	25.7	50.0	73.0
20	N.W	41	W.	33	W.	39	.316	.335	.363	.338	46.0	61.8	58.6
21	N.W.	31	N.	12	N.	27	.434	.479	.537	.483	43.8	65.8	38.3

22	N.	11	N.	27	N.W.	34	.722	.732	.742	.732	74.0	67.1	22.0
23	W.	47	S.W.	38	S.W.	22	.863	.921	.908	.897	67.1	69.2	74.6
24	S.W.	59	S.W.	42	S.S W.	56	.805	.709	.520	678	89.8	89 8	89.5
25	W.	53	W.S.W.	75	N.W.	72	.290	.206	.299	.265	100	69.2	81.0
26	S.W.	28	W.S.W.	10	S.S.W.	65	.380	.440	.340	.387	64.7	71.2	87.2
27	S.W.	52	W.S.W.	80	N.W.	92	.082	22.895	22.929	22.969	100	100	76.0
28	N.N.W.	69	N.W.	62	S.S.W.	17	.184	23.434	23.578	.362	15.6	55.3	55.3
Mean	–	–	–	–	–	–	–	–	–	23.351			

METEOROLOGICAL TABLES.

Date.	Thermograms.				Rain and Snow.	Clouds, 7 A. M.		Clouds, 2 P. M.		Clouds, 9 P. M.	
	7 A. M.	2 P. M.	9 P. M.	Mean.		Amount.	Kind.	Amount.	Kind.	Amount.	Kind.
1	15	16	11	13.2	Frozen mist.	Dense clouds	on Mt.	Dense clouds	on Mt.	Dense clouds	on Mt.
2	13	17	24	19.5	– –	1 above. 5 below.	–	8 above. 1 below.	St.	10 above Hazy below.	St.
3	33	37.5	19	27	Rain from 6 A. M. to 5 P. M.	10 above. 0 below.	–	Light clouds	on Mt.	Light clouds	on Mt.
4	18	20	15	17	– –	3 above. 5 below.	Cir.St. Cum.	5 above. 0 below.	Cir.	10 above. 0 below	St.
5	11	17.5	14	14	– –	6 above. 0 below.	Cir. & St.	5 above. 0 below.	Cum.	10 above. 0 below.	St.
6	18 5	20	17	18	Snowing from 7 A. M. to 2 P. M.	Dense clouds	on Mt.	Dense clouds	on Mt.	Light clouds	on Mt.
7	7	16.5	18	14.7	– –	0 above. 6 below.	St.	1 above. 2 below.	Cir. St.	0	–
8	24	31.5	31	29.2	– –	10 above. 0 below.	St.and Nim.	3 above. 1 below.	St. St.	8 above.	–
9	33	40	34	35	– –	Light clouds	on Mt.	2 above. 1 below.	Cir. St.	Clouds	on Mt.
10	36	35	24	29.7	– –	Clouds	on Mt.	Clouds	on Mt.	Clouds	on Mt.
11	25	29.5	30	28.6	– –	4 above. 0 below	Cir. & St.	5 above. Hazy below.	Cir. & Cir-st	10 above. 3 below.	–
12	35	85	33	34	– –	Clouds	on Mt	Clouds	on Mt.	Clouds	on Mt.
13	15	18	14	15.2	– –	5 above. 9 below.	–	3 above.	Cir. & St.	0 above. 9 below.	–
14	10	10	7	8.5	– –	1 above 1 below.	–	Clouds	on Mt.	Clouds	on Mt.
15	5	18.5	19	15.3	– –	1 above. 3 below.	Cir. St.	10 above. 0 below.	Cir. & St.	8 above. 0 below.	–

Day												
16	25	34	24	27	–	–	Clouds	on Mt.	Clouds	on Mt.	Clouds	on Mt.
17	38	43	39	39.7	–	–	Clouds	on Mt.	Clouds	on Mt.	Clouds	on Mt.
18	20	24	19	20.5	–	–	7 above. 3 below.	Cir. St.	8 above. 3 below.	Cir.St. Cum.	0	–
19	19	12	14	15	–	–	Clouds	on Mt.	Clouds	on Mt.	0 above. 3 below.	– Cum.
20	21	17.5	24	21.6	–	–	7 above. 0 below.	Cir.-cum.	6 above. Hazy below.	Cir. & St.	10 above. 5 below.	St. Cum.
21	25	32	20	24.2	Snowing all day.	–	Dense clouds	on Mt.	Dense clouds	on Mt.	Dense clouds	on Mt.
22	11	12	9	10.2	–	–	Dense clouds	on Mt.	Dense clouds	on Mt.	Dense clouds	on Mt.
23	14	22	22	20	Snowing after 9 A. M.	–	4 above. 3 below.	Cir.-st. St.	Dense clouds	on Mt.	Dense clouds	on Mt.
24	2	-4	4	.7	–	–	Clouds	on Mt	Dense clouds	on Mt.	Dense clouds	on Mt.
25	-1	4	6	3	–	–	Clouds	on Mt.	Dense clouds	on Mt.	Dense clouds	on Mt.
26	5	14	15	12.2	–	–	Clouds	on Mt.	0 above. 1 below.	St.	Hazy.	–
27	10	10.5	8	9.1	–	–	Clouds	on Mt.	Clouds	on Mt.	Clouds	on Mt.
28	8	10	5	7	–	–	Clouds	on Mt.	Clouds	on Mt.	Clouds	on Mt.
29	1	9.5	10	7.6	–	–	0	–	0	–	0	–
30	16	17	17.5	16.7	–	–	1 above. Hazy below.	–	Clouds	on Mt.	Clouds	on Mt.
31	14	10.5	3	7.6	–	–	1 above. 5 below	Clr.St. Cum.	1 above. 0 below.	St.	0	–
Mean	–	–	–	18.0								

MARCH.

Date.	Winds.						Barograms, at 32°.				Relative Humidity.		
	Direction, 7 A. M.	Miles per hour, 7 A. M.	Direction, 2 P. M.	Miles per hour, 2 P. M.	Direction, 9 P. M.	Miles per hour, 9 P. M.	7 A. M.	2 P. M.	9 P. M.	Mean.	7 A. M.	2 P. M.	9 P. M.
1	S.S.W.	42	S.W.	42	W.	64	23.301	23.187	23.379	23.289	73.0	82.9	79.7
2	N.W.	44	W.	28	S.S.W.	62	.630	.662	.613	.635	62.3	74.8	86.8
3	S.S.W.	66	S.S.W.	89	W.	82	.401	.230	.274	.302	89.3	90.2	84.5
4	Calm.	–	W.S.W.	2	Calm.	–	.605	.584	.552	.580	84.0	77.2	64.8
5	N.W.	58	W.	42	W.	8	.500	.710	.668	.626	59.6	75.7	81.6
6	S.S.W.	42	S.S.W.	14	N.W.	56	.505	.473	.480	.486	84.0	85.5	83.4
7	N.W.	42	Calm.	–	W.	12	.573	.755	.700	.676	53.8	82.9	68.2
8	W.S.W.	18	S.S.W.	10	W.S.W.	11	.793	.820	.886	.833	86.8	89.4	83.9
9	S.W.	48	S.W.	45	S.W.	54	.801	.825	.855	.827	94.7	86.3	94.7
10	S.W.	45	S.W.	56	N.W.	42	.686	.688	.775	.716	90.0	94.9	86.8
11	S.W.	29	S.S.W.	50	S.	60	.990	.863	.740	.854	87.2	83.4	88.2
12	S.W.	36	S.S.W.	28	S.S.W.	62	.705	.504	.329	.513	94.8	94.8	89.3
13	N.W.	35	N.W.	42	N.W.	24	.372	.469	.407	.416	91.0	84.0	81.6
14	N.W	32	N.W.	52	N.W.	45	.444	.510	.553	.502	58.2	79.1	79.6
15	N.W	35	S.W.	12	N.W.	9	.618	.713	.778	703	75.0	68.2	69.2
16	S.W.	7	S.W.	16	S.W.	38	.714	.773	.746	.744	87.2	89.5	94.7
17	S.W.	46	S.S W.	25	S.W.	27	.683	.625	.590	.63[illegible]	90.5	96.6	90.7
18	N.W.	24	S.W.	28	W.N.W.	54	.612	.636	.613	.62[illegible]	70.2	86.8	84.5
19	W.	34	W.N.W.	48	N.N.W.	32	.574	.588	.757	.639	84.5	81.0	90.7
20	W.S.W.	22	W.	10	S.S.W.	57	.871	.860	.765	.832	70.2	75.7	73.8
21	S.S.E.	68	S.S.E.	42	W.	19	.406	.278	.158	.281	87.2	94.8	85.0

22	W.N.W.	65	W.S.W.	87	N.W.	66	22.961	22.920	.144	.002	79.7	80.4	73.4
23	W.	61	S.W.	36	W.S.W	24	23.287	23.266	.250	.268	63.5	86.0	86.0
24	W.	72	N.W.	76	N.W.	64	.089	.069	.294	.118	43.8	64.5	48.0
25	N.W.	88	W.N.W.	86	N.	67	.059	.077	.288	.141	36.9	48.0	52.0
26	N.	52	N.	27	Calm.	–	.334	.484	.589	.469	50.0	63.5	64.8
27	S.E.	48	S.E.	37	N.E.	16	.241	.119	.207	.189	79.1	69.2	56.3
28	N.	27	W.S.W.	29	W.N.W.	48	.247	.323	.392	.321	55.3	58.2	75.0
29	N.W.	81	W.	46	W.	56	.497	.574	.650	.574	41.6	68.2	58.2
30	W.N.W.	29	W.	39	N.W.	24	.640	.566	.547	.584	65.9	83.4	75.7
31	N.W.	49	W.	43	N.N.W.	48	.450	.450	.489	.463	63.5	69.2	73.0
Mean	–	–	–	–	–	–	–	–	–	23.513	–	–	–

APRIL.

Date.	Thermograms.				Rain and Snow.	Clouds, 7 A. M.		Clouds, 2 P. M.		Clouds, 9 P. M.	
	7 A. M.	2 P. M.	9 P. M.	Mean.		Amount.	Kind.	Amount.	Kind.	Amount.	Kind.
1	11	19.5	13.5	14.4		1 above. 0 below.	Cir.	8 above. 0 below.	Cum. & St.	10 above. 0 below.	St.
2	11.5	15.5	15	14		10 above. Hazy below.	Cum.	4 above. 0 below.	Cum. & St.	0	
3	20	30	25	25	Snowing at 9 P. M.	5 above. Hazy below.	Cir.	8 above. Hazy below.	–	Clouds	on Mt.
4	25	25	22	23.5	Snowing all day.	Dense clouds	on Mt.	3 above. 10 below.	Cir. St.	Clouds	on Mt.
5	11	4	5	6.2	–	–	Dense clouds	on Mt.	Dense clouds	on Mt.	0 above. 5 below.	Cum.
6	5	10	16	11.7	–	–	0	–	3 above. 0 below.	Cir.	2 above. 0 below.	St.
7	34	41	43	40.2	–	–	Dense clouds	on Mt.	Clouds	on Mt.	Dense clouds	on Mt
8	43	47	45	45	–	–	Dense clouds	on Mt.	10 above. Hazy below.	St.	Light clouds	on Mt.
9	41	46	39	41.2	–	–	9 above. 5 below.	St. St.	3 above. 4 below.	Clr.St. St.	8 above. 4 below.	Clr.St. St.
10	30	26.5	23.5	25.9	–	–	Light clouds	on Mt.	8 above. Hazy below.	Cir. & St.	4 above. 2 below.	
11	29.5	26	26.5	27.1	Snow, sleet, and rain.	Clouds	on Mt.	Clouds	on Mt.	Clouds	on Mt.
12	29	29	15	19.8	Snow at 6 A. M.	Clouds	on Mt.	Clouds	on Mt.	Clouds	on Mt.
13	14	29.5	22	19.6	3 inches of snow during night.	Clouds	on Mt.	Clouds	on Mt.	Light clouds	on Mt.
14	32	35.5	20	26.9	–	–	0 above. 8 below.	St Cir.	Clouds	on Mt.	9½ above. 2 below.	
15	21	30.5	23	24.1	Snow at 11 A. M.	3 above. 4 below.	St. St.	10 above. 2 below.		Clouds	on Mt.

16	25	36	21	26	Snowing all day.	Clouds on Mt.	Clouds on Mt.	Clouds on Mt.
17	25	38	21	26.2	Snowing all day	Clouds on Mt.	Clouds on Mt.	Clouds on Mt.
18	20	22.5	20.5	20.8	– –	Light clouds.	Clouds on Mt.	Clouds on Mt.
19	20	30	28.5	26.7	– –	0 above. – 1 below. St.	4 above. Cum. 0 below. –	10 above. St. 0 below.
20	28	39	46.5	40	Rain 9 A. M.	Clouds on Mt.	Clouds on Mt.	Clouds on Mt.
21	29.5	35	30	31.1	Snowing at 8 P. M.	Light clouds on Mt.	7 above. Cir. & Hazy below. St.	Clouds on Mt.
22	30	31	24	27.2	Snowing at 7 A. M. and 2 P. M.	Clouds on Mt.	Clouds on Mt.	9 above. 0 below.
23	24	20	13	17.5	Snowing.	Clouds on Mt.	Clouds on Mt.	Clouds on Mt.
24	11	18	18	16 2		Light clouds on Mt.	Clouds on Mt.	Clouds on Mt.
25	19	26.5	25	23.8	Snowing	6 above. St. 0 below.	10 above. – Hazy below.	Clouds on Mt.
26	14	21	19	18.2	– –	0 above. 7 below. Cum.	3 above. St. & 0 below. Cir.	0
27	24	27	18	21.7	Snowing.	Hazy above. 3 below. St.	9 above. 2 below.	Clouds on Mt.
28	25	28	33.5	30	Snowing.	Clouds on Mt.	Clouds on Mt.	Clouds on Mt.
29	39	35	33	35	– –	2 above. St. 7 below. St.	6 above. Cir. St. 9 below. Cum.	Hazy above. 10 below.
30	31	32.5	25	28.3	Snowing at 10 A. M	Clouds on Mt.	Clouds on Mt.	Clouds on Mt.
Mean	–	–	–	24 1				

APRIL.

Date.	WINDS.						BAROGRAMS, at 32°.				RELATIVE HUMIDITY.		
	Direction, 7 A.M.	Miles per hour, 7 A.M.	Direction, 2 P.M.	Miles per hour, 2 P.M.	Direction, 9 P.M.	Miles per hour, 9 P.M.	7 A.M.	2 P.M.	9 P.M.	Means.	7 A.M.	2 P.M.	9 P.M.
1	W.	2	S.	4	S.	22	23.628	23.566	23.461	23.552	59	77	53
2	S.E.	32	N.E.	11	N.	22	.274	.286	.349	.303	70	73	64
3	W.	11	S.W.	2	S.W.	18	.408	.452	.433	.431	70	78	74
4	S.S.W.	27	Calm.	–	W.	33	.359	.411	.273	.348	87	87	86
5	W.S.W.	89	S.W.	52	W.	43	.012	.107	.355	.158	59	48	50
6	N.N.W.	53	N.W.	50	W.	27	.441	.483	.619	.514	50	68	65
7–8	S.W.	48	W.	38	W.	46	.575	.752	.668	.665	89	91	91
8	W.	50	W.	23	W.	34	.668	.747	.776	.730	91	88	92
9	S.W.	24	S.W.	18	W.	42	.786	.744	.678	.736	82	76	81
10	N.W.	42	N.N.W.	48	N.N.W.	52	.588	.582	.573	.581	89	81	93
11	S.S.W.	15	S.S.W.	28	S.	20	.585	.486	.432	.501	94	87	94
12	W.	12	W.	54	N.W.	60	.307	151	.164	.207	78	85	82
13	N.W.	46	W.N.W.	18	W.S.W.	3	.209	.305	.385	.299	81	85	92
14	W.	2	W.	2	W.	4	.441	.426	.434	.434	79	75	71
15	N.	1	W.	5	W.S.W.	12	.410	.490	.558	.486	85	73	86
16	W.	1	S.W.	1	Calm.	–	.553	.595	.599	.582	73	87	85
17	W.S.W.	4	N.W.	2	N.W.	26	.597	.613	.665	.625	87	53	85
18	N.W.	42	N.W.	16	N.W.	25	.637	.672	.701	.670	85	86	86
19	N.N.W.	24	W.S.W.	6	W.N.W.	1	.766	.836	.785	.795	85	83	88
20	W.S.W.	28	S.W.	58	S.W.	62	.689	.510	.447	.643	94	90	88
21	W	49	W.N.W.	15	W.	20	.507	.597	.564	.556	83	79	83

22	W.	1	W.	17	N.W.	18	.535	.527	.540	.534	89	89	93
23	W.	49	N.W.	62	N.W.	74	.520	.497	.433	.483	86	92	90
24	N.W.	62	N.W.	24	W.N.W.	23	.640	.796	.848	.761	79	84	84
25	W.S.W.	17	S.W.	23	N.W.	32	.808	.654	.536	066	54	81	87
26	N.W.	51	N.N.W.	17	N.	1	.527	.726	.900	.718	63	85	69
27	E.	1	S.E.	9	S.E.	39	.961	.886	837	.89	86	76	68
28	S.S.E.	16	S.	9	S.S.W.	2	.671	.658	.695	.645	100	100	94
29	W.	1	W.	5	W.N.W.	8	.554	.511	.537	.534	90	62	94
30	W.	11	W.	15	W.	30	.498	.463	.459	.473	89	89	93
Means.	–	–	–	–	–	–	–	–	–	23.514			

MAY.

Date.	THERMOGRAMS				Rain and Snow.	CLOUDS, 7 A. M.		CLOUDS, 2 P. M.		CLOUDS, 9 P. M.	
	7 A. M.	2 P. M.	9 P. M.	Means.		Amount.	Kind.	Amount.	Kind.	Amount.	Kind.
1	27	29.5	27.5	27.8	Snow at 1½ P. M	0 above. 10 below.	Cum.	Clouds on Mt.		Clouds on Mt.	
2	26	29.5	27.5	27.6	– –	0 above. 4 below.	. St.	Clouds on Mt		10 above. 0 below.	St.
3	28	32.5	24	27	Sleet at 7 A. M.	Clouds on Mt.		Clouds on Mt.		10 above. 0 below.	–
4	21	22.5	21	21.3	Snow all day.	Clouds on Mt.		Clouds on Mt.		Clouds on Mt.	
5	23	35	38	33	Rain.	Clouds on Mt.		Clouds on Mt.		10 above. 3 below.	–
6	42	45	36	39.7	– –	0 above. 8 below.	St.	2 above. 7 below.	Cir. St.	7 above. 10 below.	–
7	25	24	19.5	22	Snow.	Clouds on Mt.		Clouds on Mt		Clouds on Mt.	
8	15	18.5	20.5	18.6	Frozen mist.	Clouds on Mt.		Clouds on Mt.		Clouds on Mt.	
9	20	24	22	22	– –	1 above. 8 below.	Cir. St.	Light clouds on Mt.		4 above. 10 below.	St. St.
10	23	24	21	22	Snow at 9 A. M.	0 above. 2 below.	St.	Clouds on Mt.		Clouds on Mt.	
11	20	27	27	25	– –	0 above. 1 below, and hazy.	–	10 above. 3 below.	–	10 above. 0 below.	–
12	27	36	31	31	– –	Clouds on Mt.		6 above. Hazy below.	St.	3 above. 0 below.	–
Means	–	–	–	26.4							

MAY.

Date.	Winds.						Barograms, at 32°.				Relative Humidity.		
	Direction, 7 A. M.	Miles per hour, 7 A. M.	Direction, 2 P. M.	Miles per hour, 2 P. M.	Direction, 9 P. M.	Miles per hour, 9 P. M.	7 A. M.	2 P. M.	9 P. M.	Means.	7 A. M.	2 P. M.	9 P. M.
1	N.W.	12	N.N.W.	21	W.N.W.	28	23.538	23.592	23.607	23.579	88	94	94
2	W.	15	W.	9	W.N W.	20	.680	.762	.768	.736	87	79	87
3	W.S.W.	7	N.W.	6	E.	8	.798	.786	.829	.804	88	94	73
4	S.E.	15	E.S.E.	38	S.E.	56	.843	.834	.771	.816	85	86	85
5	S.	28	S.W.	22	W.S.W.	3	.717	.654	.608	.658	86	89	90
6	N.W.	3	N.W.	1	W.S.W.	1	.590	.533	.429	.517	84	92	80
7	S.W.	57	W.	63	N.W.	54	.160	.035	.085	.093	87	93	92
8	W.N.W.	58	W.	62	W.	32	.130	.126	.404	.220	82	84	78
9	N.N.W.	35	N.N.W.	14	N.N.W.	10	.534	.604	.634	.590	70	68	92
10	W.	8	N.W.	20	N.W.	25	.600	.548	.612	.586	93	93	85
11	N.W.	17	W.S.W.	55	W.N.W.	46	.640	.601	.573	.603	85	88	94
12	W.	18	W.	30	W.	35	.622	.651	.610	.628	88	94	80
Mean	–	–	–	–	–	–	–	–	–	23.569			

SUMMARY OF OBSERVATIONS

TAKEN ON MT. WASHINGTON, FROM NOVEMBER 12, 1870, TO MAY 13, 1871.

	November.		December.		January.		February.		March.		April.		May.	
Highest barometer	22	23.865	11	24.007	13	24.168	23	23.921	11	23.960	26	23.990	4	23.643
Lowest barometer	24	23.023	16	22.646	22	22.649	4	22.457	22	22.920	5	23.012	7	23.035
Mean	–	23.465	–	23.315	–	23.499	–	23.851	–	23.513	–	23.514	–	23.569
Highest thermometer	26	28	13	29	13 (2 A.M.)	38	– (3 A.M.)	37	17	45	–	47	6	45
Lowest thermometer	30	0	24	15	23	—45	5	—59	24	— 4	8	4	8	15
Mean	–	16	–	9.4	–	6.14	–	7.1	–	18	5	25	–	26
Prevailing wind	–	W.	–	N.W.	–	W.	–	N.W.	–	W.	–	W.	–	–
Greatest velocity	24	72	15	105	22	100	–	98	3	89	5	89	7	63
Number of calms	–	None.	–	1	–	None.	–	2	–	None.	5	1	–	None.
Number of clear days	–	None.	–	None.	–	None.	–	1	29	1	4	1	–	None.
Number of fair days	–	8	–	7	–	14	–	18	–	17	–	13	–	4
Days when clouds on Mt.	–	10	–	24	–	17	–	9	–	13	–	17	–	8

DECEMBER.

Date.	Thermograms, 7 A. M.				Thermograms, 2 P. M.				Thermograms, 9 P. M.			
	Mt. Washington.	Montreal.	Lunenburg, Vt.	Providence, R. I.	Mt. Washington.	Montreal.	Lunenburg, Vt.	Providence, R. I.	Mt. Washington.	Montreal.	Lunenburg, Vt.	Providence, R. I.
1	14	34	24	20	16	43	32	52	13	30	30	40
2	15	36	37	38	16	55	40	51	15	38	34	44
3	5	24	27	37	14	39	28	39	17	35	20	33
4	17	35	30	36	18	36	34	51	16	33	35	43
5	15	26	32	37	20	33	39	47	18	30	34	45
6	22	33	35	43	22	32	38	45	15	32	36	40
7	15	31	30	36	22	32	36	45	20	30	28	40
8	16	29	32	48	18	31	35	44	15	31	33	34
9	12	29	28	32	13	34	29	40	11	25	25	31
10	14	21	20	29	15	26	23	37	20	20	20	31
11	25	17	24	30	28	31	20	38	27	29	32	42
12	17	31	30	42	20	33	37	43	20	34	36	44
13	23	34	35	44	29	35	38	44	27	34	35	40
14	22	33	33	40	22	34	32	42	14	32	30	34
15	12	18	20	34	0.5	18	15	30	— 7	16	13	22
16	—10	15	10	19	— 6	27	19	27	—13	16	16	21
17	1	16	15	19	5	25	21	31	4	25	14	27
18	4	19	16	28	— 1	20	18	33	— 4	15	14	24
19	0	10	7	19	9	33	23	36	11	24	15	29
20	15	22	19	35	20	31	24	45	14	26	28	36
21	10	22	22	33	10	28	27	37	6	23	20	23
22	0	15	12	17	— 1	26	18	24	— 5	13	10	16
23	— 4	10	8	16	— 2	16	10	20	— 2	8	— 2	16
24	—10	— 1	5	12	—11	8	8	20	—15	— 2	— 5	15
25	—14	— 2	18	7	— 9	10	5	13	— 7	8	0	13
26	— 2	16	7	20	— 1	20	18	30	0	24	17	26
27	0	23	16	20	5	28	25	32	7	23	20	28
28	6	25	20	30	9	23	30	32	11	— 0.2	18	30
29	6	— 5	10	25	3	16	10	27	1	— 1	0	15
30	1	— 4	—15	6	8	12	10	20	5	9	18	36
31	15	23	24	34	14	33	29	40	14	19	28	33

Means of Month.

Mt. Washington . . . . 9.4   Lunenburg, Vt. 21.8
Montreal . . . . 24.3   Providence, R. I. 31.8

JANUARY.

Date.	THERMOGRAMS, 7 A. M.				THERMOGRAMS, 2 P. M.				THERMOGRAMS, 9 P. M.			
	Mt. Washington.	Montreal.	Lunenburg, Vt.	Providence, R. I.	Mt. Washington.	Montreal.	Lunenburg, Vt.	Providence, R. I.	Mt. Washington.	Montreal.	Lunenburg, Vt.	Providence, R. I.
1	0	17	16	27	—7	22	20	32	—2	13	10	25
2	10	19	4	28	9	38	26	43	7	22	25	37
3	—7	5	10	23	2	24	25	31	0	10	23	30
4	—18	—8	—6	16	—13	1	14	22	—14	—2	—2	15
5	—2	—6	5	29	10	8	29	45	18	15	28	46
6	18	32	37	44	16	34	35	45	8	27	28	35
7	—6	—6	8	25	—7	13	10	27	—8	—2	—5	14
8	—6	—8	—18	10	—4	2	—10	24	—5	—5	3	16
9	—6	—12	—6	7	—3	8	12	17	—11	—5	—7	9
10	—2	—12	—22	5	0	10	5	20	4	—1	—5	20
11	13	7	—6	17	23	7	20	30	25	11	17	34
12	31	19	22	35	33	20	31	52	33	24	82	36
13	34	28	33	34	36	40	42	46	33	40	36	34
14	32	40	34	32	34	33	45	50	34	21	38	40
15	29	17	35	37	28	30	36	40	32	33	37	39
16	32	30	38	44	33	29	33	47	31	22	35	34
17	1	7	18	25	8	19	34	37	—1	12	15	28
18	—4	7	12	25	—.5	19	19	32	0	4	4	23
19	5	—9	—8	23	9	10	15	28	10	0	6	26
20	15	5	0	23	17	27	24	27	15	29	21	27
21	13	29	20	30	15	30	31	42	7	27	27	35
22	—5	—7	—2	28	—27	1	—8	19	—41	—13	—18	2
23	—35	—23	—30	—3	—4	—7	—12	6	1	—21	—13	2
24	0.5	25	—12	6	0	—13	0	9	—8	—9	3	7
25	—18	—12	0	10	—23	3	6	23	—15	—12	—22	2
26	0	—22	—20	—4	5	—14	5	5	6	—12	—4	7
27	5	—6	—10	10	—4	14	18	28	—13	4	9	20
28	—14	—3	4	13	—0.5	8	15	23	3	—1	2	19
29	3	1	5	19	7	14	24	20	8	21	15	21
30	7	20	24	28	13	25	33	38	11	14	38	28
31	23	19	28	35	26	30	45	42	34	33	42	36

MEANS OF MONTH.

Mt. Washington . . . . 6.1 | Lunenburg, Vt. 13.5
Montreal . . . . 11.0 | Providence, R. I. 25.6

FEBRUARY.

Date.	Thermograms, 7 A. M.				Thermograms, 2 P. M.				Thermograms, 9 P. M.			
	Mt. Washington.	Montreal.	Lunenburg, Vt.	Providence, R. I.	Mt. Washington.	Montreal.	Lunenburg, Vt.	Providence, R. I.	Mt. Washington.	Montreal.	Lunenburg, Vt.	Providence, R. I.
1	19	30	38	41	20	31	35	43	15	29	30	34
2	16	30	30	27	15	42	36	37	14	17	33	39
3	—19	2	5	20	— 3	12	24	29	15	7	29	31
4	—31	—13	— 8	25	—34	5	—14	14	—40	—13	—15	3
5	—25	—27	—28	— 6	—11	— 2	—10	8	— 1	—12	—20	4
6	10	— 8	—12	5	13	14	7	20	15	1	2	17
7	14	1	— 5	14	16	16	23	30	11	8	14	25
8	15	8	20	24	14	26	28	32	18	20	24	33
9	18	24	29	32	20	35	35	36	18	33	34	35
10	0	19	24	28	— 3	29	18	32	— 9	9	10	20
11	—21	0	0	15	—13	26	12	25	— 8	13	3	22
12	— 2	2	5	19	14	9	10	23	9	9	10	26
13	0	8	8	16	5	31	15	27	4	9	7	17
14	7	— 2	0	15	14	16	20	22	8	15	18	22
15	0	11	12	16	13	36	26	31	20	23	18	25
16	14	25	18	32	17	30	26	43	9	26	28	35
17	4	19	20	28	12	35	28	42	14	27	25	31
18	13	33	24	37	27	38	36	46	17	18	25	36
19	— 5	9	10	24	5	26	15	31	3	26	18	29
20	3	16	20	24	4	23	25	39	2	15	18	33
21	2	1	20	27	— 3	28	15	27	8	7	0	16
22	4	0	—15	8	— 2	25	10	23	3	10	6	17
23	9	— 0.5	— 5	12	19	31	20	35	25	17	24	32
24	35	29	38	36	35	42	45	45	33	40	45	47
25	22	34	38	46	19	46	40	55	13	33	30	45
26	7	31	28	38	21	46	38	38	25	33	35	35
27	26	35	34	34	15	31	30	43	6	25	24	35
28	8	11	15	27	0	31	25	33	8	28	19	29

Means of Month.

Mt. Washington 7.1	Lunenburg, Vt. 17.5
Montreal. 13.0	Providence, R. I. 27.9

PART FOURTH.

WHAT THE WORLD SAID OF US.

———◆———

HE members of the expedition whose history has been narrated in the foregoing pages have been interested in what has been said of them by the public. At their respective breakfast-tables they have often wondered what was being said of them in hundreds of families where they had reason to believe the previous night's dispatch was being read aloud from the morning journal.

From time to time there have appeared in the newspapers references to our occupation of the summit, expressing the opinions of various writers, either upon the facts reported or the general prospects of the expedition. As these may represent the table-talk of the morning, we have selected a few extracts from the many before us, for preservation with our record. As the tendency to burlesque is a national American trait, we have been favored with a very large proportion of articles of an amusing character, whose perusal has raised our spirits during some of the dull days, when all was disagreeable without and dark within.

For the entertainment of the mountain party a card-basket was manufactured from birch bark grown at the base of Mount Washington, ornamented with outline sketches and pithy remarks. Both the sketches and quotations were intended as prophetic, the latter having been uttered while the project was yet untried, and the former designed early in the winter. The conflicting opinions of the doubters and believers in the ultimate success of the enterprise appear in direct contrast. Our readers may judge for themselves to which class the true prophets belonged.

Early in 1870 the following item went the rounds of the papers respecting the crime of one of the attempts at climbing Moosilauke : —

" In wandering around trying to find the house upon the summit, Mr. Huntington froze both feet solid above the ankles, rendering amputation necessary. His sufferings were of the most fearful description."

As an estimate of the way in which such a report, if true, would have been held by many persons, we quote an opinion expressed thus in our hearing not long afterwards : —

" Now if they had crippled themselves in a noble

BIRCH CARD BASKET.

SHOWING WHAT THE WORLD THINKS OF THE MT. WASHINGTON EXPEDITION.

Presented to J. H. HUNTINGTON, *Dec. 25th*, 1870.

"O, wad some power the giftie gie us
To see oursels as ithers see us."

cause, they would have had something to sustain them under the affliction ; but to deliberately throw away health and the hopes of a life-time for a mere nothing — so idiotic — so like a lunatic — perfectly chimerical ! "

RARE SNOW-FLAKE.

On the sixth of January Mr. Nelson added to the usual Press dispatch the following : " We noticed a snow-flake this morning of an hitherto undescribed form." Very shortly afterwards, the public read the following : —

" A STARTLING DISCOVERY.

" A party of fossilized scientific maniacs are wintering out on the top of Mount Washington, N. H., and a gaping world stands below in anticipation of great discoveries !

" After laying in a good store of edibles and drinkables, and other little luxuries, such as playing cards and cribbage boards (constructed on purely scientific principles, according to Hoyle), they have just got to work on their startling discovery. We palpitate as we record the first sensation which they have condescended to let loose to the world. It is that they have discovered a new and hitherto unknown species of — *snow-flake !*

" What effect this tremendous discovery will have

on the subsequent development of the resources of the country time alone can determine. It is barely possible that this new snow-flake will be adopted all over the country, and that the old-fashioned article will be done away with altogether!

" If such should be the case, the country, and those individuals who have provided these high old daddies with their elaborate outfit, can congratulate themselves on not having lived, or spent their money in vain."

THE GREAT POWDER HOUSE MILL EXPEDITION.

A long account of the organization and equipment of the expedition appeared with the above title, from which we present the following extract :—

" That 19th of December will be long remembered by those who had the good fortune to witness the procession as it started for the summit. Each individual of the party was dressed in a complete suit of seal-skins, and bore an enormous flag with the motto ' Excelsior !' A noble and fearless band of martyrs to science ; determined to freeze or perish in the attempt ! Next, after a feast worthy of Delmonico's, came our marvelous interesting observations, as soon as the party had reached the summit. During the journey up hill our best thermometer was broken. This cast a gloom over the party, until Professor Blowpipe with wonderful presence of mind suggested that we should take turns in standing out in the cold, and then 'guess' in relation to the temperature. The historian tried it first; and after roosting on top of the old house gave it as his deliberate opinion that it was about 71° below zero. The barometer was 42° in the shade; the velocity of the wind frightful to contemplate; and before we had completed our first day's experience, each individual member of the party said that the '*Relative Stupidity*' of the whole affair was at least ' 99 ' ! "

TIP-TOP HOUSE IN A STORM.

An illustrated weekly attempted to delineate the residence of our party upon the summit when the storm was raging. The building drawn was the Tip-top House, which was not inhabited at all during the winter, and a part of the text accompanying the illustration was the following : —

" The deep snows that obstruct the road to the summit, and render it impassable for months, shut them off as effectually from the rest of the world as if they were floating on an iceberg, in that famous polar main which you must first see to believe in — only that they have the telegraph with which to communicate with their fellow-men. The accounts which they send us of the state of the atmosphere are not exactly what old ladies call ' inviting.' It is a singular fact, however, that the thermometer indicates a less intense degree of cold on the very summit of the mountain than prevailed during the storm at Lowell and other places no further north. The principal discomfort arises from the violence of the wind.' "

RETARDATION OF SCIENCE.

" The progress of science in this country has experienced a heavy blow. We refer to the gale of wind which the professors and others, encamped for the winter on the summit of Mount Washington, reported December 15th, its velocity being ninety-two miles per hour."

EXHAUSTION OF SUPPLIES.

In January the sympathy of the public was excited by the following item : " Of the eleven tons of coal taken up for the winter's stock of the meteorologists at the summit of Mount Washington, over one half was consumed a week ago. Their stove contains seven dampers (!), which during the gales will not stop the draft and rattle fearfully."

A similar report prevailed in regard to the provisions. The correspondent of the Boston " Journal," who visited the party early in February, promptly denied the truth of these rumors, and they quickly disappeared from sight. At the breaking up of the expedition it was found that enough supplies were on hand to maintain the Signal Service party for several weeks.

" THE MAD MOUNT WASHINGTON PHILOSOPHERS.

" The scientific persons on the summit of Mount Washington have temporarily abandoned the scientific pastime of sliding down hill, the extreme coldness of the weather having indicated euchre and catch-penny — games which can be played within doors — as more appropriate to the season than out-of-door sports. One of their number, however, whose name is said to be Smith, recently went forth to ' measure the velocity of the wind,' — a process which we presume to be identical with the boyish sport of kite-flying, — and after an exposure of five minutes, returned to the house ' completely covered with frost two inches in thickness.' We must be permitted to have our doubts in regard to Smith. The name itself has a suspicious look. There may be a person of that name, but we wholly reject the theory of a Smith coated with two inches of frost, and yet sufficiently lively to telegraph his condition to an astonished public. Much science has probably made Smith mad. He doubtless labors under the delusion that he is a sort of plum-pudding *glace*, and with that method in his madness so often noticeable even in unscientific lunatics, invents the hypothesis of an accident occurring while measuring the wind to account for his supposed condition. This theory receives additional confirmation from the fact that Smith voluntarily took up his abode on Mount Washington, a course of conduct of which it is absurd to suppose that a sane person would be guilty. No right-minded man can excuse the scientific persons who permitted Smith to expose himself by kite-flying with the mercury twenty-five below zero. Of course no one would expect from them the same practical common sense which we look for in unscientific people, but it really was too thoughtless to permit a scientific fellow-creature to venture out in such extreme cold for the mad purpose of ' measuring the wind.' It is time that some charitable person should take measures to protect these unhappy persons from their own mad selves."

" AN ICE MYSTERY OF SCIENCE.

" What has become of the scientific persons who retired to Mount Washington at the beginning of the winter to slide down hill and fly kites in the interests of science? Since the cold morning some six weeks ago, we have heard no news of them. It is therefore possible that they have fallen victims to the inclemency of the weather, and are now sitting stiff and cold around their extinguished fire, holding in their icy hands the frozen cards wherewith they were playing strictly scientific games when the frost-king called them."

We have space for only one other extract, which purports to be the official report of the expedition, addressed to the chief signal officer : —

" It was the original design of the expedition to ascend the mountain early in November, but it was finally thought fit to defer the ascent until the mountains should become inaccessible. This occurred on the 25th of that month. On the next day, the roads being entirely impassable, the gentlemen composing the expedition proceeded to make the ascent, and starting from the Notch at seven A. M., reached the summit at 4.38 P. M. A commodious hut had been erected for their accommodation, and was already well stocked with sextants, quadrants, patent sounding lines, life-buoys, playing cards, telescopes, demijohns, cold hams, diving-bells, sleds, patent car-couples, kites, magnetic telegraphs, steam-engines, and other necessary scientific apparatus. The entire expedition being quite exhausted in point of legs by the exertions of the ascent, immediately went to bed, without making any observations except those of a strictly personal nature. On the following day the secretary began to keep a full diary of each day's proceedings, a copy of which is hereby submitted.

" *November* 27. Height of thermometer 20° ;

barometer, 1.464. Mean direction of wind, north-west. Greatest velocity of wind 2.40 per hour. Weather clear, but cloudy. At ten A. M. the expedition was mustered for sliding down hill. It was found by experiment that the sleds ran more rapidly down hill than in the contrary direction, This was accounted for by Professor Huntington upon the theory of tittlebats, and an able paper upon the subject was prepared and read by him the same evening. (See Schedule A, annexed to this report.)

" *November* 29. Snow fell heavily to the depth as measured in the pail standing at the northwest corner of the Observatory, of ten feet. Professor Smith, incautiously endeavoring to continue his experiments in sliding down hill, was buried in the snow. The expedition dug over some thirty acres of snow in the attempt to find and extricate him, but without success. Hot water was then sprinkled over the snow until it melted, when the professor was found, much exhausted, but full of ardor, he fortunately having a pocket flask with him.

" *December* 5. Hailing violently. Professor Jones became lost on the mountain, and hailed the other members of the expedition for two consecutive hours in vain. As they were listening to a paper on the " Origin of MumblePeg," prepared and read by Professor Hitchcork, no attention was paid to Professor Jones. When he was finally discovered, he was covered with a coating of ice three inches in thickness, and of great purity. With a view to making further experiments upon him, he was left in an exposed position until morning, when he was unfortunately found to be insensible. Boiling water after a time proved efficacious in reviving him. The coating of ice, however, seemed to have rendered his nervous system peculiarly irritable.

" *December* 9. The application which had been made to the Department at Washington for permission to allow the wind at the summit to exceed the velocity prescribed by Professor Maury, was returned approved. During the evening chemical experiments were made illustrating the ease with which whiskey, water, cigars, and lemon can be made to combine. The slight intoxicating effect of the mixture was unanimously attributed to the lemon. A paper enforcing that view was read by Professor Wood.

" *December* 10. Wind north by west, blowing with a velocity of one hundred and twenty miles per minute. Professor Smith venturing to stand on the windward side of the Observatory, was instantly flattened against the boarding. He was spread out over an area of eighteen square feet, and experienced considerable inconvenience from the disarrangement of his hair. Toward evening the wind lulled, and he was carefully detached by knives, and laid upon the shelf until means for his compression could be devised.

" *December* 13. Another violent wind. The spare shirt of the expedition, which was hung upon a line in the rear of the observatory, was blown into narrow strips. The question being raised, whether the wind would have the same effect upon a human being, it was resolved to secure a boy for the purpose of trying the experiment.

" *December* 18. After each member of the expedition had read a paper upon the 'Malleability of Scientific Persons, as exemplified in the flattening of Professor Smith,' an attempt to compress that gentlemen was made. He was laid upon the floor and hammered, chiefly on his edges, by large sledge hammers. After six hours of continuous hammering he had regained nearly his former shape. He was entirely satisfied with the result.

" *January* 1, 1871. The boy who had been sent for — age sixteen, weight ninety pounds — arrived, and he was fastened to the clothes line, the expedition sitting around him. The wind was blowing with a velocity of three hundred miles in thirty-nine minutes. Such was its violence that the bottom was immediately blown out of a tumbler, the mouth of which had been presented to the wind. Professor Nelson made a fine sketch in oil of the scene. In eleven minutes and eight seconds after the boy was hung upon the line he was blown into shreds of not more than the thickness of twine. The expedition then returned into the Observatory, and in the evening Professor Jones read an admirable paper upon the ' Ductility of Boys.'

" *March* 10. The last of the assimilating fluids was exhausted, and the expedition voted unanimously to descend the mountain."

APPENDIX.

SUBSCRIBERS TO THE MOUNT WASHINGTON EXPEDITION.

Nathaniel Thayer	$100.00
John Cummings	50.00
Smithsonian Institution	50.00
Edward Wigglesworth	30.00

SUBSCRIBERS TO THE AMOUNT OF TWENTY-FIVE DOLLARS.

C. J. Sprague, Kemble & Hastings, J. M. Forbes, Fuller, Dana, & Fitts, J. L. Little, and M. R. Ropes & Co., of Boston, and Frederick Billings, of Woodstock, Vt.

SUBSCRIBERS TO THE AMOUNT OF TWENTY DOLLARS.

John Ball, Grand Rapids, Mich.; S. N. Bell, Manchester, N. H.; L. H. Stone, Auburndale, Mass.; M. Brimmer, Blake Brothers, and H. Hunnewell, of Boston.

The following presented sums less than twenty and more than ten dollars : —

Pond & Dunklee, and W. K. Lewis & Brothers, of Boston ; Onslow Stearns, Concord, N. H.

SUBSCRIBERS TO THE AMOUNT OF TEN DOLLARS.

Alpheus Crosby, John Bertram, George Peabody, and Moses A. Farmer, of Salem, Mass.; Edwin Stoughton, Windsor, Vt. ; **H. A. Ward**, Rochester, N. Y.; Thaddeus Fairbanks, Horace Fairbanks, Franklin Fairbanks, and W. P. Fairbanks, of St. Johnsbury, Vt.; Geo. B. McCarter, Washington, D. C.; Charles Marsh, Woodstock, Vt.; Arthur C. Page, Eastman, Ga.; Gyles Merrill, St. Albans, Vt.; L. B. Ward, Providence, R. I.; J. C. Delano, New Bedford, Mass.; I. A. Lapham, Milwaukee, Wis.; Nathaniel White, Warde, Humphrey, & Co., George A. Blanchard, Abbott, Downing, & Co., McFarland & Jenks, E. C. Eastman & Co., and the "Daily Monitor," of Concord, N. H.; Edward L. Wilson, Philadelphia ; Henry M. Mansur, I. N. Andrews, H. P. Parker & Co., M. H. Stimpson, Tower, Giddings, & Torrey, E. Whitney, Edward Austin, W—— and C——, G. Higginson, Fields, Osgood, & Co., H. N. Clark & Co., Little, Brown, & Co., R. H. Stearns, Chauncey Smith, Freeland, Beard, & Richardson, J. W. Edmonds, S. D. Warren, John J. May, Whitton & Brothers, George Howe, W. Endicott, Jr., J. H. Lowell, William Perkins, John T. Bradlee, J. H. Pray, Son, & Co., and G. B. Putnam, of Boston; Rev. S. P. Leeds, of Hanover, N. H.

OTHER SUBSCRIBERS AND FRIENDS.

Our list shows the names of fifty-three persons, largely from Boston, who contributed sums less than ten dollars. To these should be added twenty-five other persons who signed themselves " Cash " on the subscription book.

The following firms and individuals have aided us in very important ways, often saving us the expenditure of large sums of money, besides contributing supplies of various kinds : —

Signal Service, War Department, U. S. Army.

Boston, Lowell, and Nashua Railroad.

Concord Railroad.

Boston, Concord, and Montreal Railroad.

Mt. Washington Railway Company.

Western Union Telegraph Company.

California Wine Company.

Sylvester Marsh, Littleton, N. H.

James Green, New York City.

Hamilton A. Hill, Secretary Board of Trade, in Boston.

Henry Edwards, Boston.

INDEX.

Abortive effort, 10.

Alpine region of Mount Washington, 34.

Altitudes, 29 ; of Mount Washington, 31 ; obtained, 41.

Arctic climate of Mount Washington, 32.

Approaches to Mount Washington, 60.

Ascent of Mount Washington in winter, 101 ; of November 30, 103 ; of February 8, 112.

Aiken, Walter, 71.

Aiken, Charles L., 14, 71.

Aurora, 147, 173, 242.

Adams, Mount, 231.

A day's tramp amid the clouds, 270.

Abbe, Prof., 283.

An ice mystery of science, 352.

Arctic and Mount Washington climate compared, 305.

Ball, Dr. B. L., 47, 114.

Battle of the clouds, 275.

Bemis, Dr. S. A , 41.

Boulders on Mount Washington, 73.

Boulders on Moosilauke, 90.

Bourne Monument, 46, 102, 110.

Botany of Mount Washington, 33, 38.

Brakes, 69, 78.

Bombardment of ice, 167, 178, 192.

Burbeck, C., 219.

Bureau of Telegrams, 282.

Casualties on Mount Washington, 46.

Carriage road, 15, 61.

Champlain Lake, 1.

Christmas, 171.

Clement, James, 88.

Cloud views, 91, 97, 172, 175, 178, 196, 219, 258, 283, 291.

Clough, A. F., 5, 18, 23, 90, 93, 99, 103, 108, 133, 168, 213, 216, 302.

Cogswell, 113, 189.

Cog-rail, 67, 81.

Coldest weather, 177, 182, 185.

Corona, 172, 178, 222, 224.

Culver Hall, 21.

Crawford, Abel, 39, 40; E. A., 39, 40, 43, 60 ; bridle-path, 60 ; House, 46.

Commerce benefited, 16.

Circulars, 7, 16.

Chandler, Benjamin, 47, 114.

Card-basket, 346.

Difficulties, 13.

Depot, construction of, 157.

Descent, perilous, 98.

Door blown in, 165.

Early history of expedition, 1.
Exploration of White Mountains, 36.
Engine, 68, 70, 80.
Electrical phenomena, 151.
Experience against expedition, 58.
Excitements on Mount Washington, 155.
Exhaustion of supplies, 350.
Early winter visits to Mount Washington, 50.

Funds raised, 17.
Field, C. A., 21.
Field, Darby, 36.
First visit to Mount Washington, 36.
First ladies on Mount Washington, 39.
First house on Mount Washington, 43.
First winter visit to Mount Washington, 51.
Fabyan House, 45.
Fabyan Turnpike, 61, 64.
Frost-work, 285.

Gates, G. W., 20.
Geological survey, 4, 24, 27.
Glen House, 46.
Grant. Pres., visit to railway, 85.
Giant's Grave, 40, 45, 60, 65.
Gales, 93, 177, 183, 192, 200.

Henry, Prof., 2.
Hitchcock, C. H., 1, 4, 7, 9, 11, 13, 15, 20, 23, 27, 111, 164, 169, 196, 219, 257, 264, 266, 270.
Hitchcock. Col., 4, 6, 44.
Huntington, J. H., 2, 4, 8, 12. 14, 20, 23, 87. 113, 133, 137, 147, 164, 174, 187, 206, 252, 302.
Holden, L. L., 112, 156, 189, 225, 229, 236, 238.

House creaks, 167, 184.
Hall. Alonzo, 219.
Hill, Rev. Pres., 28.

Instruments used, 310.
Ice columns, 96.

Jackson, Dr. C. T., 29, 39.
Jacob's Ladder, 67, 72, 83, 107, 150, 152.
Journal by Huntington, 163 ; by Kimball, 137 ; by Wilson, 169.

Kimball, H. A., 18, 23, 103, 136, 169 ; almost another monument, 108.
Kerite wire, 9, 10, 15, 148 ; repaired, 152, 174, 187, 199.
Kilburn, B. W., 208.

Life on the summit, 155.
Litigation about summit, 45.
Laying the cable, 148.
Little, William, 5, 130.

Moosilauke, 5, 87, 136.
Mount Cenis Railway, 75.
Myer, General, 9, 19.
Members of the expedition, 23.
Maps of the White Mountains, 27.
Model of White Mountains, by Pres. Hill, 28.
Model of White Mountains, by C. H. Hitchcock, 28.
Mount Washington, height of, 31.
Mount Washington, origin of name, 38.
Mount Washington Railway, 62 ; building of, 66 ; route of, 71 ; officers, 77.
Mount Washington, shadow of, 171, 176.
Measuring the wind, 93, 174, 177, 183, 191.

Mad Mount Washington philosophers, 351.
Marsh, Sylvester, 7, 63, 77, 82, 83.
Marshfield, 61, 105, 149, 166, 189.

Noyes, 48.
Notch House, 45.
Naming of mountain peaks, 41.
Nelson, S. A., 11, 23, 169, 257, 267, 270.
Nutter, Mr., 210.

Osgood, Sheriff, 51.

Powder House Mill Expedition, 348.
Patents of Mr. Marsh, 77.
Photographing, 132, 142.
Pendulum, 177.
Pulse by telegraph, 196.
Photographers, 18.
Physical character of White Mountains, 24.

Reports for benefit of commerce, 282.
Righi, Mount, Railway, 76.
Railway, Mount Washington. (See Mount Washington.)
Railway depot, 6, 14.
Rogers, Dr., 210.
Rare snow-flakes, 347.
Retardation of science, 350.

Sable, 140, 170.
Smithsonian Institution, 2.
Signal service, 9, 146.
Smith, Theodore, 19, 23, 140, 149, 168, 171, 174, 176.
Summit House, 43.
Spaulding, J. H., 44, 52.
Shadow of Mount Washington, 175, 176.
Sanborn, J. J., 67.
Sliding down hill, 74, 176.

Strickland, 46.
Sunrises, 137, 170, 175, 178, 264.
Scientific dispatch, 197.
Stoves, smoking, 167.
Storms, 301.
Startling discovery, 347.

Telegrapher, 19, 22 ; telegraphing, 146 ; from Hanover, 20, 249.
Topography of the mountains, 25.
Tuckerman, E., 33, 36, 39, 42.
Tip-top House, application for, 3 ; refused, 6, 44.
Turkey, 190.
Twin River Farm, 65.
Tuckerman's Ravine, 124, 217, 267.
Tower on Mount Washington, 50.
Tip-top House in a storm, 349.
Thawing and freezing, 353.
Thompson, Eben 252.

Visitors to Mount Washington, 39.
View from Moosilauke, 40, 94.
Views from Mount Washington northward and eastward, 118 ; oceanward, 123, 260 ; southward and westward, 126 ; into Great Gulf, 119 ; up the Androscoggin, 121 ; towards Winnipiseogee, 127 ; down the Ammonoosuc, 127.

White Mountain Range, 24.
Winds, severe, 141, 165, 169, 171, 174, 176, 178, 180, 182, 184, 191, 197, 293, 294.
Windows broken, 178, 192.
Western Union Telegraph Co., 154, 193.
Waumbek Junction, 66, 71.
White Mountain House, 45.
Wilson, E. L., 208.
What the world said of us, 345.